MASSES, CLASSES, IDEAS

MASSES, CLASSES, IDEAS

Studies on Politics and Philosophy Before and After Marx

Etienne Balibar

translated by James Swenson

Routledge • New York & London

Published in 1994 by
Routledge
An imprint of Routledge, Chapman and Hall, Inc.
29 West 35 Street
New York, NY 10001

Published in Great Britain in 1993 by
Routledge
11 New Fetter Lane
London EC4P 4EE

Copyright © 1994 by Routledge

Printed in the United States of America.

Library of Congress Cataloging-in-Publication Data

Balibar, Etienne
  [Essays. English. Selections.]
  Masses, classes, ideas: studies on politics and philosophy before
  and after Marx
  Ettienne Balibar; translated by James Swenson
    p.   cm.
  Includes biographical references and index.
  1. Political Science—Philosophy. 2. Philosophy—Marxist.
  3. Ideology I. Title.
  JA74.B33 1993
  320.01—dc20

                                        93-19168
                                        CIP

British Library Cataloguing-in-Publication Data
Balibar, Etienne
  Masses, Classes, Ideas: Studies on Politics and Philosophy Before
  and After Marx
  I. Title.   II. Swenson, James
  320.01

ISBN 0-415-90601-6 (hardcover)
ISBN 0-415-90602-4 (paperback)

CONTENTS

PREFACE

The essays I have collected in this book were written between 1982 (the first, on "Spinoza, the Anti-Orwell") and 1991 (the last, on "What Is a Politics of the Rights of Man?"). They are logically independent from one another and can be read separately (with the sole exception of chapter 6, "Politics and Truth," which is a continuation of the previous essay on "The Vacillation of Ideology in Marxism" [chapter 4], and would also benefit, so I believe, from a preliminary reading of chapter 5, "In Search of the Proletariat"). However, I have presented them in a successive order, which I hope will help the reader understand their common objectives and some of the underlying hypotheses.

I do not claim to present a systematic doctrine of political philosophy. But I certainly believe that the questions I have asked while rereading certain classical works or addressing current issues, the criteria according to which I have measured concepts of different origin, and the correspondences I have tried to establish between different periods and contexts all refer to some very crucial issues in our understanding of the political tradition. Like many of my contemporaries, I am trying to set this tradition to work again in the very uncertain conjuncture we are living in. This involves transforming the tradition *from the inside.*

A first and central issue is already indicated by my subtitle: "Studies on Politics and Philosophy before and after Marx." To American and English readers, it will recall a well-known book: C. E. Vaughan's *Studies in the History of Political Philosophy before and after Rousseau,* published in 1925 in Manchester. It was through this book that many of us first became acquainted with (among others) the doctrines of Spinoza, Locke, Fichte, and Mazzini. I have no pretension to match the breadth of scope and richness of content of that great classic, but I want to retain something of its method. What appeals to me in the analogy between a "before and after Rousseau" and a "before and after Marx" is not only a matter of formal characteristics. Let me explain more precisely.

We find ourselves today at nearly the same chronological distance from the writing of the *Communist Manifesto, Capital,* or the *Anti-Dühring,* as political thinkers or activists at the beginning of this century (among them the first generation of "Marxists") found themselves with respect to the *Discourse on the Origins of Inequality* or the *Social Contract.* And it could be claimed that, by virtue of their intrinsic conceptual power as well as their controversial legacies in the experiences of revolutions and counter-revolutions, the impact of Rousseauism and Marxism in their respective "centuries" (I mean the centuries that came *after* them) have been fairly comparable. (This might also suggest that a withering away of the interest in Marx in the coming decades is not any more likely than a forgetting of Rousseau was in the twentieth century). We could even trace a closer analogy between the meaning and lasting effects of Rousseau's asking the famous question, at the beginning of the *Social Contract* (I, 5): "What makes a people a people?"[1] and the impact of the questions asked by Marx, Engels, and some of their followers concerning the role of class struggles, mass movements, and the socialist/communist *Weltanschauung* in modern politics. Actually the latter set of questions concerns the revolutionary unity of *the people* (or, as I say in chapter 2, "the people's people": the working class or the proletariat) just as the former concerned the state unity of *a people* (*ein Volk*—versus *das Volk,* to recall the symptomatic oscillation which took place in the recent events of East Germany, before the fall of the Wall). So the latter appears in a sense as simply pushing one step further the inner tension of "insurrection" and "constitution" which is so typical of *modern* democratic political thought, and is clearly exhibited in Rousseau's writings.

But this takes us to the core of the analogy which I would suggest is implicit in my essays and above all in their assemblage: the fact that I want to evaluate the degree of originality of Marxist political theory with respect to its forerunners (the exact nature of the "break" it represents), and discuss the kind of irreversible constraints it imposes on its successors (that is, on ourselves), just as it once proved necessary to evaluate the degree of originality and the kind of irreversible threshold represented by Rousseau, in order to understand modern democratic thought. Because Rousseau had broken with past "constitutional" theory on a decisive point (regarding popular sovereignty, and the "immanent" nature of legislation), it would not prove possible to think of politics after him in the traditional way (as an "art" of the rulers); as a result, the very *use* of his predecessors, be it of Locke, or Spinoza, or even Machiavelli or Aristotle, would become twisted and determined by the new "paradigm" he framed. Because Marx and Engels (who in this respect are hardly separable, in spite of their very different casts of mind) had broken with past "ideological" representations of the motor forces and the orientation of history, it proved impossible to think of politics after them in the traditional way (as a realization of the "will," or the "ends" of Reason). The contemporary "crisis of Marxism" poses no objection to that; on the contrary it is the best proof of it, particularly inasmuch as it leads many of us to reread classical, pre-Marxist authors, in order to find some foundations for an alternative view of the relation between law, the state, social interests or social struggles, or more simply (an orientation which I share to a large extent) to elicit clarification of the central *aporias* of Marxism itself and ways to get out of them.

Admittedly neither Rousseau nor Marx and the Marxist tradition can be isolated from their historical destiny. Rousseau has a necessary connection to the French Revolution (although the Revolution was not exactly a "Rousseauist" process, nor was the *Declaration of the Rights of Man and the Citizen* a Rousseauist text: but who could argue that, without the *Discourse* and the *Contract*, the radical, motor forces of the Revolution could have found their genuine language?). Similarly, Marx cannot be read apart from the history of the labor movement and other revolutionary or reformist movements before and after the Soviet Revolution (although it certainly was not a Marxist revolution, but rather a revolution, and later on a counterrevolution, carried on *in the name of Marx*, which is something quite different and much more ambiguous). My objective here, however, is not directly social and political history. It is concentrated on the *intellectual* implications of Marxism and some other doctrines that can be compared with it (both positive implications, the opening of new fields of thought, and negative implications, the production of blockages or "epistemological obstacles").

In this respect, what I would like to insist on is the following general idea. If it is a question of the symmetries between Rousseau and Marx, what seems remarkable to me is above all the philosophical *reversal* which takes place when passing from one to the other. I have already mentioned the well known fact that Marx pushed one step further the "democratic" orientation arising from Rousseau.[2] But I should recall now that this new step could be taken only on the condition of *reversing* the philosophical attitude toward "politics." Rousseau is indeed a very typical representative (maybe *the* typical modern representative, in the sense that he created the conditions for this conception to survive the end of the classical era) of what we can call *the autonomy of the political.* In his view politics may have historical conditions, a complex matter to deal with ("the passions and the interests"), nevertheless it is ultimately founded *upon itself*, as a "constituent" activity of the people, and individuals within the people. In a kind of "virtuous circle" (which certainly has to do with Rousseau's conception of "virtue"), it presupposes an autonomy of political concepts and decisions for which it will itself create the conditions.[3] What became very clear with the American and French revolutions, and especially in the formulations of the *Declaration of Rights*, was that this autonomy of the political, reminiscent of a long tradition in the definition of *citizenship*, had become effective only because it expressed another autonomy—namely, the emergence of "we the people" as a political subject, or the practical imposition of popular sovereignty. Now the striking fact concerning Marx, in this respect, is that he completely reverses this position. No doubt this is one of the crucial aspects of what he calls "materialism." He typically advocates a conception of *the heteronomy of politics*, meaning that the "truth" and "reality" of politics is not *within itself*, in its own political consciousness or activity, but *outside itself*, in its "external" conditions and objects.

I am not thinking here of the reductionist or economicist views which amount to a *negation* of politics, and have been attributed to Marx by some vulgar readings. I am thinking of the fact that Marx has indeed identified the political process (in which individuals and groups are active) with the complete development of the contradictions intrinsic to its "other": the "economic" field in the broad sense. Therefore politics in Marx is not negated, or nullified; on the contrary it is dialectically *recreated* as a more effective process. It becomes a "class politics," that is to say, a social practice which, from both sides or camps (the dominant class, the revolutionary class), constantly *crosses the border* of "the political," as it was officially defined. This is the case because it has to face the consequences of the fact that labor is an antagonistic social relation, in which there is exploitation and domination, which leaves no aspect of social and personal life in the "modern," "industrial" society unaffected. Hence the apparent paradox: in order to reassert the crucial importance of (collective) *autonomy in politics*, meaning the self-determination and self-liberation of "the people" (now basically defined as the *working* people), Marx the radical democrat had to deny the autonomy of the political. He was to build the most powerful and comprehensive "heteronomic" theory of politics in the history of philosophy, which relies on a provocative "materialist" identification of politics with its "other": what I call a *short circuit* of "politics" and "economy," arising from the simultaneous economic critique of "politicism" and political critique of "economicism."

Now we are aware that this radical assertion of the heteronomy of politics was epochmaking; it has shaped the whole modern political debate.[4] But we should also be aware that it is precisely this assertion or short circuit (and the subsequent organization of democratic politics around the issue of a "politics of labor") that is put back into question by the current "crisis of Marxism" and the underlying historical phenomena. Whether this crisis, with the "post-Marxist" stance it determines, will (should) lead to a revival of political theory as a theory of the *autonomy of the political*, and particularly (in the democratic or progressive camp) to a *return* to a Rousseauist (or, in a slightly different manner, a Lockean, or a Kantian) point of view, is a crucial philosophical question. It is still by now entirely open, although it underlies much of the current debate in political theory and political philosophy.

According to the general project of testing the originality of Marxism as a political philosophy, and throwing some new light on its historical situation, I have divided the essays I am presenting here into three parts, by following a roughly chronological order of subjects dealt with, rather than the order of their actual writing.[5] I shall now propose a brief summary of these three parts, by indicating some of the key themes which could be taken as guiding threads.

In the first part, called "Dilemmas of Classical Politics: Insurrection vs Constitution," I give readings of three major texts, or groups of texts, of the classical tradition: Spinoza's philosophy (in the *Theologico-Political Treatise*, the *Ethics*, and the *Political Treatise*) inasmuch as it represents the most lucid example we have of a combination of politics and ontology; the 1789 French

Declaration of the Rights of Man and the Citizen inasmuch as it founds the potential identity of "man" and "citizen" (or the universal right and access to politics) on a revolutionary principle of "equaliberty"; finally, the enigmatic notion of the "internal (or inner, or interior) border" lying at the core of Fichte's *Addresses to the German Nation*, which were to become a model for much of the subsequent "nationalist" literature. Thus there is one seventeenth century, one eighteenth century, and one nineteenth century text. But also there is one text in which the "political subject" submitted to discussion is the *multitude*, one in which it is proclaimed to be the *nation* made up of free and equal citizens, and one in which it is identified with the *people*, as a transcendent *and* incarnate unity.

"Spinoza, the Anti-Orwell: The Fear of the Masses" is the earliest of these essays. It was undertaken in an attempt to clarify what I thought were the reasons for the unique theoretical and political importance attributed by Spinoza to the concept of "the masses," but also to clarify the high degree of ambivalence in his attitude toward what he himself considers to be the basic problem of politics—namely, the "popular" or "mass" movements as *real* phenomena in the field of the *imaginary* (hence his largely aporetic propositions intended to provide democracy, which he designated himself as the "most natural" and "most absolute" regime, with a juridical foundation, and the possibility of drawing from him both revolutionary and conservative arguments). My conclusion is that the importance of Spinoza's philosophy for democratic thinking (even today) does not arise in spite of, but rather because of these very aporias. It is precisely these aporias that allow him to frame a realistic concept of freedom, which is inseparable from the originary "transindividal" character of human nature, and a concept of community immediately associated with a dialectics of affective "fusion" and rational "communication." This latter concept is, I think, well ahead, not only of his time, but also of many of our contemporary debates on this issue.

Spinoza had a radically democratic view of the complementary functions of individual liberties and collective freedom, and also of the formidable difficulties which arise from this complementarity in practice. But he certainly had a very negative view of "revolutions," which he still considered in the "ancient" way, as mere changes in the form of a regime or in the identity of the rulers, accompanied by mass movements. This may explain his inability (or our inability inasmuch as we follow him) to express and valorize another dialectical aspect of politics, which is precisely the negative import, or negativity, of the principle on which a democratic revolution is founded (and which is best exemplified by the *Declaration of the Rights of Man and the Citizen*—namely, the fact that any effective democratic *constitution* remains dependent on the idea of *insurrection*, which itself must always take a *negative* logical form. By means of a deliberate play on words, I call it the "proposition of equaliberty," meaning that equality and liberty are "identical" in practice, because *neither* can true liberty go without equality *nor* can true equality go without liberty, and I try to show that it is literally contained in the articles of the *Declaration*, being a logical prerequisite for its new universalistic (or "infinite") definition of the *citizen*. But this leads me to emphasize the inner tensions of "equaliberty," which make it anything but a *stable* or "axiomatic" principle, and account (at least at the conceptual level) for the contradictory forms of its realization. Having been once "declared" in history (and in fact this "declaration" or "utterance" was repeated several times, in basically equivalent forms), the proposition of equaliberty could no longer be ignored, but it could also not be implemented (particularly as a *Grundnorm* or a principle of the juridical order) without mediations and conflicts.

However, it seems to me that these contradictions (in the broad sense) are of two very different kinds. One group of contradictions emerged when equaliberty was combined with the antagonistic principles of *property* and *community*, or better said, with opposite, conflictual forms of these principles (the national community versus the proletarian community, capitalist property versus property as a result of personal labor). Those are openly displayed in political discourse throughout the modern era, and in particular they provide the discourse of "class struggle" with its essential ideological references. On the contrary, another group of contradictions were mainly repressed in political discourse: which does not mean that they found no expression at all, but rather that they were institutionally marginalized and, with few exceptions, could hardly be recognized as contradictions in their own right. I suggest that this other group is underpinned by two great anthropological divisions or "differences": sexual difference, and intellectual difference, inasmuch as they are *also* immediately political. Not by chance, they are precisely the contradictions whose importance seems today either to relativize or to "overdetermine" the more classical forms of social conflict. This leads me to suggest that what is sometimes described with more or less clarity as a "postmodern" turn in the history of politics does not, in fact, so much refer to a *new stage* in a linear periodization as to a superimposition of *layers* of the "political," which can be hierarchized differently according to the conjunctures. I return later to these questions when confronting the more practical question of a "politics of the rights of man" as it can be defined today (see chapter 9).

Third, I include in this first part of the book my essay on Fichte's *Addresses to the German Nation* (which I also wrote in the mid-eighties, at the time when I was working with Immanuel Wallerstein on our book *Race, Nation, Class*)[6], both because it brings in a reference to the currently more and more crucial question of nationalism (to which I return in the third part), and because in my opinion it adds an essential example to the discussion of the notion of *community*. I was amazed to realize that the real meaning (and therefore the real reasons for the ambivalent effects) of the philosophy displayed in the *Addresses*[7] remains so completely distorted and misunderstood. The reasons could be that the text is more often symbolically mentioned than actually read. But even authors who go into detail, with a good knowledge of "German Idealism," keep picturing it as an intermediary link between what they present as "Herder's cultural particularism" (or "historicism") and nineteenth century racial theories, not to speak of Hitler's National Socialism. Behind these amazing errors, I think that we can identify on the one hand lasting prejudices (themselves nationalist, especially in France) concerning "German ideology," but also on the other hand a complete misunderstanding of the role of universalism, and especially moral universalism (of which Fichte is a brilliant representative) in politics and history. The fact that some radical expressions of nationalism (and probably *every* symbolic institutional foundation of a national community, as a crystallization of nationalist ideology) are rooted in universalistic, not particularistic, categories and principles, will remain a mystery for anybody who believes in the absolute character of such alternatives as "individualism versus holism" or "rationalism versus irrationalism." Conversely the categories elaborated by such a consistent idealism as Fichte's philosophy of history (particularly those categories which identify subjectivity with activity) are perhaps more illuminating for our understanding of nationalism and the construction of a national "identity" than any empirical sociological explanation. At least they should be integrated into such an explanation, and this is what I try to demonstrate.

Finally, this first series of critical readings leaves us with some questions. One question has to do with the Janus face of "universalism" in politics and political discourse. It is not certain that Spinoza could be considered an advocate of universalism (he certainly is not anti-universalistic, as some quick comparisons with Nietzsche would suggest), since his analysis of transindividuality as an actually existing network of all individuals in nature refers to a deeper concept of *singularity*. But on the other side, the undoubtedly universalistic proposition of equaliberty, as an expression of the conquest of personal and civic rights, and the no less universalistic notion of the national community in Fichte, can (and perhaps must) enter into sharp conflict, although they have a clear historical connection. It would be attractive to refer the first to a "formal," "negative" notion of the universal (a "universal of the void," so to speak), and the second to a "substantial" universal (which could also be labeled, in another language, an *ideological* notion of the universal). However, the way (unexpected, in many respects) in which the question of the universal and universalism presents itself in today's "unified" world suggests to us that we abandon these kinds of traditional symmetries and leave the discussion provisionally open (I return to it in the third part).

Another question which arises concerns the concept of *revolution*. At the heart of its classical meaning (in modern times) there lies not so much a metaphor of the reversal of established power (although this connotation is still present) as the idea of a process leading from oppression to resistance, from injustice to insurrection, and from insurrection to collective liberation. This is clearly a teleological scheme. If it does not necessarily become the core of a new eschatology (a theory of the "end" of history as the full realization of its "ends"), it nevertheless seems to imply the representation of a subject of history which is constituted in these successive stages (or even better, which constitutes itself by liberating itself through these stages: hence the intrinsic relationship between historical idealism, from Kant onward, and the idea of revolution, since modern "idealism"[8] is above all a theory of the active *self-construction* of the subject). Fichte's "people" (with its Jacobin origins and its mobilizing function in the national liberation struggle) is a clear expression (or possibly transposition) of this idea, closely associated with a revolutionary concept of activity (*Tätigkeit*), which appears again as the central notion in Marx's *Theses on Feuerbach*.

But what is Marx's "proletariat," precisely? Is it not another figure of the subject of history constituting itself in the process of its own liberation? Things are notoriously complicated here. There is a clear symmetry (therefore theoretical similarity) between Fichte's "nation" and Marx's "proletariat," which are also both concepts of (moral) *communities* and *identities*, just as there would be a constant symmetry in the last two centuries between the ideologies of nationalism and socialism. But there is also in Marx's "materialism," and perhaps this is his more *original* contribution to theory, a clear element of *deconstruction of the representation of the subject*, precisely in the case of the proletariat: a deconstruction which results both from his analysis of exploitation as a "natural-human" process and his concrete pictures of the class struggle. In many respects the Marxian "proletariat" is a *nonsubject* rather than a subject in history (Althusser was right on this point, and he had every reason to insist on it in the face of its massive denial). But how is that compatible, not only with the notions of insurrection and liberation, but even more profoundly with the irreversible *truth* that the revolutionary principle expresses, as a kind of "*de jure* fact"? How can there emerge in actual historical conditions a *true proposition*, that is expressed both *by* and *for* some humans or groups of humans, without these humans appearing to themselves in their very practical recognition of the truth as "a subject"? This is a very difficult question indeed, which never ceased haunting the debate around Marxism and socialism. It also crosses in a fascinating manner the questions which can be asked on a Spinozistic base concerning the nature and role of collective ideals, passions, and actions. Although it is sometimes claimed that there is a Spinozistic element in Fichte's philosophy, it would be much more logical here to analyze the Fichtean "people" as a perfect illustration of the *imaginary community* whose constitution and ambivalence were the very object of Spinoza's theory. In the case of Marx's "proletariat," it would not be very difficult either to develop a Spinozistic "deconstruction" of its teleology, and of the imaginary representation of its universal mission.

It seems to me, however, that the critique would become much more interesting if it took into account the object or problem that, in a sense, *Spinoza and Marx have in common*: namely, the problem of the "masses," or better said, of the determining role of the masses in history.[9] If we undertake this comparison (which is one of the main suggestions of this book), we may get to the idea that *Spinoza explains something that Marx does not explain* (therefore also explains something in Marx himself, which remains obscure to the Marxists). But we may as well get to the idea that *Marx explains something that Spinoza does not explain* (therefore also etc.). To put it briefly, there is a "psychological" (or psychoanalytical, in the literal sense) superiority in Spinoza's theory of the masses, but there is a "historical" superiority in Marx's account of their social and economic constitution. But just as Marx was "dialectical" enough to at least indicate the necessary function of the imaginary in his picture of political-economic processes, Spinoza was "dialectical" enough to at least indicate the necessity of economic "real" conditions in his discussion of the political effects of imagination. Could it then be the case that the crucial determinations of "politics" are precisely the horizon of this complementarity, which, however, must take the form of an opposition (at least initially)? I will formulate a more precise hypothesis on this point after I have given an account of what my essays on Marxism in this book deal with.

As I have said above, these three essays ("The Vacillation of Ideology in Marxism," "In Search of the Proletariat," "Politics and Truth") are in fact complementary. They were written in the course of the same investigation, often as a result of pedagogic activity with my students,[10] and actually in more favorable circumstances would have become a small book, which I have nearly reconstructed here. Literally speaking, they find their point of departure in simple "philological questions," which to me are anything but secondary, since a good many of the false dilemmas which have been maintained by generations of "Marxists" (and antiMarxists), with the over-simplifying conclusions they have produced concerning the content of Marx's theory, result from, or become justified by, pure mistakes concerning the *actual content* of Marx's writings, and above all his *terminology*. Marx's *real text*, as it was written by him, is full of surprises for anyone who was educated in classical "historical materialism" (both in the tradition of the Second and the Third International, which equally maintained the idea of a coherent, albeit uncompleted "system"—an idea which was hardly challenged by the various brands of "critical Marxism" in the twentieth century, from Lukacs and Korsch to Gramsci, the Frankfurt School and the early Habermas, or Lefebvre and Althusser in France).[11] The discrepancies however between Marx's actual formulations and what he is believed to have "demonstrated" or explained are not only significant testimonies of the distance separating Marx's real thought from its idealized "Marxist" picture. More profoundly they are symptoms of the deep antinomies which characterize his analyses of the political process in modern "class societies," which is his true object.

To name but two examples, which are examined at length in the following essays, one begins to measure the difficulty and relevance of these antinomies when one realizes that Marx's major theoretical work, i.e., *Capital* (Book I), contains hardly any explicit references to *the proletariat* (except in some "marginal" locations, which I will explain), in spite of its being centered on the social conditions of the revolutionary mission of the working class in history; and contains no references at all to *ideology*, in spite of its being centered on the critique of "bourgeois" political economy as an "apology" of the capitalist system. I should add that such notions as "the subject of history" or "class consciousness" are indeed completely absent in all of Marx's writings, which is not to say that the problems usually referred to under these names bear no relation at all to Marxism.

From these initially purely *negative* and rather enigmatic statements, I move to a more developed inquiry about Marx's "materialist" conception of the class struggle in capitalism, which I see as an adventure, a process of experimental and theoretical discovery which never ceases to displace its initial assumptions while developing its critique of the "dominant" picture of politics, but also repeatedly stumbles on the same basic obstacles. First of all I want to establish a clear link between the successive stages of Marx's (and Engels's) intellectual history, and precise episodes of their political involvement in nineteenth century social movements, which meant in practice a need for successive contradictory tactics. But above all I want to relate this history to what I feel are the intrinsic *aporias* of "historical materialism" as theory of politics, on which I think we are still dependent. It seemed to me that they are concentrated around two crucial, and not unrelated, difficulties.

One concerns the notion of "dominant ideology," or more precisely the latent aporia of "domination without dominated" in the field of "ideology," which appears not only as a blind spot in Marx's and Engels's discussion of contemporary political struggles, but also as the missing link in their account of historical causality. This difficulty culminates in the persistent obstacles (which have tragic consequences) to properly conceptualizing the nature of "proletarian ideology" and "party ideology" (or Weltanschauung), and above all in the kind of (limited, but not inexistent) effectiveness which "revolutionary" or "scientific" *ideas* should have in the history of proletarian politics.

The *second* basic difficulty concerns the presence of an aborted dialectics of the *proletariat as class* and the *proletariat as mass*, which already emerges with Marx's early writings, virtually acquires a structural function in *Capital*, and almost becomes recognized as the very "essence" of politics in the brilliant essays of the "later" Engels, but eventually becomes concealed and neutralized by historical "determinism" or teleology.

Far from concluding from these "aporetic" inquiries that Marxist theory was, after all, collapsing due to its internal contradictions, I suspect that the difficulties in Marx are closely connected with problems that remain open in the present—particularly with problems which concern the new forms and functions of racism in the "world-economy," "world politics," and "world communications" of the late twentieth century. (Obviously this way of expanding and reformulating the import of my textual readings in the field of political philosophy, did not arise only from its internal logic, but also from civic or activist concerns.) To these questions, my third part, "Frontiers of Contemporary Politics: Questioning the Universal," is largely devoted, although more from a conceptual than an empirical point of view. It seems to me that the present conditions of political "practice" are characterized, notably, by two major facts or tendencies.

One is the fact that the *universalization of politics* has been realized in practice as a result of world wars, colonization and decolonization, capitalist "development" and its crisis, the rise and fall of "socialism," and so forth. The universalization of politics in practice is a crucial *philosophical* fact too, i.e., it changes the conditions of theoretical thinking—just as the realization of "abstraction" in practice (in the expansion of monetary circulation and commodification of human activities) was a crucial philosophical fact, to which Marx devoted his analyses of "fetishism" and "real subsumption." Indeed we suspect that the two facts are connected, although they develop unevenly in history. It is a *positive* fact in a sense, which provides an opportunity for political practice to tackle some of its *real* conditions, particularly the "economic" conditions, which, as Marx clearly explained, are never "natural," but "social" (and also never "local," but "global"). In my essay "What Is a Politics of the Rights of Man," I try, for example, to show how this situation is likely to set up a new dialectics, or political questioning, of the "individual" and "collective" aspects of property, *within* capitalism itself. Nevertheless, as a consequence, the "universal" or universalization *are no longer ideals*: something which deeply affects their ethical function.

This is the more so because the very same world in which "universality becomes concrete" (as Hegel would say), or an actual fact, is also the world where "humankind" as such is *structurally divided* along racial, cultural, sexual, and intellectual lines. What Fichte had called the "interior border" becomes economically relativized and institutionally blurred in many places (not to speak of the military "world order" which transcends it). But in reality it becomes multiplied and diversified: as Foucault would have said, it passes from the level of "macro-politics" to the level of "micro-politics" or micro power—without simply abandoning the level of state powers or apparatuses, but nevertheless profoundly transforming their functions. Borders, boundaries, or limits are no longer mainly (or apparently) on the *fringes* of every political "community," they are located *everywhere* (just as the "peripheries" of the world economy are more and more in its "center"). It is, therefore, a world in which the *projective mechanisms* of identification or (imaginary) recognition of the "human" and the "infra-human" (perhaps even the "superhuman," since there is no stable "measure" of humanness in this respect, or better said, the "mismeasure" is the actual rule), which classical psychoanalysis described mainly at the *individual* level (although they are in reality profoundly *transindividual*) become direct stakes and objects of politics.

But this leads us immediately to what I consider to be the *second* crucial fact concerning current historical conditions. To borrow once again the terminology which emerges from a critical reading of Marx (and from oblique comparisons between Marx and Spinoza, Marx and Fichte, Marx and Freud), the dialectics of "class struggle" seems to have given way to—better said, it has become apparently integrated into—a more complex and ambivalent dialectic of "mass conflict" (with, notably, a corresponding multiplication of "violence" as an "irrational" or "uncontrollable" phenomenon).[12] As I have argued elsewhere,[13] the "class struggle" in history is not a quasi-natural base underlying political processes. It is a *conjunctural form* (which can be very crucial indeed, and plays a decisive role for long periods in significant areas of the world) taken by mass movements and mass conflicts when definite political conditions are realized. To put it provocatively, *class struggles organized as class struggles* (with the corresponding institutions) in history are not the rule, they are the exception, and this should be accepted as a *Marxist* (or revised Marxist, or "generalized Marxist") thesis. But the "basic" structure underlying the conjunctures, which is able to take a number of different forms (including ethnic, national, and religious forms, none of them a single "essence," but on the contrary with infinitely many varieties) is precisely "mass conflict," whose *matter*, so to speak, is precisely *ideology* (as collective consciousness, but to a much greater extent as the transindividual imagery, which simultaneously works at the conscious and the unconscious level). As I suggested above, it should lead us, not to renounce the idea of causality in history, but to develop a pattern of historical causality in which the "complex unity" of the real and the imaginary, or of economy (in the broad, social sense) and ideology (in the broad sense, including the unconscious) is not something derived, but something *originary*. It is a pattern in which, so to speak, each of these "inverse" aspects of collective human life mainly produces its effects "on the other stage": ideology making economy effective, and conversely economy making ideology effective—usually in an unpredictable manner.

This indeed poses a difficult problem for politics, and above all for *democratic* politics. From the late nineteenth century onward, recognizing the "mass factor" in history, and therefore also the causal function of the imaginary and the unconscious, was mainly the privilege of either conservative (sometimes very reactionary, including parafascist) political theories, or "libertarian," *antipolitical* doctrines and moral currents. It is now a question for the "masses" themselves to practically control, regulate, and understand the dialectics of mass ideologies and mass movements (of which they are constitutive parts themselves) both in terms of everyday experiences, and in terms of abstract notions, which are a necessary condition for collective action. On the other hand, organized class struggle, with its political and geographic conditions, and its typical successive stages (ranging from the initial open hostility of the state—the antithesis of "state and revolution"— to the final relative integration or recognition, in the form of "national social" states) was no doubt one *particular*, but very effective, form of the *universalization* of political practice.[14] Now the paradox, but probably also the unavoidable result, of a conjuncture in which the material conditions of politics become universalized is precisely that this specific form of "subjective" universalization (which was nothing else indeed than a new implementation in practice of "equaliberty") has today lost most of its capacity to shape reality, at least as an *autonomous* form. To put it in other terms, there is currently a huge gap between the advance of "passive" universalization and the regression, or crisis, of "active" universalization, at least in its traditional forms. And there is a corresponding withering away of the public sphere (*Öffentlichkeit*) under the triumphant impact of "communication."

This is an uneasy, even worrying conjuncture indeed, which bears all the marks of a kind of "zero point" of political practice. But of course it is mainly an appearance, coming from the fact that once again politics exists, or re-creates itself, in the forms of its "others," in forms which are not recognized *as such* (in my essay on "Politics and Truth," I try to elaborate the reciprocal notion of *politics working as its own mask*, which seems to me to emerge directly from an internal critique of Engels's periodization of the "dominant" forms of "domination"). However the appearance of a crisis does much to reproduce the crisis itself.

Because I am convinced that some of the germs of this situation and of the attempts to understand it are not recent, or that there might be historical "cycles" taking place, I devote a special discussion to the propositions of "Freudo-Marxism" (more precisely: Wilhelm Reich's description of the "mass movement" which fascism had manipulated in the 1930s, in my essay on "Fascism, Psychoanalysis, Freudo-Marxism"). But of course I do not imagine that we could or should *repeat* this intellectual experience, however stimulating it can still be. We had better learn from its limits.

In reality what I believe is that we find ourselves in a situation in which the very concept of "politics" has to be *re-created*, possibly *beyond* the dilemmas of the "autonomy" and the "heteronomy" of the political.

As always, it is both a question of interpreting the "signs of the time" and confronting the critical legacy of past conceptualizations. This legacy now includes, at the very least, not only the "classical theories" of individuality, property, and community, centered on the democratic insurrections and constitutions of the bourgeois era, but also the "antinomies" of class politics, especially Marxist class politics; and not only the development of these antinomies, but also ongoing reflections on the "political unconscious" of modern mass conditions and mass movements. My aim in this book is to provide some materials for the confrontation of these heterogeneous, often conflicting, but equally necessary sources.

It is my pleasure to finish this preface by acknowledging the help and friendship of several people who directly and indirectly made this book possible. The first idea of collecting some of my recent historical and philosophical essays and presenting them to the American audience came from John Rajchman. He was also very helpful in establishing the selection of essays which has now been adopted. His first suggestion was warmly received at Routledge, which had already published some of my essays in collective volumes, for which I am very grateful. I want especially to thank my editor, Maureen MacGrogan, who throughout the preparation of the volume has kept me in the right direction, and her assistant Katherine Lieber. My translator James Swenson has, so it seems to me, done very fine work: I did not make things very easy for him, both because I share some of the well known stylistic habits of "Continental" philosophers, and because I wanted to take advantage of this English version to make corrections in my own texts. Although the complete volume has been revised and harmonized in its style and terminology, some of the essays included (or a previous version of them) had been already translated and published in American journals. I want to thank very warmly the translators, editors, and publishers (they are indicated with a footnote in the corresponding chapters), with particular reference to the journal *Rethinking Marxism*. Among the many American friends and colleagues who, since my first visit in the United States in 1983, have so generously contributed to introducing me to their background and debates, taught me the vitality of American intellectual life, and rewarded me with a keen interest in the continuation of my own work in philosophy, I would like to say here how particularly indebted I am to Warren Montag, with whom I share many interests and passions, and to John Rosenthal, then a postgraduate student at the New School for Social Research, who struggled hard to have my visit there leave a written trace.

While revising this book and writing this preface, I benefited from a Fellowship-in-Residence at the Netherlands Institute for Advanced Study in Wassenaar, which offered me the best possible environment.

Wassenaar, 25 February 1993

PART ONE

DILEMMAS OF CLASSICAL POLITICS

Insurrection vs. Constitution

1

SPINOZA, THE ANTI-ORWELL
The Fear of the Masses

For Emilia Giancotti

With this intentionally untimely title, I shall attempt to formulate the problem on the basis of which it would be possible to understand and discuss what makes Spinoza's political thought (or better, if we share on this point the conception brilliantly put forth by Negri, Spinoza's thought, inasmuch as it is thoroughly political)[1] indispensable for us today, however aporetic it might appear. In fact, I believe that it is impossible to reduce the positions of the "renegade Jew" from the Hague, despite their deductive appearance, to a single definition, even if considered as a tendency which would progressively prevail over others in his intellectual itinerary. It seems to me, on the contrary, that what he is heading toward, or what we head toward when we undergo the experience of reading him and attempt to think in the concepts he offers us, is a complex of contradictions without a genuine solution. But, not only can the problems he poses not be returned to a time irretrievably past; it is precisely this complex of contradictions that makes them unavoidable for us today, conferring on his metaphysics a singular critical power and constructive theoretical capacity. Perhaps this is the sign by which we can recognize a great philosopher.[2]

As a result, there is no question of fictitiously resolving these contradictions by taking a position beyond the point reached by Spinoza in his inquiry, or the place that he occupies in a historical evolution whose meaning we believe we possess. In this respect, the demonstration produced by Pierre Macherey in his *Hegel ou Spinoza*[3] seems decisive to me. Every reading is certainly a transformation. But the only effective (and therefore instructive) transformation is one that rejects the ease of retrospective judgment, which refuses to project onto Spinoza's contradictions a schema (dialectical or otherwise) that he himself would have already invalidated. As a result, it is the inverse that is important: to bring to the fore, if possible, contradictions characteristic of his thought that turn out to be at the same time entirely current, and in this way enable us to understand both what there is for us to think in Spinoza's concepts, and how the latter, in their turn, can be active in our own inquiry, without any pre-established solution.

The Ambivalence of the "Mass Standpoint"

French translators, although often less than rigorous on this point, have rendered Spinoza's *multitudo*, in certain contexts, as "mass." They have sought neither to emphasize systematically the relationship that brings together different uses of *multitudo*, nor to clarify the successive or simultaneous utilization of notions which interfere with it, such as *vulgus*, *plebs*, *turba*, and also *populus* (to which I shall return). But they have been sensitive to that which, in the use that Spinoza makes of it, calls for a confrontation with much more recent problematics—crossing over at least a century-and-a-half of "individualist" philosophy—which have been formulated in what has been called the age of masses or crowds, and of mass movements. On the condition that all the nuances of Spinozist argumentation and terminology are taken seriously—which will lead to the perception that it is not a matter of a finished concept but of a persistent problem, reformulated several times—this comparison is justified and illuminating.

Spinoza is centrally inscribed in the context of a period in which the transformations of the state, the formation of the modern "absolutist" state in the midst of revolutionary troubles and violence, caused the emergence of the problem of mass movements as such, and hence of their control, their utilization, or their preventive repression. Neither this preoccupation, nor the corresponding reference to the theoretical pair *imperium/multitudo* belongs to Spinoza alone: it is enough to read Hobbes to see that. But

Spinoza's originality appears from the outset in the fact that for him the "mass" is itself the principal object of investigation, reflection, and historical analysis. In this sense, one can say that Spinoza is, in his time and beyond it, one of the very few political theorists who does not take as his central problem the constitution of the state (or of the state order or even of the state apparatus) and thus reduce the existence of mass movements to a pre-existent "nature" or horizon which threatens the security and stability of the state. Spinoza seeks above all an *explanation* of the causes and logic proper to mass movements. This goes well beyond the fact of conferring on the *multitudo* a symbolic positivity, in order to make it the other name for the "people" or for "civil society," and to proclaim in it the foundation of political and juridical order. In Spinoza the "mass," or to put it better, the masses, become an explicit theoretical object, because in the last analysis it is their different modalities of existence, according to historical conjunctures and according to economies or regimes of passion, that determine the chances of orienting a political practice toward a given solution.[4]

This is why we must reach the point of inquiring, problematically, whether or not the originality, the irreducibly subversive aspect of Spinoza's thought, confirmed by the reactions that it provoked right from the beginning—in short, to borrow Negri's striking expression, the "savage anomaly" of Spinozism—consists in the fact of having adopted in theory the "standpoint of the mass," or the "mass standpoint," on politics and the state. This standpoint is neither that of the state itself in its different variants nor a popular or democratic standpoint, nor, strictly speaking, a class standpoint.

If we must nevertheless adopt a deliberately ambivalent formulation, it is also for another reason. "The fear of the masses" should be understood in the double sense of the genitive, objective and subjective. *It is the fear that the masses feel. But it is also the fear that the masses inspire* in whoever is placed in the position of governing or acting politically, hence in the state as such. So that, arising in the context of the power (*puissance*) of the masses and their movements, the problem of the constitution or reform of the state is first posed in the context of that fear—which may be as extreme as panic or may remain rationally moderated, but which never purely and simply disappears. We must try to understand how this reciprocal fear might be balanced, so as to make room for other, more constructive forces (those of love, admiration, devotion, as well as those of common, rationally perceptible utility), or else on the contrary how it can maintain itself to the point of threatening the dissolution of the social body. For the masses are all the more frightening and uncontrollable the more they are terrorized by natural forces or by the violence they suffer, and this violence in its turn is all the more immoderate in that tyrannical power, in fact, feels secretly disarmed before them.

Two observations may thus be formulated.

First, by taking as his object the very dynamic of the fear felt and inspired by the masses, with its possible reversals, Spinoza did not fail to conceptualize the affective ambivalence that characterizes it. Neither fear without hope nor hope without fear: this proposition is deduced immediately from the primitive division (joy and sadness) to which the concept of "desire" is submitted as the "very essence of the human." Now, it is this concept of desire—complex from the start—that in the *Ethics* becomes the explanatory principle of all emotional life.

Spinoza's whole effort certainly tends to define a "path" which permits this life, individually or collectively, to be oriented toward increasing the power of acting, toward the preponderance of joyous passions, thus reducing as much as possible the empire of sadness, fear, and hate. Yet it is doubtful that, at least at the collective level, a complete reduction of psychic conflict would ever be possible, bringing an end to the *fluctuatio animi* in the soul of the masses. This reduction is always something we strive for, a *conatus*, as Spinoza puts it. Hence it is only in a limit situation, entirely problematic and probably utopian, that we could escape this determination, and that political practice could cease to be governed by reciprocal fear and the vacillation between love and hate.

And yet—this is the second observation—it is not any more possible to ignore everything in Spinoza's text that evokes the ideal, or at least the model (*exemplar*) of the neutralization of the passions, and strives to define its conditions in relation to both the individual and the collectivity. This is the case each time Spinoza traces the program of institutions conforming to nature, in which each person's desire to conserve his own being would be directly expressed in a rational recognition of the collective interest. This is also the case in the figure of Christ.

Further, we cannot help but notice *another ambivalence*, all the more remarkable in that it can in certain respects be formulated in Spinozist categories, and as such thereby authorizes a sort of self-criticism of the system itself. I mean *the ambivalence betrayed by Spinoza's attitude, his own position regarding the "masses."* Let us recall how it is manifested in some decisive moments of Spinoza's writings.

First there are the scholia of proposition 37, part IV of the *Ethics*, which are echoed by chapter IV of the *Theologico-Political Treatise*, and which formulate the hypothesis of a city directly constituted by persons "living according to the guidance of reason,"[5] who are consequently free from the desires and fears that the *vulgus*—that is, the vulgar or the crowd—obey, but who are capable of ruling themselves directly by the perception of the "common notions" of all humanity. Without entering here into the never-ending discussion regarding the exact nature of the "wisdom" defined in the *Ethics* by the third kind of knowledge and by the "intellectual love of God," we may nevertheless pose the following question: once it is possible to find a path, however arduous it might be, to *free oneself* from the passions, that is, to combat sad passions not only by reinforcing joyous passions but by developing *active* affections, which would immediately result from an adequate knowledge of causes, does not the hypothesis posed one moment but just as quickly rejected (since "men" in general *do not live* according to the guidance of reason) become in turn a reality, either as the "end" of history or as the project of a society of free persons, bound together by friendship and by the common enterprise of knowledge and living together, without internal or external conflict, in the midst of the crowd of others? But such a society would thus reconstitute, whether or not one wishes it, a "state within the state (*imperium in imperio*)." This is true even without taking into account that by projecting a pure exercise of intelligence for a small number that would coincide with a retreat from the collectivity, or at least with a neutralization or negation of the effects of society on the individual, Spinozist "wisdom" would once again become the watchword of an asceticism, of an absolute autonomy of the individual, in short, the fantasy of a "self-mastery" that completely contradicts Spinoza's analysis of the concatenation of natural causes and the development of the power of bodies.

More plainly still, the guiding thread of the argument of the *Theologico-Political Treatise* leads to a definition of a regime by which antagonistic passions—essentially the religious passions that are generated by the inevitable difference of opinions regarding the divinity (that is, the supreme subject from whom the moral commandments of love and justice seem to emanate), and which thus transform this love into mutual hate—may be neutralized. But this neutralization, which is indeed at this point explicitly a reduction of the "mass" as a form of social existence, is equally problematic.

It leads Spinoza to define—not only regarding Mosaic theocracy, but also regarding Dutch democracy such as it is or should be—a modality of obedience to the law in which love and the conscious choice of the lesser evil would be entirely substituted for the fear of punishment. Must we, then, represent such obedience as the resurgence of the limit case that we evoked a moment ago (as *Ethics* IV, proposition 73 moreover suggests), and which we might be tempted to define, according to a dialectic that is hardly Spinozist, as an "obedience/nonobedience," a "state/nonstate" (as Lenin would later say), or, if one wishes, a withering away of the state in the fulfillment of its end? Or must we generalize the surprising formula of chapter XVII, which evokes the "constant practice of obedience" of the Hebrews ("by reason of habit it must have no longer seemed like servitude to them, but freedom"), while combining it with the initial thesis of the same chapter, and thus approaching the idea of a political freedom which consists essentially in the imagination (hence the illusion) of freedom—called love (or obedience through love?[6] In other words, must we recognize Spinoza as one of the classic theorists of "voluntary servitude"?

We know that this neutralization of antagonism is concentrated in the statement of the "doctrines of universal faith" and of their practical function (since they must permit everyone to practice justice and charity *in his works*, whatever his opinions, and thus institute a sort of equivalence of theological hypotheses under the control of public powers). But how are we to think of these dogmas themselves? Are they an outward appearance common to different religious conceptions and, as a result, immanent in imaginary thought? Are they in this sense accepted by everyone by virtue of the collective practice of men who communicate amongst themselves in spite of their differences, and thus themselves produce the conditions of their coexistence and their mutual commerce? Or on the contrary, do they result from an idea of the understanding that the philosopher produces apart from the crowd by abstracting himself from its conflicts and by applying to it a method of historical critique based on scientific axioms, and which he proposes to the state (that is, to its magistrates or regents) to impose on the crowd and on itself, in the perspective of an arbitrage (*jus circa sacra*) and of a reasoned progress, as it will be envisaged by the *Aufklärung*?

The very meaning of Spinozist theology and ecclesiology clearly depends on this alternative. At the limit, it is either a radical, popular version of the *Imitation of Jesus Christ* in the tradition of the medieval *Devotio moderna* and of all "liberation theologies," or a bourgeois, pre-Rousseauian and pre-Kantian "natural religion."

Certainly the sterility of this sort of alternative is in one sense precisely what the *Theologico-Political Treatise* seeks to displace. But it is doubtful that its final chapter produces in this regard anything but an aporia to the extent that it is led back to a double interpellation, directed toward both the citizens and the state, so as to ask them to recognize the interest they would have in making these doctrines the limiting rule of their behavior. The acknowledgment of this aporia can be read clearly in the note that figures at the end of the preface: Spinoza reserves this book—intended and composed as a direct intervention in the political conjuncture of the crisis of the Republic, in order to defend a certain form of state given as democratic, by helping it to reform itself—for philosophers and dissuades "others" from reading it, that is, he fears seeing it read by the *vulgus*, the man of the crowd, "from whom nothing is to be hoped," because superstition and fear cannot be extirpated from his soul.

Doubtless these are at bottom the very difficulties that pervade the use Spinoza makes in the *Theologico-Political Treatise* of the concept of "common notions," about which the text of the work never clearly permits us to decide if they are defined *theoretically* as axioms of natural reason, or if they are defined *practically* as the perception of utility, similar for all men, at the heart of the imagination. This is perhaps—we must here be content to formulate this as a hypothesis—the index of the fact that, by transplanting the thesis of the *Ethics*, according to which inadequate ideas themselves have a reality and a truth in relation to those who think them, to the terrain of concrete analysis and political intervention, the *Theologico-Political Treatise* is led in practice to modify the apparently rigid and intellectualist definition of the first two kinds of knowledge (hence implicitly of the third as well, moving even further away from the intellectual elitism that characterized the *Treatise on the Improvement of the Understanding*, to which, as Deleuze clearly explains, the theory of "common notions" is opposed).[7]

But these difficulties are also quite obviously those derived from Spinoza's position on the movement of the religious mass described in the *Theologico-Political Treatise* and in the *Ethics*, and through it, of the religious mass that threatens the Dutch Republic from within at the moment that Spinoza is writing. For this mass is at the same time the force that must be dissolved in order to deprive the monarchist subversion of its "mass base" and the force that must be constituted in order to enlarge the democratic base of the Republic. Perhaps it is even the force that would have to be developed, on account of the vigor of its faith in the Gospel and its morality, while being purged of its superstitions and its intolerance.

Death in the Life of the People

Before going further, it is necessary to look at the quite striking evolution of

Spinoza's terminology, which eventually leads to the concept of the "masses" getting its name: *multitudo*.[8]

It is no accident that the term is completely absent from the *Ethics*. More precisely, it appears only once, in the sense of the numerical indefinite: "*in multitudine causarum*" (*Ethics*, V, scholium to proposition 20). But even in this sense, which is as important in the characterization of the relation of the modes to substance as it is in exposing the physics of the "agreement" (*convenientia*) and "disagreement" of bodies, everywhere else Spinoza uses other formulations: *multi, plures, plurimi,* and so on. *A fortiori* the *Ethics* does not designate as *multitudo* the sum of the individuals who constitute the human species or a definite community. As we shall see, this absence signifies that the problem of the human "mass" is present in the *Ethics* under another modality which is both more indirect (or more complex) and more essential than numerical determination.

No less significant, however, is the constant reference in the *Ethics* to the *vulgus*, which is generally translated in an indefinite way as "the vulgar," but which always also designates *the crowd*. This reference is present only in the *scholia* (whose strategic function Deleuze has shown), beginning in part II. But the appendix to part I had already referred in this sense to the *ignari* ("the ignorant"). The *Ethics* combines two correlative approaches: first, to relate the whole system of anthropomorphic and teleological illusions, which naturally result from ignorance of natural causes, to the standpoint of the "vulgar"; and second, to explain the necessity of this standpoint in an anthropological way.

The term *vulgus* is obviously derogatory, which would reinforce our suspicion that to escape ignorance is also to extricate oneself from the crowd. However, it can be given an analytical and not merely a polemical signification, since the imagination is simultaneously a kind of knowledge and a kind of life to which everyone's affective forces contribute. Ignorance is, positively, a first kind of (inadequate) knowledge, whose sources are both immediate experience and "hearsay"—that is, the process of circulation of the signs of language and of collective rumors. But the content of the imagination appears from the outset as having a political connotation, since it associates the illusion of human free will with the representation of God as "master" and "king" of nature, or as legislator. Such a representation implies that humanity perceives itself as God's "people," as a set of individuals who enter into a personal relation of love and hate (devotion, divine reward, vengeance, etc.) with him. At the same time that it elicits an inadequate idea of individuality, it has already come to constitute an anticipation, an inverted guarantee of the representation which submits the crowd to a monarchical political power by conferring on this power the appearance of "divine right."

It is only in the *Theologico-Political Treatise* that a strict connection among *plebs, vulgus,* and, for the first time, *multitudo* is established. But this connection remains very ambivalent, as we shall see.

At first glance, all these terms are reserved for the aspect that is negative, antagonistic, and "violent"—destructive of social life, as opposed to the positive aspect of natural right designated by the *populus,* the collection of the *cives.* In chapter XVI in particular, which is quite remarkable in comparison with the *Political Treatise,* Spinoza never speaks either of *multitudo* or *plebs* or *vulgus,* not even in relation to democracy, which he presents as "the most natural" state—that is, both as one form of state among others (the *imperium populare*) and as the originary truth of the different constitutions. But although *vulgus* (which essentially has an epistemological connotation: it is the ignorant, if not backward, crowd, characterized by its prejudices) and *plebs* (which has a sociopolitical connotation: it is the mass of the people in opposition to those who govern, and thus, whether by right or merely in fact, "inferiors") are present from beginning to end in the *Theologico-Political Treatise, multitudo,* which represents the unity of the two aspects, intervenes only at three strategic points which are worth examining more closely.

The first occurrence is in the preface, in the analysis of the mechanism of popular superstition. Here it is a question, as we know, of a system, or better, of a political and ideological apparatus for the subjugation of thought:

> The cause that engenders, preserves, and fosters superstition is therefore fear....All men are by nature subject to superstition....As the crowd (*vulgus*) always remains at the same level of misery, so it is never long contented....This inconstancy has been the cause of many upheavals and terrible wars....Nothing is as effective in ruling the masses as superstition (*nihil efficacius multitudinem regit, quam superstitio*)....The greatest care has been taken to invest religion, whether true or false, with pomp and circumstance (*cultu et apparatu*) to give it more weight than any other motive....No one has surpassed the Turks in the use of such measures....The greatest interest and the greatest secret of the monarchical regime is to deceive all men. (preface to *TPT*)

These indications will later be confirmed by the description of the Hebrew state and by references to the catastrophic history of the English monarchy. Exploiting a natural fear in each individual, the monarchical and ecclesiastical apparatus of superstition reproduces it and so expands it as a mass phenomenon, thus rendering it uncontrollable. The monarchical regime, for this reason, is a regression to the initial barbarism of humanity, or, more precisely, it is a production of the only barbarism that seems truly without hope: *Ultimi barbarorum!*

Men, then, "fight for slavery as if for salvation, and count it not shame but the highest honor to risk their blood and their lives for the vainglory of one man" (*ibid.*). This is a surprising thesis on Spinoza's part, since this inversion of the natural *conatus*[9] of individuals goes so far as to give substance, in the fury of mass movements, to the desire for their own death, to self-destruction. In fact, this extreme, in which nature seems to contradict itself *qua* instinct of self-preservation, must be connected to the veritable circle of death described later by Spinoza when he analyzes the concatenation of tyrannical monarchies and popular revolutions:

> It is no less dangerous to overthrow a monarch even if it is established by all means that he is a tyrant....For how will [the new king] be able to endure the sight of citizens whose hands are stained with the blood of the murdered king and yet rejoice in this parricide as a good deed that they cannot fail to consider as an example for him....He will not be able easily to avenge the death of the tyrant by executing those citizens unless he defends the cause of the tyrant he has succeeded, thus approving of his actions and consequently following in his footsteps. So it happens that the people (*populus*) have often been able to change tyrants but never to remove tyranny or change the monarchical government (*imperium*) into another form. The English people have furnished a fatal example of this impossibility....After much bloodshed they could do no better than to salute a new monarch under another name (as if the question were simply the name given to the sovereign)....Too late, the people perceived that they had done nothing for the good of the nation but violate the rights of the legitimate king and change the existing order into something worse. (*TPT*, XVIII)

The revolution devours its own children and leads to restoration.

Here Spinoza is naturally thinking about Cromwell, and more generally about the contemporaneous controversy over regicide. What is significant is not only that he does not adopt the theocratic perspective (illustrated, for example, by his contemporary Racine in *Athalie*), but that he shows that such a perspective is internal to the affective mechanism that encloses the monarchy and the people within a circle of death. Nor, consequently, is it a question of a "war of all against all" in Hobbes's sense, that is, of an essentialist anthropology. The violence and the threat of death that civil or external wars imply do not express a "primitive," originary condition, situated prior to the civil state and more or less well repressed by its constitution. The negativity they introduce is not the antithesis of the rule of law, each term excluding the other by definition, but rather the extreme consequence of its own history, the effect of an inversion of human desire brought about by its immanent antagonisms, in determinate conditions. We are—I shall return to this—poles apart from Hobbes.

After this overture, *multitudo* appears again only in chapters XVII and XVIII of the *Theologico-Political Treatise*:

> All, those who govern as much as those who are governed, are men, and as such are inclined to abandon work and seek pleasure (*ex labore proclives ad libidinem*). Whoever has experienced the inconstant temperament of the multitude will be brought to despair by it. For it is governed not by reason but by the affects alone. (*TPT*, XVII)

Such is the danger and the problem that every state must confront by combining affective means (piety, patriotic devotion) with rational ones (utility, hence private property).

But at the end of political corruption the danger arises again, uncontrollably:

> In a state of this sort, it is the wrath of the people that rules over all. Pilate, by giving in to the anger of the Pharisees, ordered the crucifixion of Christ....Following the example of the Pharisees, the vilest hypocrites, moved by the same rage, everywhere began to persecute men of signal intelligence and striking virtue, whose very qualities made them odious to the mob (*plebi invisos*), by denouncing their opinions as abominable and inflaming the anger of the ferocious mob against them. (*TPT*, XVIII)

These passionate, if not themselves "passional" formulations are at the heart of the political and historical argumentation of chapters XVII and XVIII of the *Theologico-Political Treatise*, which alone provides the complete meaning of the contract theory explained in chapter XVI, and confers on it after the fact a properly dialectical function.[10] It is, in fact, exactly the same system of causes that, under new conditions, explains first the remarkable stability of the Hebrew state (in particular, the institutionalization of patriotic hate, "stronger than any other feeling, a hate born of devotion, of piety, believed to be pious—the strongest and most persistent kind" [*TPT*, XVII]), and later its progressive and total ruin. This is why such a ruin can only appear to those who provoke and suffer it as the anticipated, already foreseen "vengeance" of the divine legislator. This is also why its genuine explanation requires a *history* of the Hebrew people, in particular of the evolution of institutions toward a conflict of political and religious powers. The concept of *multitudo* becomes, then, *par excellence*, the element that allows Spinoza's political thought to move from abstraction to the concrete unity of theory and practice, as the beginning of chapter XVII indicates.

We thereby come to the most important aspect of his demonstration: to show that, in all cases, *the principal danger for the state is always internal*, always constituted by the people itself.

> It has never come to the point that the security of the state was less threatened by its citizens (*cives*) than by external enemies (*hostes*) and that those in power (*qui imperium tenent*) feared the former less than the latter. The Roman Republic is testimony to this. (*TPT*, XVII)

In other words, it is the natural conditions of the *civitas*, of the constitution of a people in and by the state (since there is no "people" outside of the state) that imply the tendency to civil war. Whence comes the necessity (taken over from Machiavelli) of arming the people, who themselves represent the principal danger, on the condition of being able to create a devotion and a discipline which become for them like a second nature. Whence comes above all the necessity of limiting the violence of the state against individuals so that it does not lead to the counterviolence of the masses.

Therefore the people (*populus*) and the *multitudo* are not something essentially different: a historical process makes the people exist as *multitudo*, that is, as its apparent negation, the "crowd"; and a certain practice controls its evolution. But the conclusion remains entirely aporetic: from the fact that the causes of ruin are always internal, Spinoza concludes that every revolution is by nature detrimental. The form of the existing state, whatever it might be, must above all be preserved with the habits of thought that it has implanted in the popular soul (*populi animus*) and to which the disposition (*ingenium*) of each is adapted. Every mass movement is synonymous with internal slavery and can lead only to replacing one tyranny with another. It is, in this sense, already internally "monarchical" by nature. No collective means or political practice corresponds to the practical task that is imposed on the citizens: to conserve or develop for themselves the constitution, the form of agreement or mutual relation which liberates them to the greatest degree from fear and violence. Democracy is desirable, but it is unarmed.

The Return to the Mass

After the tragic event of 1672 (the Orangist Revolution) that "verifies" his foresight while contradicting his efforts, Spinoza, consistent with himself, will not modify this conclusion. But he will try to reconsider the whole problem of the state's "foundations" in a way that is both more radical (by making *multitudo* the very concept of the people who must be governed, and from whom the governors must be chosen) and less "savage" (by displacing the analysis from imaginary processes to juridical institutions and administrative statistics). The aporia will not disappear, but the *multitudo* will become the fundamental concept of his political theory, as Negri has brilliantly demonstrated.

In fact, we may see in the *Political Treatise* a genuine explosion of the concept of "mass" which now covers all aspects of the political problem, both at the "theoretical" level of natural right and at the "practical" level of the regulation of each political regime. This innovation in relation to the *Ethics* and even to the *Theologico-Political Treatise* (both of which Spinoza refers to as presupposed by the *Political Treatise*) reflects the fact that natural right is now, for the first time, thought explicitly as the *power of the mass* (*potentia multitudinis*), hence as the "right of number" (since *jus* = *potentia*), not, of course, in the sense of an arithmetic sum but in the sense of a combination, or rather, an interaction of forces. The different forms of the state are so many modalities of this interaction, which permits Spinoza, while preserving their traditional distinction, to go beyond arithmetic formalism (power of one, of several, of all) and to analyze them according to the dialectical progression of a more fundamental question, that of "absolute power" (*imperium absolutum*). Let us say more explicitly that what is at stake is the question of the *absoluteness of power*: to what extent it is absolute, and under what conditions. The connection between *multitudo* and *imperium*, between modalities of the existence of the "mass" and modalities of the functioning of the "state," therefore, constitutes the internal workings of all politics, and is thus the guiding thread of the argument of the *Political Treatise*.

The divergence between Hobbes and Spinoza appears in its greatest clarity here, as does the reason for which Spinoza finally renounced the use of the concept of an original *contract*, even under the already very different form that he had given to it in the *Theologico-Political Treatise* (since this form was not purely juridical, or metajuridical, but from the outset historical, and included an analysis of the imaginary "guarantees" that overdetermine the pact and make it effective).

Hobbes no less than Spinoza, of course, is a theorist haunted by the fear of the masses and their natural tendency to subversion. His entire organization of the state, including the way in which the distinction between the public and the private spheres operates, can be understood as a system of preventive defense against the mass movements that form the basis of civil wars (of classes and of religions) and of revolutions. It is in this context that the *multitudo* becomes in his writings the initial concept in the definition of the contract (see *De Cive*, chapter VI, and *Leviathan*, chapters XVII and XVIII), in order to constitute the system juridically, and establish it ideologically (on equality). *But in Hobbes's writings it is only a question of a point of departure*, which is immediately left behind. Hobbes carefully separates the two elements that Spinoza wants to bring together (thus intimately combining democratism and Machiavellian realism). For Hobbes the "multitude" that establishes the contract is not the concept of the "mass"; it is the concept ("methodologically" individualist, as current Anglo-American sociologists say) of a "people" always already decomposed, reduced in advance (preventively) to the sum of its constituent atoms (people in the state of nature), and capable of entering one by one, through the contract, into the new institutional relationship of civil society. It is this Hobbesian "multitude," let us remark, whose concept Locke—the philosopher of "tolerance" in a sense diametrically opposed to Spinoza, despite certain verbal similarities—will transform in chapter VIII of the *Second Treatise*, in order to show that majority agreement takes the place of the act of all, or of unanimity, both by right and in fact.

Spinoza, on the other hand, immediately combines these two elements. He speaks from the outset of the role of the "multitude" in the constitution of the state, understanding it not as the abstraction of the people, but as the historical and political reality of the mass and of crowds in movement. This is why the role of the concept in his case is not that of an abstract presupposition immediately denied, superseded in a teleological dialectic, but that of a principle of concrete analysis, which proceeds by expanding continuously within a constructive dialectic. This is why, above all, the question of *unanimity*, which is no less central for Spinoza than for Hobbes, acquires a diametrically opposite significance. For Hobbes, unanimity is the essence of the political machine, implied logically in its very apparatus. For Spinoza unanimity is a problem.

The existence of the state is that of an individual of individuals that cannot exist without forging for itself a "quasi-soul," that is, the analogue of an individual will: "the body of the state (*imperii corpus*) must be directed as if by a single soul (*una veluti mente duci*), and this is why the will of the commonwealth (*civitatis voluntas*) must be taken for the will of all (*pro omnium voluntate*)" (*PT*, III, 5). But this unanimity is not acquired automatically (*a fortiori* it is not guaranteed *a priori* as in Rousseau, in the metaphysical idea of the general will, at the risk of seeing the initially repressed specter of "fractions" and "particular societies" re-emerge afterward on the terrain of practice).[11] It must be constructed as a function of the constraints that constitute the movements of the minds or souls of the mass (*PT*, VIII, 41: *multitudinis animos movere*) and of the greater or lesser knowledge or information about the commonwealth that their own instruction and the form of institutions procure for different individuals. The problem of unanimity is identical to that of the material conditions of obedience, hence to that of the conditions that make possible a representation of the multitude in the state, and to that of the condition of an effective power of decision-making.

And yet the constitutive role of the *multitudo* very much risks, in spite of everything, appearing as purely theoretical, in the bad sense of the term, in the sense of a theory which remains irreducibly inadequate to practice. It is clear that this is a permanent preoccupation in the *Political Treatise*. Chapter X constitutes in my eyes the proof and practically the admission of this difficulty: before even coming to the aporia characteristic of democracy, it is the very construction of the aristocratic state, the stability (the "absolute" character) of which is after the fact once again put to the test and is found to be inadequate *in its own kind*. A new moral principle which confers on this construction the "supplement" of a necessary stability must then be invoked: civic virtue, the love of laws after the Roman manner, "for laws are the state's soul. As long as they are preserved, the state is necessarily preserved. But the laws cannot remain inviolate unless they are under the protection of both reason and affects common to all men" (*PT*, X, 9).

Now, the heart of the argument of the *Political Treatise* (and of its own particular "realism") had been on the contrary the principle posed at the beginning, according to which:

> If human nature were so constituted that men most desired what is most useful, no art would be needed to maintain harmony and trust. But as it is certain that human nature is otherwise constituted, the state must be so ordered that all, those who govern as well and those who are governed, willingly or unwillingly, act to benefit the common good; that all, whether by their own will or by force or necessity, are compelled to live according to the dictates of reason. (*PT*, VI, 3)

Stated at the opening of the analysis of the monarchy, this principle nonetheless has a general scope. We must therefore assume that it has in the meantime been modified or corrected. It remains the case that chapter X ends with what can only appear as a pious wish: faced with the critical situations in which the mass is terrorized by the dangers it must confront, and in which it tends to throw itself into the arms of a providential man, "it would be necessary to return to pre-established laws, accepted by everyone" (*PT*, X, 10). But what, if not a petition of principle, proves that we will not instead see the state sink into an inexpiable civil war?

If one is willing to consider the *Political Treatise* not as the execution of a pre-established, perfectly coherent plan, already certain of its conclusions, but as an experiment in thought, or better yet, a theoretical experiment fraught with its own internal difficulties, then the absence of a theory of democracy, which has always aroused the irritation of exegetes and which has given rise to occasionally ingenious attempts to supply what is missing, will appear to us in a new light. We shall not be able to remain content with the accident that the death of the author constitutes, still less with proposing to put ourselves in his place in order to deduce this theory from the general lines of the initially posed principles. We should indeed ask ourselves what, in the very definition of concepts, finally leads to theoretical blockage, and makes the constitution of a coherent theory of "democracy" impossible, inasmuch as its concept would be fundamentally equivocal. Such a reading would not constitute—far from it—a "refutation" of Spinoza or a disqualification of his standpoint, of which there have been so many. It might on the contrary reveal the power of this standpoint even more, if only because it would forbid our finding in him a kind of circular thought in which initial theoretical principles are never anything but the abstract anticipation of the conclusions. In this case such a circle would make the initial definition of natural right, the foundation of the state on the agreement of the multitude of individuals, into the advance guarantee of the final "discovery," namely that the democratic state is by nature the best, the most "natural" or most stable state, according to the line of thought characteristic of all bourgeois liberalism.

Let us say things differently. The constitutive relation between the masses and the state (*multitudo* and *imperium*) is thought in a rigorous way from the outset by Spinoza as an internal contradiction. The argument of the *Political Treatise* is thus the most explicitly dialectical of his writings: exploring the ways to resolve a contradiction means first of all developing its terms.

The thesis that appeared in the *Theologico-Political Treatise* as a statement of historical fact this time becomes the very principle of analysis (and Spinoza rereads Machiavelli in order to search the latter's work for everything that already reflects the implications of this thesis): "it is certain that the commonwealth is always threatened by citizens more than by external enemies, for good citizens are rare" (*PT*, VI, 6). I will return later to the essential correlate of this thesis: that the dissolution of the state under the effect of its internal contradictions is never total.

By the same token, the following political thesis is reaffirmed (after 1672): changing the form of the state by a revolution or counterrevolution is always the worst solution (which is why it is important to show that every form of the state can be stable, "absolute" in its kind, or, if I may be permitted the expression, "relatively absolute" or historically viable).

The fear of the masses, in its ambivalence, is more than ever the fundamental question: the entire inquiry of the *Political Treatise* is devoted, therefore, to the attempt *to find the point of equilibrium* (or points of equilibrium) between the power of the mass and the power of those who govern, it being understood that it is a question precisely of the *same* power, caught up in a process of division and combination, hence at the same time one or concentrated, and multiple or dispersed, expressed in both obedience (or rebellion) and decision (or indecision). Or again: this inquiry seeks the point of equilibrium, of "political balance," that permits *both* the mass and those who govern to master the terror that they reciprocally inspire, instead of allowing themselves to be led by it into a whirlpool of death. Then the concept of a *libera multitudo* (a free mass or a mass "in freedom") can no longer designate only an external political datum (the fact that a state is constituted by itself and not by conquest), but would express the intrinsic quality of a social existence which has the "cult of life" (*PT*, V, 6).

Since I cannot follow here in detail the paths of this inquiry from one chapter to another of the *Political Treatise*, according to its unfinished dialectical progression, I wish only to recall what can clearly be seen in the insistence of a characteristic theme introduced in relation to monarchy: that of the "return to the mass," the risk and even the inevitable occurrence of which is implied by the nature of a state which constructs its "soul" by representing all wills by the will of a single mortal individual:

> The form of the state must remain the same, and thus there must be only one king, always of the same sex, and sovereignty must be indivisible. As to my saying that the king's oldest son should succeed him...it is clear that the election of the king by the mass (*quae a multitudine fit*) should be, if possible, eternal. Otherwise, it will necessarily happen that sovereign power will pass on to the mass of the population, the greatest possible change and for that reason an extremely dangerous one....In the civil state everyone maintains the same right after death that he had in his lifetime, not by his own power but by the power of the commonwealth, which is eternal. The case (*ratio*) of the king is completely different: the king's will is the civil law itself, and the king is the commonwealth itself. When the king dies, the commonwealth also, in a sense, dies, and sovereign power thereby returns by nature to the mass (*summa potestas ad multitudinem naturaliter redit*), which then has the right to pass new laws and abolish old ones. (*PT*, VII, 25; the entire paragraph is essential)

A little further on (chapter VIII, section 3), Spinoza summarizes his argument by writing: "kings are mortal, assemblies are eternal; power once transferred to a sufficiently large assembly will therefore never return to the mass (*nunquam ad multitudinem redit*)....We conclude, therefore, that power conferred on a sufficiently large assembly is absolute or comes very close to being absolute."

Let us pause here for a moment. Such is indeed the thread of the argument that seeks a stable equilibrium which would confer a kind of eternity on the state: to find the construction that will prevent forever, insofar as it is humanly thinkable, the "return to the mass" by making the representation of the people no longer physical and individual but juridical and collective.

But Spinoza continues: "If there exists an absolute power, this can only be that which is possessed by the entire people (*quod integra multitudo tenet*)." *One more step*, after monarchy and aristocracy, according to the logic of this political calculus, and we would have the democratic solution to the problem. But this final step is a contradiction in terms: *what, indeed, would be the concept of a power definitively removed from the risk of the* "*return to the mass*" because it would always already have belonged to this entire mass? Or perhaps: if the mass is by nature "frightening to those in power (*multitudo imperantibus formidolosa est*)" (*PT*, VIII, 4), which means that "in practice power is not absolute," *to what extent can the passage to the limit (democracy) guarantee that the mass in power will not be frightening to itself*?

Let us go even further. Seeking progressively to construct the conditions of unanimity (hence the obedience of the social body to the law that is "like a soul" for it), the *Political Treatise* weaves together several threads, it pursues several unequally developed ideas.

One of these ideas, which remains secondary, echoes the interest of the *Theologico-Political Treatise* in the life of the imagination, by examining the conditions under which the government will not provoke "the indignation of the largest part of the population (*maximae partis multitudinis*)" (*PT*, III, 9; VII, 2; etc.), whether because the king or the aristocracy seduce the crowd, or because they surround their own figure with prestige, or because a combination of tolerance and state religion is established in the state.

But the main idea is henceforth quite different: it concerns the recognition of the "common notions" that express both public utility and the interest of each person, that is, the very preservation of the social body. Spinoza's thought here divides once again according to antithetical "affective" postulates.

On the one hand, a series of texts (in which, significantly, *plebs* and *vulgus*, indeed *turba*, once again come to connote *multitudo*) states a "pessimistic" thesis, according to which the crowd is incapable of governing itself, of moderating itself, for the divisions in its midst from which seditions arise are always being reborn:

> It is obvious that the whole mass (*multitudo integra*) will never transfer its right to a few men or to one alone if it could be in agreement with itself and if the controversies that often occur in large assemblies (*ex controversiis quae plerumque in magnis conciliis excitantur*) did not lead to sedition. (*PT*, VII, 5)

And again:

> Men, as we have said, are by nature enemies (*natura hostes*), and their nature persists despite the laws that bind and unite them. It is for this reason that democratic states change into aristocracies, and aristocracies into monarchies. I am persuad-

ed that most aristocratic states used to be democracies. (*PT*, VIII, 12)

And finally:

> The first possible cause of the dissolution [of aristocracies] is indicated by that most astute Florentine in his *Discourses* on Livy (III, 1): *every day in a state*, as in a human body, *there are certain elements that join with others (quotidie aggregatur aliquid) and from time to time require medical treatment*: it is therefore at times necessary for something to bring the state back to the principles on which it was founded. If this does not occur in time, the infection will spread until it cannot be suppressed except by suppressing the state itself. (*PT*, X, 1)

This thesis therefore leads us tendentially toward a Platonizing logic of the degradation of the political "absolute" or of the power of states.

But on the other hand Spinoza rediscovers the "optimistic" postulate already stated by the *Theologico-Political Treatise* (XVI): "It is almost impossible for the majority of a single assembly, if it is a large one, to agree on an absurdity." When solitude threatens (*PT*, VI, 1), when their vital interest is at stake, a *large number* of individuals cannot err in the majority; better yet, *the multitude as such cannot become absolutely delirious* (see, for example, *PT*, IV, 4; VII, 4 and 7): "human nature is so constituted that each man ardently seeks what is useful to himself...and defends another's cause to the extent that he thinks by this to improve his own situation.... Although a council composed of a great number of citizens will necessarily include ignorant men it is nonetheless certain that ...the majority of this assembly will never want to wage war, but will always love and pursue peace."[12] Referring whether explicitly or not to this thesis—which is not so much "utilitarian" as vitalist—Spinoza constructs a model of the equilibrium of powers, a hierarchical system of "councils" of government which maximize the possibilities of deliberation and of rational decision. Whence this astonishing sentence: "the number of patricians can be much greater than that of the mass. It is only in their too small number that peril lies" (*PT*, VIII, 13).

Here we are at the heart of the endeavor of the *Political Treatise*. The constructions it proposes to us are not so much juridical as numerical or, if you will, *statistical* (preserving for the term its initial double meaning, which Spinoza could have received from mercantilism, and which he seeks to elaborate in a constitutional sense). These functional relations (*rationes*) between parts of the multitude, between the leaders and the led, between executive power, deliberative power, and power of oversight, always have simultaneously a triple function: first, to *fix* the state's structure or to individualize its form; second, to *decompose* the existing multitude in order to rationally *recompose* it with respect to existing conditions ("economic" conditions such as commerce, wealth and poverty, for example, are evoked in passing, but especially important are the "cultural" conditions of knowledge and ignorance); finally, to set out the conditions of an effective political *decision-making* (for example compelling the patricians to form a unique body directed by a common thought) and to constitute the instances charged with overseeing its rationality.

Spinoza's "statistics" must be able to be read both as a "science of the state" and as a "science of the population," both from the standpoint of the *imperium* (security, regulation of obedience and of deliberation) and from that of the *multitudo* (effective decision-making, concentration of its power to act). It is a sort of political version of double-entry bookkeeping. Several recent interpreters have seen the importance and the originality of this enterprise: for example, Mugnier-Pollet speaks of a "veritable political metrics," which is still too Platonic a term. Matheron puts into play and brilliantly develops the calculations indicated by Spinoza, seeking a passage from "static equilibrium" to the "dynamic equilibrium" of the social body. On this point Negri is wrong, in my view, to argue that the Spinozist notion of "constitution," insofar as it represents the development of the power of the multitude, does not leave any room for the idea of mediation. Certainly Spinoza challenges the juridical mediation of the contractual type as the real or imaginary foundation of sovereignty. But this is in order better to develop, in the *Political Treatise*, an analysis of institutional mediation. This makes him one of the first theorists of the modern *state apparatus* (I agree on this point with Pierre-François Moreau's interpretation), whereas Machiavelli, notwithstanding his reflection on the organization of the army, limited himself to an analysis of state power as a source or object of political strategy, and Hobbes, as we have said, limited himself to the distinction between the public and the private *spheres* (in order to determine which "societies," distinct from the state itself, can legitimately exist without constituting "fiefdoms" or "states within the state").[13]

But once again the result is theoretically aporetic, just as it is politically equivocal (in particular in the use of the notion of *absolute*). How does this construction, however significant it may be from the historical point of view, actually respond to the question posed?

To organize numerically the relationship *imperium/multitudo* (state or state power/masses) is indeed to introduce into *each* form of the state a principle which is in fact democratic. This would not be an ideal foundation of sovereignty, but a regulative mechanism and a natural tendency. Even a monarchy is stable or "absolute" only if—repudiating the tyrannical practices that, under the apparent omnipotence of a single person, in fact hide a disguised aristocracy and the ferment of anarchy (*PT*, VI, 5)—it becomes not only a constitutional monarchy—limiting itself by imposing constraints, like Ulysses before the Sirens (*PT*, VII, 1)—but a monarchy which makes maximum room in its midst for the democratic element (if only William of Orange could understand this warning, Spinoza perhaps was thinking!). The same is true, *a fortiori*, for aristocracy: whence the demonstration that establishes the superiority of urban "federative" aristocracy (*PT*, IX) over centralized aristocracy (the domination of a city over its "countryside") in which the subjects remain foreigners (*PT*, VIII, 9-12)—which perhaps reveals the causes of the collapse of the republican regime in 1672, to the extent that federalism tended to deteriorate into Dutch centralism (*PT*, IX, 2).

But, once again, *what is democracy itself,* if it must finally be defined as a fully functioning regime, a concept in its own right, and not only as an "element" or a stabilizing "tendency" at work within the institutions of other regimes? From the moment that Spinoza—wishing to link theory to practice—begins to reflect on institutions, democracy is no more than the *limit* of the perfecting of aristocracy, according to the same "statistical" principle of decomposition and recomposition of the *multitudo*. As a result, paradoxically, democracy is never able to find its own principle.

The aporia is once again inevitable, from the moment that the very nature of the concepts used implies both the necessity of multiplying the institutions that *fix* the aristocracy by incorporating into its hierarchy of "councils" the entire *multitudo,* and the necessity of radically transforming its principle, which is always based on external control, still prisoner of the rule expressed by the "*terrere, nisi paveant*": the mass terrorizes if it is not afraid![14] The initial definition of aristocracy already entirely contained it:

> It thus appears that the best condition (*conditionem optimam*) of
> such a state will be if it is as close as possible to an absolute state,
> that is, by making the mass as little to be feared as possible, and
> granting it no other freedom than that necessarily accorded it by
> the constitution of the state. This freedom is less the right of the

> mass than that of the state as a whole (*non tam multitudinis, quam totius imperii jus*), which only the nobility (*Optimates*) can demand and maintain as their own. (*PT*, VIII, 5)

And Spinoza adds: "It is in this way that practice will best agree with theory...as is self-evident." Perhaps, but how can this affirmation be reconciled with the perspective of an identification of the sovereign assembly and the entire people without the fundamental definition of natural right as *potentia multitudinis*, "power of the mass," quite far from being "conserved in the civil state itself," being emptied of its effective content?

Every state is "absolute" to the extent that its structure realizes the democratic tendency. But democracy itself can never be defined except as a *perfect aristocracy*: an intrinsically contradictory concept. Or to put it another way, the concept of a noncontradictory state (and correlatively of a noncontradictory mass) *is itself contradictory*. Commentators have not ceased to turn in this circle.

From this follows the extreme importance of the troubling formula that specified the meaning of these terms with regard to the selection of patricians from the outset:

> We have named aristocratic the form of state power (*imperium*) which is held not by one man but by a certain number of individuals chosen from the mass (*ex multitudine selecti*) whom we shall from now on refer to as patricians. I say deliberately: a certain number of individuals who are chosen; for this is the principal difference between this state and the democratic state....Thus, even were it the case in some state that the entire multitude (*integra multitudo*) were admitted to the ranks of the patricians, provided that this admittance were not a hereditary right...the state would nonetheless remain an aristocracy in the strict sense that no one was admitted to the ranks of the patrician without having been expressly chosen (*nisi expresse selecti*). (*PT*, VIII, 1)

Here once more the old ideal makes itself heard, the old utopia of a government which would be "best" because it is (and to the extent that it is) the government "of the best," even if it is a question of demonstrating that it is the majority that must be this "best." How can we avoid confronting these formulations with the rough draft of chapter XI concerning the democratic, "absolutely absolute" (*omnino absolutum*) state? This is indeed the crucial moment in which this dialectic, like others, however different they may be, must turn to face its own intellectual challenge. *Hic Rhodus, hic salta*! Here we see Spinoza renounce giving an initial definition of democracy as a particular form of the *imperium/multitudo* relation as he had done for previous regimes. The very fact that it would be tautological (which, in Rousseau, for example, would give it foundational value) obviously constitutes for him an insurmountable obstacle, a sign of the return of the long-deferred utopia. Thus, the evasive maneuvers, the appeal to preliminary considerations: first we must distinguish "various kinds of democracy." We see him finally bogged down in a search for the "natural" criteria of citizenship, justifying the a priori exclusion of this or that "class" (above all, *women*, whose seductive weakness, the final refuge of the passions of the multitude, always poses a mortal danger to the state).[15] And, if I dare say it, we watch him die before this blank page.

Individuality and Communication

I said above that it is not a question here of claiming to "refute" Spinoza, but of seeking to disengage that which constitutes the singular power of his thought, by trying to rescue him from the retrospective confusions that seek by any means to make him the "precursor" of Rousseau, Marx, or Nietzsche. It is a question of trying to understand how, animated contradictorily by his own fear of the masses and by the hope of a democracy understood as mass liberation, Spinoza was able to end up conferring on this concept an importance and a complexity unequaled among his contemporaries or his successors, in historical conditions which, in any case, condemned him to a complete theoretical solitude. This is why, to conclude, I would like to return to concepts which, in advance of the explicit naming of this problem in the *Political Treatise*, express this originality and this actuality in the clearest manner. It is indeed in the *Ethics* and in the *Theologico-Political Treatise* that we shall find them, on the condition that we do not attempt to find in them the coherence of a definitive political or philosophical "solution."

It is not enough to remark, as has already been said, that the theory of the passions in the *Ethics* rests on the development of their ambivalence, from the initial division of the *conatus* to the analysis of the *fluctuatio animi*. Again we must ask ourselves what the "object" of this analysis is.

This object is not the individual but *individuality* or, better, *the form of individuality*: how it is constituted, how it tries to preserve its own form, how it is composed with others according to relations of agreement and disagreement or of activity and passivity. If it is well known that Spinozist individuality is not at all "substance," it is no less important to recall that it is no more "consciousness" or "person" in the juridical or theological sense. Men, finite singular modes, are conscious of their desires and unconscious of the causes that produce them; that is, they "think," which is something quite different. All human individuality is caught up in this way in the *in-between* of the inferior forms of individuality that are composed in it—but which are not for all that dissolved in it—and of the superior forms of individuality into which it can enter—a gradation which could be expressed metaphorically in the language of mathematics by recalling that the "power" of an (infinite) set and that of the set of its "parts" are always incommensurable. This is why, if the soul (the set of thoughts) must be defined as the "idea of the body," individuality not only has nothing to do with a "union of the soul and the body," it completely excludes this mystical representation.[16]

If we return, then, to the analysis of the passions, or to the life of the imagination, we see that the vacillation of the mind is explained both by the complexity or multiplicity of the body and by that of external relations with other "ambiant" (Gueroult) bodies: it is in the encounter of these two multiplicities—which it is utterly impossible for man to know adequately, but of which he always perceives a part—that the conflict of affections emerges.

Still more remarkable is the analysis of the mechanism of this encounter: men—who try to preserve themselves and increase their power of acting—associate love and hate to *quod simile* (*Ethics*, III, propositions 15-17), that is, to the *trait of resemblance* that they perceive between themselves and external "things," which turn out to be other men. In other words, love and hate are not relationships of "recognition" between subjects: they are *concatenations of affects* which are always *partial*, which are reinforced by the repetition of encounters, by the collision of words and images, and which separate or reunite individuals in the imagination. These concatenations by similarity between parts (which Lacan would call "*morcelées*") are not a modality of the relationship between "ego" and "others." They are transversal (not to mention transferential) relationships which pass from one object to another, below the threshold of corporeal individuality and beyond it. They are not the product of a "consciousness" but rather produce the effect of consciousness, that is, an inadequate knowledge of our corporeal multiplicity, which is inseparable from desire itself, therefore from joy and sadness, fear and hope, and so forth.

Doubtless the most astonishing illustration of this principle of the analysis of the mechanism of affective identification (and of its ambivalence) is to be found in the following definition of *jealousy*:

> If someone imagines that a thing he loves is united with another by as close, or by a closer (*arctiore*), bond of friendship than that with which he himself, alone, possessed the thing, he will be affected with hate toward the thing he loves, and will envy the other...because he is forced to join the image of the thing he loves to the image of him he hates. This latter reason is found, for the most part, in love toward a woman. For he who imagines that a woman he loves prostitutes herself to another (*alteri sese prostituere*) not only will be saddened, because his own appetite is restrained (*ipsius appetitus coercitur*), but also will be repelled by her, because he is forced to join the image of the thing he loves to the shameful parts and excretions of the other (*rei amatae imaginem pudendis et excrementis alterius jungere cogitur*). (*Ethics*, III, proposition 35 and scholium, 1:514)

From that moment it is not arbitrary to affirm that the *Ethics* (essentially in the third and fourth parts) performs a genuine reversal of point of view (anti-Copernican, by anticipation). The process that it studies appears at first to refer to and to be supported by an individual—who is certainly complex but relatively autonomous, indeed isolated—considered abstractly as exemplary of the human species, who would be affected from the outside in diverse and contradictory ways, by both similar and dissimilar things, which it does not master and which in that sense threaten its integrity. In reality, without the idea of individuality (that is, of the stability of a composite) disappearing, without which there would be neither desire nor force (*conatus*), *it is the process itself*, the affective network cutting across each individual, which soon becomes the true "object" (or the true "subject"). Each man, each individual, as such singular, is always both similar and dissimilar to himself and to others, and his subjective isolation is only a fiction. This fiction culminates in the imagination of others' freedom, from which I imagine a certain assistance or obstacle to my own and which carries the passions of love and hate to an extreme (see *Ethics*, III, scholium to proposition 49).

The constitution of individuality and that of the multitude in the imaginary are one and the same problem, one and the same process: what Spinoza calls *affectuum imitatio*. This is why it is not abusive to maintain that the object of Spinozist analysis is, in fact, a system of social relations, or of mass relations, which might be called "imagination," and the concrete example, or better the singular historical form of which, for Spinoza, has always been constituted by religion (and morality). The concept that he proposes for it escapes both "psychologism" and "sociologism." It is not reducible either to the idea of an original intersubjectivity (such as can be found, for example, in Fichte), or to the idea of a conditioning of individuals by their social conditions of existence (which Marx did not escape).

It is on this basis that Spinoza can demonstrate how passions that are bad in themselves are nonetheless necessary for the commonwealth to discipline the mob (*vulgus*). For, once again, "the mob is terrifying, if unafraid" (*Ethics*, IV, scholium to proposition 54, 1:576). The ambivalence here is in full play, since the esteem (*gloria*) on which the knowledge of power rests, if it can draw its origin from reason, is most often only a "self-esteem (*acquiescentia in se ipso*) that is encouraged only by the opinion of the multitude…and since the struggle is over a good thought to be the highest, this gives rise to a monstrous lust of each to crush (*opprimendi*) the other in any way possible" (*Ethics*, IV, scholium to proposition 58, 1:578).

It is on this basis, finally, that Spinoza can examine in detail the contradictory consequences that continually result from the way in which, identifying others with "representatives" of a general idea of man, each individual always "wants the others to live according to his own temperament" (*Ethics*, III, proposition 31, 1:512) as if it were the condition of his own existence, from which result these practical universals, "vulgar" *par excellence*, that are the ideas of *class* and of *nation* (see *Ethics*, II, scholium I to proposition 40; III, proposition 46).

In other words, Spinoza's object is the relationship through which affects communicate between themselves, and therefore the relationship through which individuals communicate through their affects. In this sense, affective communication is the very concept of the mass. But the effort that traverses this communication from the desire of every person to the desire of all in the commonwealth, signifies that it is always necessary to analyze it according to a polarity. At one of the poles, corresponding to superstition, communication is governed entirely by a process of identification, that is, a misrecognition of real singularities. At the other pole, corresponding to the affirmation of the "common notions" that, like all ideas, are practical actions, communication is the unity of adequate kinds of knowledge and of joyous affects which multiply the strength of individuals. The difficulty—or aporia, it seems to me—of Spinozism comes from the fact that, having from the beginning thought the imagination and the weakness of the "ignorant" human being as an always already social process of collectivization and not as the imperfection or original sin of a "subject," it appears, however, incapable of thinking in its own concepts the knowledge and the mastery of the conditions of existence that the process procures for human beings as an equally collective practice. The crowd vacillates; it does not truly transform itself in order to pass from one "kind of knowledge" to another (or when *one* effects this passage according to the "path" described by Spinoza). The crowd's "history," however requisite from the origin, remains problematic. And this is so in spite of the fact that the Spinozist conception of the objectivity of the idea (the identity of the order and the connection of things and the order and connection of ideas) had posed from the outset that knowledge is not subjective: neither a "becoming-conscious" nor a "will to know," but a process that is immanent in the real itself.[17]

However, if there is on this point an aporia, it is only the counterpart of an idea of immense novelty, not only for its time, but perhaps for our own time: that of a *communication* which, insofar as it is a contradictory relationship, no longer has anything to do with the idea of *communion* (whether in its mechanistic or organicist variants). Not only does the reality of *bodies*, and their internal/external multiplicity, thus definitively replace the fantasy of the "mystical body," but the analysis of the affective ambivalence that structures their reciprocal relationship, on the other side, prevents us from ending up in a mysticism of the body. We may appreciate, in passing, that the violence of excommunication, initially imposed on Spinoza, had thus been overcome by a radical transformation of the very idea of communication. And it can be established that, under these conditions, the question of his historicity rebounds one more time.

The imagination of the masses is the very field within which the argument of the *Theologico-Political Treatise* is inscribed, essentially under the form of prophetism, which is entirely governed by the mechanisms of transference, of identification, and by what might be called the anticipated response of the "prophet" to the demand in which the "temperament" of his people is expressed. This is only a way of saying that those who are recognized as prophets are individuals whose imagination reproduces the collusion of words and images within which a nation lives its identity. This is why the whole history of nations, as Spinoza understands it, is inscribed within the contradiction of a convergence, both necessary and improbable, of religion and the state, of prophetism and rational communication. But if that is so, the final aporia of the *Theologico-Political Treatise* can be read in a way that, at least theoretically, has nothing purely negative about it.

Doubtless the *Theologico-Political Treatise* culminates in the pious wish for a society within which the governors and the governed would hear at the same time the reasonable voice that explains their common interest to them; doubtless the "pact" that is thus proposed to them has as its content a "universal faith" which appears at first to differ little from a "natural religion," which would only lead us back to the ideology of the Enlightenment. But this is only a secondary aspect. The principal aspect is, on the contrary, the fact that Spinoza never stopped analyzing the historicity of religion (and of "superstition"). Therefore the "universal faith," whose practical function is what is important here, has to be produced on the basis of a mass practice and a mass theological tradition. In short—and here we are not only poles apart from the ideology of the Enlightenment, but in opposition to its positivist posterity, whether "secular," "materialist," or even "dialectical materialist"—Spinoza had the audacity to think and to justify theoretically the project of a *collective transformation of religion*, from the inside, as a fundamental *political* task, and to inquire under what conditions such a problem might have a rational meaning.

It may be recalled that one of the sensitive points in the reasoning of the *Theologico-Political Treatise*, in which its aporia is best demonstrated, is to be found in the difficulty of giving a precise meaning to the final "solution" concerning the freedom of thought, which is, however, the very objective of the entire book. In fact, Spinoza says to us that all must agree to "leave human beings the freedom to judge," while denying them the "right to act by [their] own decree," which must be entirely transferred to the sovereign in the interest of all, leaving it up to the sovereign to cede back a part of such right if he judges it possible. Hence, this solution consists—or should consist—in *drawing a line of demarcation* between "private freedom" and "public right" which coincides with the *division between thought and action*.

However—and Spinoza's own text is enough to show it—the drawing of such a line has never occurred except in theory, and in reality it is not rigorously thinkable in Spinozist terms. It is therefore out of the question that "individuals" and "the state" should ever manage to reach an agreement on the modalities of such a demarcation. The distinction between "thought" and "actions" is immediately called back into question, in fact, both by excess and by default. It is called into question by excess, for the freedom to think (to reason, to judge) is nothing without the freedom to communicate one's opinions: *no one*, in practice, *can think all alone*, without expressing his opinions, without communicating, if only with a circle of friends. *The "place" of thought is not the "private" individual* or the "secrecy of conscience" which is its philosophical hypostasis; it is communication itself, whatever its limits or its extension. (We can understand why the *Ethics* does not postulate that "I think" but that "man thinks," and goes on to show that he thinks all the more as his notions become more "common notions.")

On the other hand, the distinction postulated is just as untenable by default for, even when it is not "corrupted," *the state cannot not pose* (and neither can Spinoza) *the question of "seditious opinions"*: "which opinions are seditious in the commonwealth? Those that cannot be posited without nullifying the pact" (*TPT*, XX). Of course, Spinoza tells us that "the one who thinks thus is seditious not on account of his judgment and his opinions in themselves, but on account of the action that such a judgment implies (*propter factum, quod talia judicia involvunt*)" (*ibid.*). But in practice, from the moment that the problem no longer concerns merely isolated individuals but the crowd—or the mass—by what means (other than grace...) can a division be carried out? For in reality since individuals—generally "non-philosophers," and even if they are philosophers—live in and not outside the crowd, *they do not have it in their power not to act in conformity with their opinions*, or to "restrain" the actions that they "imply." The state, therefore, cannot be content to "define" logically which opinions are subversive; it must still seek out *who* thinks subversively, in order to take precautions against them. That is, unless it recognizes that the criterion is inapplicable or insufficient. Spinoza moreover said it clearly: "obedience doesn't concern external action as much as it does the soul's internal action (*animi internam actionem*)" (*TPT*, XVII), and it is on this internal action that the recognition—or lack of it—of the necessity of the commonwealth's laws depends.

It is not difficult to see that, in every case, these difficulties are not sophistical objections but result from what is strongest, most original, and in a sense, most liberating in Spinoza's thought. The reasons for this are to be found in the *Ethics*, as I have indicated in passing. If the individual cannot think without acting in some way (taking account of the fact that in the terminology of the *Ethics* certain actions are only "passions"—but also that every passion, even inadequately, expresses an affirmation, that is, an action), it is because, adequately or not, it is of the essence of the individual to affirm its own being. The individual is by nature desire and therefore *conatus*. It is moreover this same term that Spinoza uses in the *Theologico-Political Treatise*:

> The crime of treason can only be committed by citizens or subjects....A subject is said to have committed this crime when

> he has attempted for whatever reason to seize the sovereign
> power or to transfer it to another. I say *when he has attempted*
> (*dico conatus est*), for if the condemnation were only to follow
> the commission of the crime, the commonwealth would be too
> late, the rights of sovereignty having already been seized or
> transferred to another.... Whatever the reason for the attempt
> (*conatus est*), treason has been committed, and he has been
> justly convicted. (*TPT*, XVI)

The "attempt" to act (for good or evil) begins *always already* "within"
thought; it is "implied" in it. That is, in no way is there, as Spinoza never
ceases to demonstrate, a "decision to act," a "will" coming to be added *after
the fact* to the proper act of understanding, in order either to execute or to
suspend it. This is a proposition which, once more, takes on its full significance only by recognizing the proper object of the *Ethics*: neither the
Cartesian nor the empiricist "subject" but the process or the network of the
circulation of affects and ideas.[18]

With respect to the impossibility of thinking outside of the process of
communication—even if it implies some remarkable difficulties for Spinoza
regarding language—I have already recalled how it is based on the very way
the *Ethics* conceptualizes "thought." But the meaning of these difficulties,
then, is reversed: they deliver a lesson and a positive knowledge. On this precise point I, for my part, would take the risk of proposing that we can try to
read Spinoza by transforming him, against his own "conservative" theses,
but in close conjunction with his own transformational tendency. We can
try to read him, then, not as a failed attempt to *define* the democratic state,
but as an unequaled effort rigorously to think democracy as the *transformation of the state*. And the latter, again, not in its imaginary "chronology" but
in its conditions and its objects.

The Incompressible Minimum

If that which makes the "solution" proposed by the *Theologico-Political
Treatise* impossible—from the moment that we seek to think of it as a fixed
(indeed, codified) reciprocal limitation—is the expansivity of the *conatus*
itself, is it not really because such a juridical solution, or such a juridical
understanding of the solution, is entirely heterogeneous to the problematic
in which it appears? Spinoza, it should not be forgotten, summarizes his
analysis by showing that it is impossible and dangerous for the state to seek
entirely to abolish citizens' or subjects' freedom of thought and to claim that

it is identical with the thought and opinions of the sovereign—not only in its verbal expression but within the images it forges—thus becoming indiscernible from its own. It is as if the state were truly only a single individual in the anthropomorphic sense (a Leviathan) and not an individual of superior strength, complexity, or multiplicity. Rejoining the themes of the Preface, Spinoza is here thinking especially, but not exclusively, of "absolute" monarchy, with its murderous dream of a politico-religious uniformity in the national space:

> Whoever seeks to regulate everything by laws irritates men's vices rather than correcting them. What cannot be prohibited must necessarily be permitted, even if harm often results from it....But let it be granted that freedom may be suppressed (*opprimi*) and that men may become so subservient that they dare not utter a word except on the bidding of the sovereign; nevertheless, they will never be made to think as the sovereign wants, and so as a necessary consequence (*necessario sequeretur*) men would everyday think one thing and say another; the good faith that is necessary to government will thus be corrupted.... Men as they are generally constituted resent more than anything else the labeling of the opinions that they believe to be true as criminal and the branding as wicked that which inspires them to feel piety towards God and man (*ipsos...movet*). This leads them to detest the laws and to conspire against the authorities and judge it not shameful but the highest honor to plot sedition in the name of such a cause, and to attempt any act of violence. Given that such is human nature, it is obvious that laws concerning opinions do not threaten criminals but independent thinkers (*non scelestos, sed ingenuos*)...and cannot thus be maintained without great danger to the state. (*TPT*, XX)

This is a causal change that strongly merits being compared to the one that Thomas More put forth in *Utopia* (from private property to oppression, from oppression to crime, from crime to sedition and civil war): each has its implication and its theoretical posterity.

Hobbes, it should be remembered, maintained the contrary: that men can believe whatever they want provided they move their lips in the same movement as the sovereign, and this opinion appeared scandalously cynical, even and especially to the defenders of the established order.[19] Now Spinoza does not attack this from a moral standpoint. He shows that it is dangerous because it is physically impossible: that means that every attempt—and God knows they have not been lacking—to identify opinions absolutely, can only turn against itself and provoke an explosive reaction. For it ignores the fact that individuality is not a *simple* totality which could be circumscribed in a unique discourse, a unique way of life; there always remains an indefinite multiplicity of "parts," relationships, and fluctuations which exceed such an imaginary project, and wind up subverting it.

Here we see Spinoza applying, in full agreement with his theory of human nature, a principle of the *minimum* of individuality or of the *maximum of compressibility of the individual*, which is really the opposite of classical individualism.[20]

This principle has other equivalents in his writings. For example, in chapter VII of the *Theologico-Political Treatise*, which is concerned with the minimum of signification of language ("no one, in fact, has ever been able to profit (*ex usu esse*) from changing the meaning of a word, whereas there is often profit in changing the meaning of a text"), this principle is deduced from the fact that the use of language, which determines the meaning of words, is not individual or "private" but common: "language is preserved by both the vulgar and the learned" (*TPT*, VII).

But this principle especially joins the one that, in the *Political Treatise*, states the *limits of a possible dissolution of the state*, which we have already encountered as the counterpart of the theses bearing on civil war:

> Since all men fear solitude, because in solitude none of them has the power to protect himself or to procure what is necessary to sustain life, it follows that men naturally desire the civil state, and they can never entirely destroy it. The conflicts and seditions that break out in the commonwealth never result in its dissolution (as often happens in the case of other societies) but simply in a passage from one form to another, if dissent cannot be diffused without changing the form of the commonwealth (*servata civitatis facie*). (*PT*, VI, 1-2)

Just as there is an incompressible minimum of individuality, there is also a minimum of social and even political relationship, equally incompressible, even under the effect of the most anarchic popular revolutions. Contrary to what the abstract individualism of theories of original social contract imply, Spinoza, while searching for the stability of the state as an "absolute," thinks that there is always a politics beyond its instability.

Our age is itself haunted by a "fear of the masses," which joins together the images of state absolutism—indeed of electronic control of opinions—and those of revolutionary violence or terrorism. In the mythical figure of "totalitarianism"—resting on some real enough but quite heteroclite facts—this fear has given substance to the fantasy of a "total" mass movement, aroused from inside or outside by a threat of death, by a radical negativity, and capable of imposing an absolute uniformity on individuals: in this way the multitude is identified with solitude without leaving any space for the "human." Hannah Arendt has proposed its metaphysics, but George Orwell (in *1984*: we are already there!) has given it a much more effective presentation in fiction (hence, fiction on a fiction), whose relevance history never stops intimating. The literary genius of this fiction consists, in particular, in the fact of having pushed the idea of domination to the point of absolute conditioning and, *simultaneously*, the idea of political propaganda to the point of the creation of an artificial language, whose very words annul freedom of thought.

Spinoza is the anti-Orwell. A reduction and absolute control of the meaning of words is not thinkable for him, any more than either an absolute reduction of individuality by the mass or of the mass by absorption into the individuality in power. These extreme cases, which would be radical negations or figures of death present in life itself, are also fictions which are physically impossible and, as a result, intellectually useless and politically disastrous.

It is true that Spinoza, if he retreated before the idea of an absolute delirium of a crowd capable of preferring death to its own utility and its own preservation, encountered, but without exploring it on account of fear of falling himself into "superstition," the problem of a delirium of the individual:

> No reason compels me to maintain that the body does not die unless it is changed into a corpse. Indeed, experience seems to urge a different conclusion. Sometimes a man undergoes such changes that I would hardly have said he was the same man. I have heard stories, for example, of a Spanish poet who suffered an illness: though he recovered, he was left so oblivious to his past life that he did not believe the tales and tragedies he had written were his own. He could surely have been taken for a grown-up infant if he had also forgotten his native language. (*Ethics*, IV, scholium to proposition 39, 1:569)

But would this question, if he had examined it, have led him toward a more psychological and juridical individualism? Would it not rather have distanced him even further from the mirror-games of consciousness (or freedom) and conditioning (or necessity)?

By showing that individuality and the multitude are inseparable, Spinoza shows also in advance the absurdity of theories of "totalitarianism," which see in mass movements only the figure of a radical historical evil and know how to oppose to it only faith in the eternal refounding of "human consciousness" and its capacity to institute the reign of the "rights of man." Quite far from being a "democrat" in the sense that we could give to that term, Spinoza finds himself perhaps furnishing thereby for our own time some ways of thinking against subjection which are more durable than if he had "succeeded" in describing the institutions of democracy. His fear of the masses is not that totally irrational fear that paralyzes the intelligence and serves only to stupefy individuals. The effort to understand that lives in him is enough to help us to resist, to struggle, and to transform politics.

2

"RIGHTS OF MAN" AND "RIGHTS OF THE CITIZEN"
The Modern Dialectic of Equality and Freedom

The relevance for today of the text of the *Declaration of the Rights of Man and the Citizen,* despite having been reaffirmed in recent years, is still presented to us in the form of a paradox. It is accompanied by the consciousness of an apparently irreducible split between concepts (freedom and equality) that are nonetheless felt to be equally necessary. Contemporary liberalism is not alone in positing that, outside of very narrow limits (those of a juridical form), "freedom" and "equality" are mutually exclusive. This conviction is widely shared by socialism at the very moment that claims for freedom and equality can be clearly seen to depend upon one another in practice. This is as evident in the struggles for democracy in the former "socialist countries" as in the antiracist movements of Western Europe or in the struggles of the Black people of South Africa.

This very deep contradiction feeds upon several axioms whose self-evidence is rarely questioned, in particular the idea that equality is essentially economic or social, whereas freedom is above all juridico-political in nature. But there is yet another seemingly self-evident axiom about which liberalism and socialism have ended up in agreement, even if they draw opposite consequences from it, namely that the realization of equality occurs through state intervention, because it is essentially a matter of redistribution, whereas the preservation of freedom is tied to the limitation of this intervention, even to eternal vigilance against its "perverse" effects. It seems to me that it is this omnipresent but uncritical reference to the state, designated as a block, that permanently reproduces both the distinction between "formal" and "real" (or "substantial") rights, as well as the representation of equality as an exclusively collective goal, while freedom (in any case the "liberty of the moderns") would be essentially individual freedom, even in the realm of public freedoms (which would then be best thought of as public guarantees of private freedoms).

From these axioms it is a very short step to the fundamental paradox, the split between the discourse of the "rights of man" and that of the "rights of the citizen." The discourse of the rights of man (above all formulated as the defense, rather than the conquest, of the rights of man) today covers a very broad spectrum, ranging from freedom of conscience or individual security to the claim for the right to existence or for the right of peoples to self-determination. But it remains entirely distinct from the discourse of the rights of the citizen, which itself oscillates between proposals to enlarge the political sphere to new domains (such as ecology) and attempts to revalorize classical politics—synonymous with the collective institution of deliberation and decision—against the invasion of economism and technocracy. It seems to be very difficult, perhaps more and more so, to uphold the equation (to which I will return) typical of the formulations of the revolutionary text of 1789: that of "man" and "citizen." There is near-universal agreement that equating man and citizen invariably leads to totalitarianism, to what is often designated as the imperialism of "everything is political and politics is everything (*le tout politique*)." The counterpart of this agreement, however, is the proclamation that the rights of man, however naturally and universally necessary they might be, essentially represent an ideal, not to say a utopia.

The reasons for this split, which seems flagrant at a time that reference to juridical universalism is being reactualized, need to be interrogated. Several well-known explanations can be put forward. One invokes human nature: between the "rights of man" and the "rights of the citizen" there would be the same gap as there is between the essential, theoretical goodness of human nature, without which a true community would be unthinkable, and the practical malevolence of empirical individuals submitted to the compulsion of their passions, interests, and conditions of existence. *Homo homini deus, homo homini lupus.* Another banal and frequently used explanation is the historicist one: time has passed, thus the conditions which gave the text of 1789 a constitutive self-evidence no longer exist. Doubtless, we are no longer "men" of the eighteenth century, and it is doubtful that we are still "citizens" of the nineteenth. We are more in one sense (for example the world of global communication and culture in which we live relativizes national citizenship, the unsurpassable horizon of the members of the Constituent Assembly of 1789); we are less in another, because our "differentiated" societies are organized not only by class but above all by status.

I will, however, privilege another, more intrinsic mode of explanation, suggesting that the statements of the "founding" text, by virtue of their simplicity and revolutionary radicality, hide within themselves from the outset a contradiction that prohibits them from becoming vested in a stable order. Or better yet: that the contradiction, in the second degree, lies in the instability of the relation between the aporetical character of the text[1] and the conflictual character of the situation in which it arises and which serves as its referent. The result is that every attempt to reactivate the text of the *Declaration*, despite being founded upon its truth, cannot help but run up against the effects of the development of its internal tensions. This path seems to me to be the most fruitful, but there are several different ways to take it.

In a recent and remarkable book, *La Révolution des droits de l'homme,*[2] writing from a neo-liberal perspective, in search of the reasons for which the revolution, for us, would be "over" (but also those that "put off" this result for so long), Marcel Gauchet has followed from text to text the development of what he sees as the fundamental aporia: that the kernel of the *Declaration* of 1789 would be that it puts in place an *absolute* notion of national sovereignty, a mimetic inversion of the monarchical sovereignty that it opposed in order to legitimate the representation of the people. To the "one and indivisible" will of the absolute monarch the Constituent Assembly had to make correspond a "general will," equally one and indivisible, equally the depository of all authority, but founded in the last analysis only upon the individuals who make up the nation. Such a notion is condemned to oscillate between direct democracy and revolutionary dictatorship: it turns out to be incompatible with the pragmatic institution of a juridical framework for modern politics, whether it is an issue of the balance of powers between the legislature and the executive or of that between the prerogatives of the state and the independence of individuals. This is why the Revolution, immediately, was a failure, while in an entirely different context, at the end of a century of political confrontations and governmental crises, its symbolic statements took on the function of a more or less consensual regulatory ideal.

Symmetrically, in a series of recent articles,[3] Florence Gauthier, rediscovering and renewing the tradition of revolutionary idealism (as it can be retraced from Robespierre and Fichte to the young Marx and, in our own time, Ernst Bloch), has tried to show that a rupture occurred between the Montagnard, Jacobin phase of the Convention and its moderate, Thermidorian phase. The articles of the text of 1789, centered on the primacy of *freedom* and on the pursuit of its universality, and those of 1793—which developed the latent *egalitarianism* of this conception as universal reciprocity or universal reciprocal recognition of freedoms, up to and including the fundamental freedom to exist (the "right to existence" with its economic consequences)—form a continuity. They proceed from the classical, essentially Lockean idea of a *declaration of natural right* that founds association or citizenship, and that draws the limits of the political sphere and the role of the state on the basis of human nature. On the contrary, the Thermidorian *Declaration* of 1795—centered on the untouchable character of *property* and on the reciprocity of "rights" and "duties"—substitutes a determinate "social" foundation for the natural, universal foundation of citizenship: there would thus be a rupture and even a reversal. This reversal of course expresses the counterrevolutionary reaction to the development of social conflicts, and in particular to the way in which the popular, non-"bourgeois" components of the Revolution continually made a *political* use of the universalism of the rights of man against the practical restrictions that their own framers had placed on them: the distinction between "active" and "passive" citizenship on a censitaire basis, and the exclusion of "*de facto* equality" from the domain of natural rights.

I will not, for my part, adopt exactly either of these two ways of interpreting the intrinsic contradiction of the revolutionary moment. Both of them seem to me, for entirely different reasons, to miss its specificity. To put it schematically, *neither* do I believe that the concept of the "sovereignty of the Nation" forged in 1789 is the reversal, within the frame of a fundamental continuity, of the concept of monarchical sovereignty, substituting as it were one transcendence for another; *nor* do I believe that the reference to man and to the universality of his nature as "founding" the rights of the citizen can here be simply brought back to the average tenor of its ideological sources, which can generically be designated by the name of classical "natural right."

As far as sovereignty is concerned, as I have tried to show elsewhere,[4] the revolutionary innovation consists precisely in subverting its traditional concept by posing the highly paradoxical thesis of an *egalitarian sovereignty*: practically a contradiction in terms, but the only way radically to expel all transcendence and to inscribe the political and social order in the element of immanence, of the auto-constitution of the people. Whence nonetheless begins the immediate development of the whole series of contradictions that proceed from the fact that so-called civil society and *a fortiori* the state are entirely structured by hierarchies or dependencies that should be both indifferent to sovereignty and essential to its institutionalization.

As far as *declared natural right* is concerned, I believe the revolutionary moment of the "declaration" and its uninterrupted efficacy in the course of sociopolitical struggles to be in fact essential. In other words I do not doubt that the materiality of this act of enunciation was the anchoring point for the series of claims that, from the morrow of the *Declaration*, begin to base upon it their claims for the rights of women, of workers, of colonized "races" to be incorporated into citizenship. But I do not at all believe that it is inscribed in the continuity of classical natural right, whether Lockean or even Rousseauist, as its culmination or radicalization. Historically and epistemologically, whatever the "self-consciousness" of its drafters, struggling with their own Old Regime intellectual formation, may have been, the core of the *Declaration of the Rights of Man and the Citizen* does not stem from pre-existing ideologies. It is no longer inscribed in the framework of the theories of "human nature" as foundation or guarantee of a juridical order that, from the sixteenth to the eighteenth century, formed precisely the alternative to theories of "divine right" and furnished opponents of absolute monarchy with the basis of their arguments. It only takes up—partially—their terminology in order to invalidate their logic. Thus what is immediately determined by it is not the triumph but the irreversible beginning of the crisis of classical natural right, the opening of the new ideological field in which the politico-philosophical ideologies of the nineteenth century will take their places.[5]

Classical natural right is characterized by the extreme diversity of its conceptions of human nature and schemes of the original foundation of civil society, corresponding to equally many strategies for reforming political institutions. The text of 1789 (the result of a veritable *coup de force* in the debates of the "national representation" working under the triple constraint of its own interests, the open but not yet declared conflict with the monarchy, and the "Great Fear" of popular insurrections) is on the contrary characterized by a remarkable *simplicity* (what I have elsewhere called a *de jure* fact), whose foundation, as we shall see, is purely negative, short-circuiting the problematic of the origins and modalities of association. It is in particular remarkable that the notion of the "contract" is absent from the *Declaration*.[6] But the complexity and heterogeneity of the theories of classical natural right, whether they be contractualist or anticontractualist, statist or economistic, "correspond" to the relative homogeneity of a rising social class, which can be called bourgeois, whereas the unitary simplicity of the *Declaration of Rights* represents, in the field of ideas, or rather of words—of words that immediately escaped the control of their authors—the real social *complexity* of the French Revolution: the fact that the Revolution, from the beginning, is not, is already no longer a "bourgeois revolution," but a revolution made jointly by the bourgeoisie and the people or the nonbourgeois masses, in an ongoing relation of alliance and confrontation. The revolution is immediately grappling with its own internal contestation, without which it would not even exist, and always chasing after the unity of its opposites.

Let us then come to the core of the revolutionary text. It lies, it seems to me, in a double identification, one identification explaining the other and giving it its content.

The *first identification* is that of *man* and *citizen*. Here a choice must be made in reading, since a long, quasi-official tradition interprets the content of the original seventeen articles as the expression of a *distinction* between the "rights of man" (universal, inalienable, subsisting independently of any social institution, thus virtual, etc.) and the "rights of the citizen" (positive, instituted, restrictive but effective), leading in turn to a *foundation* of the latter upon the former. And doubtless in order to "found," it is necessary to distinguish what founds and what is founded, but the whole question here is to determine whether, in the text itself, we are indeed dealing with the statement of a "foundation." Doubtless as well, the duality of the terms "man" and "citizen" bears with it the possibility of a dissociation whose effects we shall observe. But, in its context, it can and should be interpreted otherwise. Reread the *Declaration* and you will see that between the "rights of man" and the "rights of the citizen" there is in fact no gap, no difference in content: they are *exactly the same*. As a consequence there does not exist any difference between *man* and *citizen*, at least insofar as they are practically "defined" by the nature and extension of the rights to which they are entitled: but this is precisely the object of the *Declaration*. I recall that *free-*

dom, property, security, and resistance to oppression (art. 2) are enumerated as the "natural and imprescriptible rights of man," that is, exactly those rights that the rest of the *Declaration* will show to be given a juridical organization by the social constitution.

What then poses a problem at this level? First of all, *the presence of resistance to oppression*, about which the least that can be said is that what follows does not institute it very explicitly. But it can also be said that it is the corollary of freedom, the guarantee of its effectiveness—to be free is to be able to resist any compulsion that destroys freedom—and that it represents the verbal trace of the revolutionary struggle that imposes this freedom as a conquest.[7] Second, *the apparent absence of equality*. But this impression should be corrected by a rereading of articles 1 ("Men are born and remain free and equal in rights…") and 6 ("The law is the expression of the general will. All citizens have the right to contribute to it.… It should be the same for all.… All citizens being equal in its eyes are equally admissible…"). These articles do more than compensate for the "absence" of equality in the enumeration in article 2; they reverse its meaning, making equality the principle or the right that effectively *ties* all the others together.

The treatment of equality in the *Declaration* is precisely the site of the strongest and most precise identification of *man* and *citizen*. Indeed it will soon be reproached for this fact, leading quickly to the dissociation in one way or another of man and citizen, "rights of man" and "rights of the citizen", whereas we find here the confirmation of their coincidence in the revolutionary moment, from which the act of enunciation (the "declaration") is indissociable. The *Declaration* does not posit any "human nature" *before* society and the political order, as an underlying foundation or exterior guarantee. Instead it integrally identifies the rights of man with political rights and, by an approach that short-circuits theories of human nature as well as those of theological supernature, identifies man, whether individual or collective, with the member of political society.

It might be useful here to reflect briefly on what radically distinguishes such a notion from the (precisely "naturalist") propositions of the tradition of antiquity. The equation of man and citizen in 1789 *is not* a revival of the *zôon politikon*. Indeed the idea of the *zôon politikon*, if it is in fact the case that it corresponds to the institutions of the Greek or Roman "city-state," is not based on the identification of equality and freedom, but on the entirely different thesis of equality within the limits of freedom, considered as a social *status*. This status is variously conceived of as founded on a tradition, a constitution, or a natural quality of individuals. Equality here is only a consequence, an attribute of freedom. No reversibility is possible between the two terms. This explains the strange limitation of the concept (or at least what can retrospectively only appear that way to the modern reader) even in the texts that plumb the most profoundly the democratic virtualities of the notion of citizenship, for example certain passages of Aristotle's *Politics*. Aristotle "defines" citizenship by the alternative exercise of the functions of ruling and being ruled, thus as a strong form of the generalized reciprocity of free, adult male individuals (which is also the basis of their *philia*: a generic concept of "social bond"). From this reciprocity is derived a cosmological placement of the "citizen" between the two limits of excess and insufficiency that form *the anthropological limits of the political*: the different figures of the subhuman (woman, slave, child), the superhuman in the figures of the wise man, the god, and the hero. But where today we see a contradictory combination of an outline of universality and its arbitrary limitation, in reality there is only the application of a different logic, in which "freedom" represents a status, a personality, and "equality" is a function and a right of this status.

Inversely, it would be equally erroneous to adopt, under pretext of historical consciousness, the classical opposition that has come to us from liberalism: in opposition to the Greek (and even more, Roman) unity of the social and the political, the *Declaration* of 1789 would have instituted their separation—or their "bourgeois" separation—itself founded on the distinction of a public sphere and a private sphere. That Marx, in a famous text of his youth (*The Jewish Question*), took up this contemporary reading on his own account does not prevent it from being fundamentally a complete misunderstanding with respect to the letter, the materiality of the text. Man in the *Declaration* is not a "private individual" in opposition to the citizen who would be the member of the state. He is precisely the citizen, and recognizing this fact should, on the contrary, lead us to question how it could have happened that the very notion of the state should be so problematic in a revolutionary text whose purpose—at least in the eyes of its drafters—was to establish a new state. This question can only be answered by examining the subversive effects of a radically new idea that concerns precisely the relation between equality and freedom, and that is stated as a universal.

What is this idea? Nothing less than the identification of the two concepts. If one is willing to read it literally, the *Declaration* in fact says that equality is identical to freedom, is *equal to freedom*, and vice versa. Each is the exact measure of the other. This is what I propose to call, in a voluntarily baroque turn of phrase, *the proposition of equaliberty:* a portmanteau word that is "impossible" in French (and English) but that alone expresses the central proposition. For it gives both the conditions under which man is a citizen through and through, and the reason for this assimilation. Underneath the equation of man and citizen, or rather *within it,* as the very reason of its universality—as its *presupposition*—lies the proposition of equaliberty.

This proposition has the status of a "self-evident truth," as the Americans had said. Or, more precisely, it has the status of a certainty, that is, its truth cannot be put in doubt. How is it then that it is put in doubt, even constantly, although in forms of denial that never stop admitting its insistence and manifesting its irreversibility?

It cannot be simply on account of the fact that there are two words. Their formal distinction is obviously necessary for an identity of signification to be posited. To put it better: for *freedom* and *equality* to be thought of as identical, an initial difference must be reduced, a difference inscribed in the relatively distinct histories of the words "freedom" and "equality" *before* the text of 1789, before this meeting point that changes the whole picture with a single stroke. From another point of view, it is simply the trace of the fact that the revolutionaries of 1789 were fighting against two adversaries and two principles *at once: absolutism,* which appears as the negation of freedom ("the royal will is law"), and *privileges,* which appear as the negation of equality ("might makes right"). The politico-social unity of monarchy and aristocracy is immediately thought by the revolutionaries in the concept of the "Old Regime," an amalgam that has been continually attacked by critics of the Revolution, today still, particularly by dissociating within the Revolution a "revolution of freedom" and a "revolution of equality."

But it is the Platonizing reading of texts that forms a more profound obstacle to the recognition of this radical thesis: equality and freedom are seen as ideas or essences and their common *nature* is sought. There is yet another reason: a feeling that it would be necessary, in order to give an "empirical content," a "reference" to this identity, to be able to indicate *which* freedom, *which* equality are identical, or rather *within what limits* they are identical. In a word, one stumbles over a stupefying indeterminacy here. There are two related but nonetheless distinct problems at issue. The answer to the first is simple, but has extreme consequences in that it engages nothing less than the *truth*-value of the proposition of equaliberty. The answer to the second is practically impossible, or rather is destined to remain indefinitely open, which is doubtless of no less import, since what is at stake is simply the application, the passage from "theory" to "practice," of a proposition that has come out of (revolutionary) practice itself.

Let us take the question of nature first. My position is brutal: the reasoning that underlies the proposition of equaliberty ($E = F$) is not essentialist. It is not based on the intuitive discovery or revelation of an identity of the *ideas* of equality and freedom, if only because they are entirely transformed by their revolutionary equation. What it is based on is the historical discovery, which can legitimately be called experimental, that their *extensions* are necessarily identical. To put it plainly, the situations in which both are either present or absent are necessarily the same. Or better yet, the (*de facto*) historical conditions of freedom are exactly the same as the (*de facto*) historical conditions of equality. My claim is that, understood in this way, the proposition of equaliberty is well and indeed an irreversible truth, discovered by and in the revolutionary struggle. It is precisely the universally true proposition upon which, at the decisive moment, the different "forces" making up the revolutionary camp had to agree. In turn, the historical effects of this proposition, however contradictory they may be, can only be understood thus, as the effects of a truth or as truth-effects.

You will say to me: where is the proof? Since it is an issue of a universal truth in this sense (an *a posteriori* universal, or better, a historical universal), the proof can only be *negative*, but it can be carried out at any moment, in situations as diverse as can be desired. If it is absolutely true that equality is *practically* identical with freedom, this means that it is materially impossible for it to be otherwise, in other words, it means that they are necessarily always *contradicted together*. This thesis itself is to be interpreted "in extension": equality and freedom are contradicted in exactly the same "situations," because there is no example of conditions that suppress or repress freedom that do not suppress or limit—that is, do not abolish— equality, and vice versa. I have no fear of being contradicted here either by the history of capitalist exploitation, which by denying in practice the equality proclaimed by the labor contract ends up in the practical negation of the freedom of expression, or by the history of socialist regimes that, by suppressing public freedoms, end up constituting a society of privileges and reinforced inequalities. Clearly, the distinction between "individual" and "collective" freedoms, like that between "formal" and "real" equality, is meaningless here: what would instead be at issue would be the *degree* of equality necessary to the collectivization of individual freedoms, and the *degree* of freedom necessary to the collective equality of individuals, the answer being the same every time: *the maximum* in the given conditions.

Whence comes yet another way to express the negative experience that constitutes the proof—the only possible proof, but sufficient as such—of the proposition of equaliberty: that the diverse forms of social and political "power" that correspond to either inequalities or constraints on the freedom of man the citizen necessarily converge. There are no examples of restrictions or suppressions of freedoms without social inequalities, nor of inequalities without restrictions or suppressions of freedoms, even if there are degrees, secondary tensions, periods of unstable equilibrium, compromise situations in which exploitation and domination are not homogeneously distributed upon all individuals. Such is the very mechanism of the formation of classes or dominant elites, which inevitably transforms power into superpower, or hegemony.

We can then understand why the text of the *Declaration*, the circumstantial work of the bourgeois mouthpieces of the revolution, does *not* have as its essential content their own domination or control over the process in which they are participating, and further why a struggle is immediately joined whose stake is the application of the "principles of 1789," that is their universal extension or limitation in practice.

But it can also be understood that the signification of the equation man= citizen is not so much the definition of a political right as the affirmation of a *universal right to politics*. Formally at least—but this is the classic example of a form that can become a material weapon—the *Declaration* opens an indefinite sphere of "politicization" of rights-claims each of which reiterates in its own way the demand for citizenship or for an institutional, public inscription of freedom and equality. In this indefinite opening come to be inscribed—and attempts to do this can be seen beginning with the revolutionary period—the rights-claims of salaried workers or dependents, as well as those of women or slaves, and later of the colonized. Such a right would later be reformulated as follows: *the emancipation of the oppressed can only be their own work*, which emphasizes its immediately ethical signification.

But here is the second aspect. An intrinsic part of the truth of our text is its "negative universality," that is its absolute *indeterminacy*. Since we are talking about a truth-effect in history, it is more than ever necessary to articulate the level of the wording of the statement and that of the act of its enunciation, or if one prefers its signification and its reference. All the force of the statement comes from its indeterminacy, but this is also the source of the practical weakness of the act of enunciation—or rather, of the fact that the consequences of the statement are themselves indeterminate: they are entirely dependent on "power relations" and the evolution of the conjuncture in which it will always be necessary in practice to construct individual and collective referents for equaliberty, with more or less "prudence" and "precision," but also "audacity" and "insolence" against established powers. There will be a permanent tension between the conditions that historically determine the construction of institutions that are in conformity with the proposition of equaliberty, and the hyperbolic universality of the statement. Nevertheless, it will always be necessary for this universality to be repeated, and to be repeated *identically*, without change, in order to reproduce the truth-effect without which there is no revolutionary politics. There will thus be a permanent tension between the universally political signification of the "rights of man" and the fact that their statement leaves it entirely up to "practice," to the "struggle," to "social conflict," to construct a "politics of the rights of man."

I now come to the following point in my exposition. I will propose the following hypothesis: to determine equaliberty, or to inscribe it in practice at the cost of struggles directed in a concrete form against the historical *negations* whose theoretical negation this proposition itself represents, is to put its truth into effect. Such an effectuation, however, depends on two factors: first, a determination of the real *contradictions* of postrevolutionary politics, that is of the given power relations and conflicts of interests in the successive conjunctures in which it is carried on, or even reconstituted; but also a determination of the *forms* in which such real contradictions are thinkable in the ideological space opened by the revolutionary proposition. Our discussion should thus take on the form of the construction of a configuration or topography of the ideological tensions of modern politics as restructured by the revolutionary proposition. It is *within* such a configuration that we must try to locate the statement of contradictions, in order to take the measure of their heterogeneity and distance.

Here, presented schematically, is the hypothesis I shall follow in constructing this topography:

1. The equation of freedom and equality is indispensable to the modern, "subjective" recasting of right, but is powerless to guarantee its institutional stability. A *mediation* is required, but it takes the antithetical forms of "fraternity" (or community) and "property."

2. Each of these mediations is in turn the object of a conflict, and is practically divided, the former into national community and popular community, the latter into labor-property and capital-property: the combination of

these two oppositions is the most general ideological form of the "class struggle."

3. Each of these mediations, as well as their conflictual expressions, *represses* another kind of "contradiction": in the case of fraternity/community, sexual difference; in that of property (labor or capital), the division of "intellectual" knowledge and "corporal" activity. As a consequence there are *two* entirely heterogeneous kinds of "contradictions," which not only do not allow themselves to be reduced to unity, but which in a certain way have to give rise to incompatible but rigorously inseparable discourses—at least for as long as the discursive matrix of political action continues to be founded on the concept of man the citizen from which we began.

Let us begin with the question of the mediations. We must begin again with the constitutive instability of the equation man = citizen, implicitly based on the identification of equality with freedom, that is on the affirmation of a potentially universal right to politics. Elsewhere I have tried to show, following others (and, if one is willing to read the texts, following the revolutionaries themselves), that this affirmation introduces an indefinite oscillation, induces a structural equivocation between two obviously antinomical forms of "politics": an *insurrectional politics* and a *constitutional politics*. Or if one prefers, a politics of permanent, uninterrupted revolution, and a politics of the state as institutional order. It is clear that such an antinomy divides the very concept of politics, with no possible synthesis (which is perhaps the typical characteristic of modernity). It also signifies that "freedom" and "equality" will permanently tend to be dissociated, to appear as distinct principles or values that can be invoked by mutually opposed forces or camps, *unless* their identity—particularly their juridical identity—is guaranteed by or, if one prefers, founded upon the introduction and the primacy of a third term. Then there would no longer be an immediate identity but a mediated one: E = F inasmuch as they are expressions or specifications of *another* principle, which would thereby appear as their common essence.[8]

Nevertheless the fact is that such a mediation cannot be made in a single form. Historically, it in turn took on two antithetical forms: mediation by *property* and mediation by the *community* (which was typically expressed during the French Revolution in the terms of the triptych Liberty-Equality-Fraternity, to be laid out on the three poles of a symbolic triangle: but the "Lockean" triangle Liberty-Equality-Property is no less decisive).

Let us pause a moment on this point. Of course, none of the notions involved—freedom, equality, property, community, or fraternity—is radically new. But what is new is the way that they are configured and defined with respect to one another, and the tension established between the two possible "foundations" for freedom and equality, which are like two alternative ways to *socialize the citizen*: property, whether individual or collective; community, whether conceived of as natural or historical (or even spiritual). This forms the matrix of the political ideologies characteristic of modernity, from socialism and liberalism (each of which in its own way emphasizes property) to nationalism and communism (each of which in its own way emphasizes community, and in France, more particularly, fraternity). Recognizing the insistence of this structure is also a way to clarify the stakes of the contemporary discomfort with respect to politics. It is widely believed that this discomfort concerns the terms of freedom and equality, but in fact it seems to have more to do with their "complements." For, as an anchoring point of individuality and thus of the relation between men and things or man and nature, "property" in all its forms has today lost its self-evidence, its simplicity, and has become a complex, opaque notion (what, for example, does it mean to be the owner of an entitlement or of a credit?). Meanwhile fraternity or the community has lost both its univocity (for there is not one but several collectivizing social relations: competing groups or bonds of belonging with which individuals are called upon to identify) and its consistency (there are social relations that, after having bound together individuals *too well*, seem no longer to bind them together *at all*: for example the professions and the family, and doubtless it is becoming more and more of a question for social class and the nation).

What is striking here is that neither property nor community can "found" freedom and equality (and consequently the kinds of politics that are deployed around these "rights" of man the citizen) without reasoning by antithesis. This is what I will call the argument of *the danger of the opposite excess*. Thus it will be claimed that the excess of community, the absolute primacy of the whole or of the group over individuals would be the suppression of individuality, which is why the relations of freedom and equality must be controlled, "measured" by the principle of the *guarantee of property*. Symmetrically it will be argued that the excess of property, the absolute primacy of individuality, would be the suppression of the community, which is why freedom and equality must be essentially defined as expressions of the *communal being* of man, of the institutions in which the community pursues its own realization.

But above all this dialectic cannot develop without each of the two great "mediations" being tendentially split, divided in two. This doubtless has to

do with the fact that, initially borne by the convergence of entirely heterogeneous social groups and practices, the notion of universal citizenship
becomes the very object of the confrontation between rulers and ruled, as
well as between the violent and the juridical or legal forms of politics. There
are always either rulers or ruled to brandish violence against the law, against
juridical forms, but also to brandish legality against violence.

What then happens historically on the side of the Liberty-Equality-
Fraternity triangle, and in fact very early, beginning with the phase of the
Convention, simultaneously "agitated" by questions of the foreign war
and public safety, as well as by the patriotic revolutionary cult and the class
differences that led to talk of a "new aristocracy" and "new privileges"? The
system of fraternity is tendentially doubled into a *national* and, before long,
state-centered fraternity, and a *revolutionary* fraternity in which extreme
egalitarianism becomes translated into communism. The term *nation*
changes its meaning: it no longer means the set of all citizens, but the idea
of a historical *belonging*, centered on the state. At the extreme, through the
mythification of language, culture, and national traditions, this was to
become the French version of nationalism, the ideal of a moral and intellectual community founded upon institutional traditions, the continuity of
royalty and republic. Opposed to it one finds on the contrary the notion of
the *people* drifting toward the general idea of the proletariat as "the people's
people," depository of its authenticity and of its veritable communitarian
aspirations.

What happens symmetrically on the side of the triangle Liberty-Equality-
Property? There too a scission is at work, which turns on questions like the
right to existence and the right to employment. It could be said that there
are tendentially two ways to justify the rights of the citizen by referring to
property, thus two ways to think the individual as bearer of the values of
freedom-equality: either by the *property of labor* (and particularly the appropriation "of oneself," of the means of existence, by labor), or by *property
as capital* (whether it is an issue of money capital or symbolic capital, for
example, entrepreneurial capacity, know-how, etc.). On the ideological level
these notions are astonishingly ambivalent (as we saw a moment ago with
the "people"). The capitalist is defined as a worker, as an "entrepreneur"; the
worker, as the bearer of a capacity, of a "human capital." The notion of property can be formally conserved in both cases, just as it appears to be what
is common to the ideologies of individualistic liberalism and collectivist
socialism, which formally agree in saying that *it is property* that is socially
decisive.

It can also be seen that these two manifest contradictions in some sense fused politically very early. From 1789 to 1793, what had been dominant was the question of the community of citizens, the problem of fraternity evoked in the complete wording of the Montagnard formula, which—once it had been cut down to acceptable dimensions—would become the "republican motto": "Unity Indivisibility of the Republic Freedom Equality Fraternity or Death." From 1789 to 1795, and to the Civil Code, the other contradiction developed, ending up in the symbolical scission of bourgeois proprietors and egalitarian communists. Throughout the nineteenth century what I have called the general ideological form of the class struggle would develop: not simply the opposition between individual and collective property, labor and capital, but the *addition* of the two contradictions. From the ideological point of view, not to speak of that of material interests, the "bourgeois camp" is both one *form of property* against another and one *form of community* against another:[9] it is liberalism *plus* nationalism. And in the same way the "proletarian camp" is a form of property, collective or social, or planned, *plus* a form of community: precisely communism, which draws its heritage from the fraternal ideal of the revolutionary crowds, and from the idea that the only citizens in the proper sense of the word are the men of the people, the workers.

I do not believe that we can be content to remain there. And this is one of the reasons for the relative inadequacy of the idea of revolution at the end of the twentieth century, which thus goes back to its very origins. The contradictions we have just been discussing are manifest contradictions that have been made explicit during the past two centuries in the discourses that make up modern, postrevolutionary politics. This means that they are perfectly well formulated in the language of freedom and equality, or, if one prefers, in the language of the struggle against oppression and injustice. But we are recognizing more and more today the existence of another type of "contradiction" or "division" that is very difficult to formulate in this language (or that always brings along a remainder that is irreducible to formulation in terms of oppression or injustice). At least we have become more conscious of its existence. A sign of the times? Perhaps.

I believe that there are fundamentally two of them—both of which those of us who were engaged in politics in what used to be called the "revolutionary party" encountered as insurmountable obstacles to the formation of a free community of individuals struggling together against social inequalities. For precisely what these contradictions or divisions of an entirely different type, generally repressed out of consciousness and political discourse, do is to call into question the model of individuality, or if one prefers "human nature," that is, the very possibility of representing the individual in general as an example of the human race. They are the *division of the sexes* (not only as a division of social roles, but more profoundly as an absolute difference, the duality of man and woman that separates the human race—and with it any community—into two "dissymetrical halves without a mediating term"); and the intellectual difference, or the division of body and mind (this "Platonic" opposition of the two sides of individuality, that Spinoza, to the contrary, had tried to think as "identical," and which is to be found from one end of the social field to the other as the division of "manual labor" and "intellectual labor," of technique and reflection, of execution and knowledge, of sport and art or culture, etc.).

Doubtless it is an issue of inequalities, or more precisely of the foundations constantly invoked in order to institute inequality, and thereby limit or annul the freedom of an entire "class" of humanity. Yet behind these inequalities there is a kind of difference that cannot be overcome by the institution of equality: which does not mean that equality is not here too the formal condition of liberation, but that it remains purely external. Here, it seems, there is no "political solution" purely in terms of equaliberty: neither by the "separation" of groups nor by their "fusion" (the myth of the total man, manual/intellectual, is worth about as much as that of the androgyne, and moreover they are related). These are repressed contradictions that haunt modern politics: in this sense, even though they are constantly presented as exterior to it, they are constantly present in the hollow of its discursive, legislative, organizational, and repressive practices. Perhaps it is only from today that the beginning of their *own* enunciation can be dated, to the extent that the inadequacy of specialized discourses on the family, education, and professional training becomes manifest.

These two differences thus have in common, negatively, that they are other than inequality, even though they are always already inscribed in a relation of power. More precisely they are inscribed in a relation of collective inequality (men and women, the elite and the masses) which is reproduced, exercised, and verified as a personal relation, between one individual and another, whereas modern society has formally abolished all dependence of one man on another. This is why they always appear out of line with respect to the notion of an inequality of rights and status: short of or beyond the "social," in the contingency of individualities or in the necessity of transindividual destinies. They have in common, positively, that they have to seek their liberation as a "right to difference in equality," that is, not as a restoration of an original identity or as a neutralization of differences in the equality of rights, but as the production of an equality without precedents or models, which would be difference itself, the complementarity and reciprocity of singularities. In a sense such a reciprocity is already virtually included in the proposition of equaliberty, but—paradoxically—it can only claim to be inspired by this proposition on the condition of *reopening* the question of the identity between "man" and "citizen": not in order to regress toward the idea of a citizenship subordinated to anthropological differences (as in antiquity's idea of citizenship), but in order to progress toward a citizenship overdetermined by anthropological difference, explicitly oriented toward its transformation, distinct from both an institutional naturalization and a denial or formal neutralization (which in fact functions as the permanent means of its naturalization). These two "differences" are not thereby similar to one another. The power that they institute does not subject the same individuals, or rather the same "classes" of individuals, and above all it does not subject them by the same means, even though it never stops adding to itself.

With sexual difference we are dealing, as it were, with a *supplement of singularity*, which prohibits the same content from being attributed to the freedom of men and to the freedom of women, and consequently either of them from being reduced to a model of common subjectivity. One can desire, as a condition of their freedom of action, that women should have "equal rights," equal access to knowledge, to the professions, to public responsibilities (which supposes a more or less profound transformation of the conditions in which they are exercised); one cannot think that they thenceforth act as generic individuals. Equality here is not the neutralization of differences (equalization), but the condition and requirement of the diversification of freedoms.

On the contrary, in the inequality of knowledge, which is both the differential reproduction of a "mass" and an "elite," the use of educational institutions to compartmentalize and hierarchize social activities, and the legitimation of the "intellectual" way of life (even in a purely formal way, outside of any acquisition of actual knowledge) to the detriment of the "manual" way of life, we are instead dealing with a subtraction of singularity. If one is willing to admit (here again, with a philosopher like Spinoza) that individuality is a function of communication, and that communication develops most not between predetermined social roles but between singularities, between "practical" experiences each one of which can learn something from and teach something to each of the others, it must be recognized that, paradoxically, the expansion of knowledge as a support of power is *disindividualizing*. The universality of the function of knowledge in modern societies, the positive condition of the constitution of a common language of politics (and also of its "secularization"), is paid for by a restriction of the real possibilities of communication—the institutional form of which is precisely the specialized monopoly of "communications." From this point of view, it is inequality that creates difference, practically irreducible, but the struggle against inequality can culminate in neither the annulling of differences nor their "democratic" reproduction in the form of a generalized selection of individuals. In order for a greater freedom for both individuals and for communication itself to develop, it would be necessary to institute at the same time a neutralization *and* a redistribution of knowledge, an "equivalence" of knowledgeable and nonknowledgeable individuals with respect to the right of expression in public space *and* a symbolic dissociation of the institutional equivalence between "intelligence" and "knowledge." In truth this egalitarian requirement has never stopped being the aporia of the political utopias of intellectual emancipation.[10]

From these considerations I will draw the following hypothesis about the inscription of "anthropological differences" in the topography of equaliberty: sexual difference maintains a privileged relation with the institution of community, whereas intellectual difference takes on its critical significance for politics above all in its relation with the institution of property.

Once all human individuals are reputed to be citizens, free and equal in rights, and virtually demand the effectivity of those rights, the division of sexual roles *directly* becomes a necessity for society to be able to represent itself as a "community" (and not as a juxtaposition of "unrelated" individuals). It can certainly be posited that every historical community, an institution that is both real and imaginary, rests on the relation between the sexes (that is on kinship, the division of masculine and feminine tasks and roles, the determination of the symbolic "character" of each individual as a repression of bisexuality). But the modern political community, not only because it is a state but because it is a state whose juridical structure is founded on the proposition of equaliberty, is *never*, as such, a sexed community: what underlies it, as a national community, is not the simple relation between the sexes (except metaphorically, it is not an extended family), but rather practical and ideological *sexism* as a structure of interior exclusion of women, generalized to the whole society. It is thus the unstable equilibrium of the denial and the universalization of sexual difference. Thus the affirmation of this difference as a political force becomes the most sensitive point of the crisis of the community (or of the communal identity crisis).

On the other side, intellectual difference maintains a privileged relation with property as a social mediation. It could be shown that the concept of an intellectual capacity has always been part of the representation of a human appropriation of things, precisely as (ontological) *difference* between a human personality and a "body" which itself is only a "thing." Its trace could be found *a contrario* in the constant legislation identifying intellectual tutelage or derangement with an incapacity to possess. To possess things one must, in effect, first "possess oneself," and this self-possession is nothing other than the generic concept of intelligence. Nevertheless, when, in opposition to community, property—individual or collective—becomes the mediation of equality and freedom, the guarantee of individual humanity and the condition of citizenship, this capacity/incapacity changes meaning: here again, it leaves the purely "private" sphere and acquires a "public" value. Every property is inscribed in the codes and equivalences formalized by the knowledge of political economy; every individual is a "proprietor" (and measured by his property) insofar as he understands the practical and theoretical science of the exchange of value, or is recognized by it (that is, is himself inscribed in its account books). Individuals or classes only have a relation to their being or their having by the mediation of this abstract knowledge that is becoming more and more autonomous and "intellectualized," even as it becomes more and more "materialized." This process of autonomization-intellectualization-materialization of "knowledge" determines more and more directly the exercise of the "property rights" and thereby individuality. But at the same time it renders more and more uncertain the identity of proprietors, the identity of the "subject" of property. Then we are no longer dealing merely with a mechanism of division of human nature that *practically contradicts* the requirement of freedom and equality. Instead we are dealing with a *dissolution* of political individuality. The "rights of the citizen" find themselves deprived of substance, inasmuch as they should be exercised by proprietors, whereas the *question* of equality and freedom finds itself led back to its original formulation, without a pre-established response: which "men" are then citizens?

Thus we can suggest that a second configuration, coming slowly to light, can be deduced from the first one, and that it is like its underside or the return of what it had repressed: instead of disposing of "mediations" for the institution of equaliberty and its ideological foundation, this topography disposes of *points of uncertainty* for the preceding mediations and foundations, which are at the same time the points where anthropological difference makes modern individual and communal identity vacillate. In these points precisely the requirement for freedom and equality (or for equal freedom) is *greatest*, but the concrete forms (whether juridical or practical) of its satisfaction are, today, the most aporetical. They are thus, by definition, the sensitive points of a recasting of politics.

By situating these points with respect to the universal truth contained in the text of the *Declaration* of 1789, we have thus finished laying out the historical and ideological "dialectic" of equaliberty, which does not give forth upon an end of history but on a question posed in and by history and in view of its continuation. It permits three "epochs" of politics to be laid out end to end: an *ancient* epoch in which the concept of the citizen is subordinated to anthropological differences, to the unequal statuses of the free man and the slave, the sovereign and the subject, "adult" and "tutelary" humanity; a *modern* epoch in which the concepts of man and citizen are virtually identified, opening the right to politics to all humans; finally a *postmodern* epoch in which the question of going beyond the abstract or generic concept of man on the basis of generalized citizenship is posed. Let us nonetheless note here that, if these epochs succeed upon one another, or engender one another, they do not supplant one another like the scenes of a play: for us, and consequently in our relation to the political *question*, they are all still present in a disunified totality, in a noncontemporaneity that is the very structure of the "current moment," which means that we are simultaneously dealing with the state, with the class struggle, and with anthropological difference. Our burden is to construct a practical conduct for ourselves on all these levels at once without being able to synthesize them. But this does not mean that we have no guiding threads at all. At the turning point between "ancient" politics and "modern" politics we have the *de jure* fact implied by the revolutionary break: the proposition of equaliberty and its universal truth-effect. At the turning point between modern politics and the politics that is in the course of being born within it and against it, we have the *problematic* of a recasting: how do we move from universal truth to singular truth, that is how can we inscribe the program and the very name of equaliberty in singularities? From that fact to this problem there is not continuity, simple progress, even less deduction, but there is necessarily connection, since without the fact the problem could not even be posed.

3

FICHTE AND THE INTERNAL BORDER
On *Addresses to the German Nation*

The ambivalence of Fichte's political philosophy is one of the great common-places of our culture. Few intellectual generations in the last hundred and fifty years have been able to avoid the question of whether this "master thinker" should be grouped among the heralds of freedom or the forerun-ners of totalitarianism, the defenders of law and rational consciousness, or the precursors of irrationalism and organicism (not to speak of racism).

One of the interests of this discussion, in which the same arguments and the same sensitive points are periodically repeated, is that it is itself an ideological phenomenon in the history of the Franco-German problem:[1] extending from the question of the articulation of the *internal* and *external* meaning of the French Revolution to that of the sense in which modern nationalisms find their prototype (if not their origin) in German reactions to the Napoleonic conquest, whether or not one thinks of it as a necessary consequence of the revolutionary event. Another interest is the constant interference between the issue of the proper meaning of Fichte's thought and that of the uses to which some of his statements have been put. It is a privileged case in which the letter of his texts cannot be analyzed in abstraction from the contradictory signification that usage has conferred upon them. Fichte has indeed been indeed "taken into the trenches";[2] at best he can move from one trench to another. But his thought also doubtless contains, if only we can understand how to explain it, one of the keys to the problem of trenches in general: why, despite the clarity with which they are marked on the map, are the battles waged there so doubtful?

This ambivalence can be presented on the basis of a problem of intellectual evolution. Are there *several Fichtes?* Two or even three successive "systems"? From a philosopher of practice, of the moral ideal, do we then move to a philosopher of the absolute? from a secular Fichte to a religious Fichte? from an individualistic Fichte to an organicist Fichte? from Fichte the theorist of natural right to Fichte the theorist of the historical mission of peoples, or rather of *one* quite determinate people? from Fichte the enthusiastic propagandist (and perhaps agent) of the Jacobin revolution and of egalitarianism, to a Fichte who appeals to the authority of the Prussian monarchy as the "*Zwingsherr*" of German unity? from a "cosmopolitan" Fichte to a nationalist Fichte? Between these different formulations, is there simply a juxtaposition due to circumstances or is there rather a term-to-term correspondence that reflects a single determination? And yet: should we really be speaking of breaks, on account of the radicality of expression that the philosopher's positions always adopt, or should we rather see in these positions themselves the symptom of a permanent contradiction that would be translated by incessant displacements?[3] Fichtean philosophy in itself would then be only a process of transition. Several interpreters have seen it in this way, retrospectively of course, and in the light of their own time's questions, even if, in order to determine where this transition is coming from and where it is heading, it has to be put back into the context of an entirely conventional history of ideas: for example, that of "German idealism" or "the birth of nationalism." It is tempting to reverse this perspective, and rather than seeking the reflection of these (too) well-known traditions in a historicist way, to try instead to pick out, amongst the paradoxes of Fichte's text, some of the reasons that constitute the persistent equivocation, both theoretical and political, of the categories of "idealism" and "nationalism" in which this history occurs and is recounted.

I propose here to undertake this analysis beginning from an astonishing expression used in the *Addresses to the German Nation*, where it holds a strategic position, "internal border." I would like to use it as a term that can reveal the tensions that give the text its particular dynamic and its value as a provocation (a very Fichtean term: *Anstoss, Anregung, Anruf*). I would also like to use it as the touchstone of a practice of reading and analysis of philosophical texts that would overcome the traditional alternative between reconstituting systems, by which philosophy gives itself an imaginary autonomy, and using the philosophical text as a document, as only one "expression" or "component" among others in the history of ideas, in the archive of a period. My contention is that the philosophical text carries to an extreme contradictions that go beyond it, but that nowhere else find so constricting a formulation.

Not every formulation is equally liable to such an analysis. "Internal border"—provided we can show that it does indeed have a central function—presents a particular advantage in this respect: it can be said that this expression is in itself a symptom, the condensation of contradictions. First of all, this is on account of the ambivalence of the very notion of "border": the border (*Grenze*) is both what encloses, even what imprisons, and what puts in touch. The site of a passage or a communication, the border constitutes both an obstacle to any ulterior progression and the starting point of an expansion, the essentially provisional limit of an exploration. But above all, there is the necessary equivocality of the apposition "internal borders" (in the plural): whether by this we understand the borders that *divide* the interior of a territory or empire (*Boden, Reich*) into determinate domains (*Gebiet*), or the borders that isolate a region from a surrounding "milieu" and thus individualize it, as expressions of the very constitution of the subject. "Internal borders" represents in some sense the nonrepresentable limit of every border, as it would be seen "from within" its lines. This expression thus brings to the fore all the classical aporias of interiority and exteriority. In the context of a reflection on the identity of a people, of a nation, or more generally of a human group, it necessarily refers to a problematic of purity, or better, of purification, which is to say that it indicates the uncertainty of this identity, the way in which the "inside" can be penetrated or adulterated by its relation with the "outside," which here we will call the foreign, or simply, thought without communication. We will observe the interplay of these connotations in Fichte's text, and will have to ask whether he masters them completely, conceptually. Naturally we can also suppose that he is deliberately *playing* with them in order to provoke a critical effect.

Let us then turn to the text. It is situated at the end of the next-to-last (thirteenth) Address, which recapitulates the lessons of the preceding addresses and begins the appeal Fichte wants to make to his listeners and through them to the entire German nation in the situation of distress it finds itself in (after Jena and Tilsitt):

> the first, original, and truly natural borders (*die ersten, ursprünglichen und wahrhaft natürlichen Grenzen*) of states are beyond doubt their internal borders (*ihre inners Grenzen*). Those who speak the same language (*Was dieselbe Sprache redet*) are joined to each other by a multitude of invisible bonds by nature herself, long before any human art begins (*vor aller menschlichen Kunst vorher*); they understand each other and have the power of continuing to make themselves understood more and more clearly; they belong together and are by nature one and an inseparable whole (*es gehört zusammen, und ist natürlich Eins, und ein unzertrennliches Ganzes*). Such a whole cannot absorb and mingle with itself any other people of different descent and language (*Ein solches kann kein Volk anderer Abkunft und Sprache in sich aufnehmen*) without itself becoming confused, in the beginning at any rate, and violently disturbing the even progress of its culture. From this internal border, which is drawn by the spiritual nature of man himself (*durch die geistige Natur des Menschen selbst gezogenen*), the marking of the external border by dwelling-place (*die äussere Begrenzung der Wohnsitze*) results as a consequence; and in the natural view of this (*in der natürlichen Ansicht der Dinge*) it is not because men dwell between certain mountains and rivers that they are a people (*welche innerhalb gewisser Berge und Flüsse wohnen, um deswillen Ein Volk*), but, on the contrary, men dwell together— and, if their luck has so arranged it, are protected by rivers and mountains—because they were a people already by a law of nature which is much higher (*weil sie schon früher durch ein weit höheres Naturgesetz Ein Volk waren*).[4]

As can be seen, this synthetic presentation of what "makes a people a people" (as Rousseau would say) combines four essential ideas:

a) the natural unity of a people, which determines that of a state, and makes it an indissociable whole, is not territorial but linguistic;

b) a language is the essence of the social bond, because it naturally (before any "artifice," any application of an "art" of politics, any deliberate "convention") forms the element of comprehension or understanding (*Verständigung*) among the parts of the whole (designated by the neuter *Es*);

c) the nature of a language's natural character is spiritual: in this sense linguistic borders, or borders that are manifested by linguistic identity, are "internal" and not "external";

d) the outside can react upon the inside: the mixture (*Vermischung*) of historically and culturally heterogeneous peoples (even simple contact with what is foreign: how is "*in sich aufnehmen*" to be understood? where does the mortal reception of the foreign begin?) destroys spiritual identity, the *meaning* of a people's history: it closes off its future.

I will first examine the meaning of these statements in the context of the thirteenth Address, and more generally in the context of the appeal made by Fichte to his compatriots, before seeking to understand how the notion of "linguistic border" is defined on the basis of the properly Fichtean concepts of the *Ursprache* and the *Urvolk*, that is, of the originary unity of a people and a language.

The thirteenth Address includes a very beautiful passage that, on account of the similarity of circumstances, reminds us of Vercors's *Silence de la mer*:

> We are defeated; whether we are now to be despised as well, and rightly despised, whether in addition to all other losses we are to lose our honor also—that will still depend on ourselves. The fight with weapons has ended (*Geschlossen*); there arises now, if we so will it, the new fight of principles (*Grundsätze*), of morals (*Sitten*), of character (*Charakter*). Let us give our guests (*unsern Gästen*) a picture of faithful devotion to friends and fatherland, of incorruptible uprightness and love of duty, of all civic and domestic virtues (*aller bürgerlichen und häuslichen Tugenden*), to take home with them as a friendly gift from their hosts (*als freundliches Gastgeschenk mit in ihre Heimat*), for they will return home at last at some time or other. Let us be careful not to invite them to despise us; there would, however, be no surer way to do this than if we either feared them beyond measure or gave up our way of life (*unsre Weise dazusein aufzugeben*) and strove to resemble them in theirs. Be it far from us as individuals to be so unmannerly as to provoke or irritate individuals (*die Ungebühr, dass der einzelne die einzelnen herausfordere, und reize*); but, as to the rest, our safest measure (*die sicherste Massregel*) will be to go our own way in all things, as if we were alone with ourselves (*als ob wir mit uns selber allein wären*), and not to establish any relation that is not laid upon us by absolute necessity (*durchaus kein Verhältnis anzuknüpfen, das uns die Notwendigkeit nicht schlechtin auflegt*); and the surest means to this (*das sicherste Mittel hierzu*) will be for each one to content himself with what the old national conditions are able to afford him (*was die alten Vaterländischen Verhältnisse ihm zu leisten Vermögen*), to take up his share of the common burden (*die gemeinschaftliche Last*) according to his powers, but to look upon any

favor from foreigners (*jede Begünstigung durch das Ausland*) as
a disgrace and a dishonor. (13th Address, 217/235-236)

It is a moral attitude that is being described here, which once again refers
to the drawing of a "internal border." But it can be read, understood, in two
ways, with two different accents. The context will not remove this equivocation. The debates it has caused until the present day in Germany itself even
assure us that it is insurmountable in practice. Let us look a little more closely.

The first possibility is that the external borders (or what held their place:
the fragile sovereignty of the German states, the fiction of the Holy Roman
Empire) are broken (crossed) and destroyed. Napoleon is in Berlin, he has
proclaimed the dissolution of the Holy Roman Empire and incorporated
part of Germany into the Confederation of the Rhine. *But the internal borders remain*: provided that the Germans remain invincible within themselves—something which is always within a man's power—this fortress
cannot be taken (like Luther's faith: *ein' feste Burg*), these borders cannot be
crossed. With his language and his culture, each individual bears within
himself the whole of the community; but each individual is also responsible, by his moral attitude, for the whole community. Whence comes the idea
that if, among the occupying troops (*Gäste!*), the Germans live alone, as if
they were only amongst themselves, if—anticipating Gandhi—they practice
an absolute "noncooperation," an "invisible border" will separate them from
the conqueror, moving the line of defense within, to a place which is everywhere and thus nowhere, inaccessible. Inversely, an internal border through
the mind or the soul of each German, separating resignation from pride,
assimilation of foreign ideas (becoming Frenchified) from Germanness: it is
the latter that must be fortified and defended, by means of a *resolution*
(*Entschluss*) renewed at every moment, if necessary against oneself (in an
inner combat between *Selbst* and *Selbstsucht*).

In this first reading, the idea is that of resistance (*Widerstand*), of a citadel
(one could even say that the true fortifications in war are internal, which
removes Machiavelli's objection against fortified places). Not only is this
resistance not incompatible with a call to arms, but it can be considered as a
preparation for it, a "moral rearmament" preceding and conditioning military rearmament. Likewise, the plan of national education at the heart of the
program for the regeneration of Germany precedes and conditions an
armed struggle, for war is only ever the continuation of politics by other
means: or rather it would continue politics only to the extent that politics is

founded upon a civic mysticism, if the soldiers—as at Valmy—are the citizens of an ethical community. Similarly, the political unity of Germany (the foundation of a national state) presupposes the consciousness of its spiritual unity. The drawing of the internal borders of freedom is the condition of the liberation of the external borders, which will come in its own time.

But this possible reading—which supposes that the letter of the text be filled out by a few elements of the context—can be placed in opposition to another one, no longer centered on the idea of resistance but on that of *refuge* (*Zufluchtsort*: a key term in the Protestant tradition, and particularly in the history of Prussian relations with France, which plays a central role in the *Addresses*). Doubtless we are defeated, our territorial states have been made into satellites, but this is secondary and in truth is only *external*. A refuge always exists for national identity, which, as an essentially moral identity (of the order of *Gesinnung* and *Sittlichkeit*), never had anything but a secondary and artificial (*künstlich*) connection with these states and their borders, and this refuge is precisely the "self" (*Selbst*) of the Germans. Or rather this refuge is the invisible liaison woven between them by the bonds of language, the invisible unity of what will soon be called the *Kulturnation.* Not only is this refuge the only one that *deserves* to be defended (for it does not concern the past greatness of states, irremediably destroyed, but, beyond all power politics, a greatness to come, the *destiny* of man); it is also the only one that *can* be defended, on the basis of the defeat itself. This then is a moment of truth and a unique opportunity that must be seized: for this refuge is not delimited by an "external border" at which the Germans would run up against other peoples; it consists in the invisible reality of their inner world, where they can progress indefinitely while encountering only themselves, running into only their own inertia (*Trägheit*) or moral indolence. The meaning of the *call* is not to prepare a reconquest or a revenge, but to incite to *reflection and meditation* (*Andacht, andenken*), in which exteriority loses all importance. It is not a reconquest of the borders (in the usual sense), but a conquest of morality and culture.

Can the context resolve this equivocation, or does it rather reinforce it? What are we to understand (what must Fichte's listeners have understood) when he cries:

> In the addresses which I conclude today, I have spoken aloud to you first of all, but I have had in view the whole German nation, and my intention has been to gather round me, in the

room in which you are bodily present, everyone in the domain of the German language (*so weit die deutsche Zunge reicht*) who is able to understand me. If I have succeeded in throwing into any heart which has beaten here in front of me a spark which will continue to glow there and to influence its life, it is not my intention that these hearts should remain apart and lonely; I want to gather to them from over the whole of our common soil (*über den ganzen gemeinsamen Boden hinweg*) men of similar sentiments and resolutions, and to link them together, so that at this central point a single, continuous, and unceasing flame of patriotic disposition may be kindled (*eine einzige fortfliessende und zusammenhängende Flamme vater-ländischer Denkart*), which will spread over the whole soil of the fatherland to its utmost boundaries. (14th Address, 228/248)

And what "resolution" does he have in mind when he continues:

Go not from your place this time without first making a firm resolution....Make it on the spot, this resolution (*Geht nur dieses Mal nicht von der Stelle, ohne einen festen Entschluss gefasst zu haben....Fasset ihn auf der Stelle, diesen Entschluss*)? (14th Address, 229/249)

History has recorded that the *Addresses* were unanimously applauded by "Germans" many of whom, perhaps most of whom were the enemies of Fichte's republicanism (still recalled in the text). It also tells us that among the organizers of the corps of volunteers who prepared the 1813 war of "national liberation" (the historical origin of this expression) were many young listeners who had been inspired by the speeches of 1808. If the need for limitations imposed by the censorship is taken into account, there is no need for a scholarly decoding to hear a call to arms in the call to moral resolution.

The fact remains, however, that Fichte insistently describes the latter as purely internal:

let everyone who hears my voice make this resolution by himself and for himself, just as if he were alone and had to do everything alone. If very many individuals think in this way, there will soon be formed a large community which will be fused into a single close-connected force....You must make a resolution of a kind which each one can carry out only by himself and in his own person....No, you are called upon to make a resolve that will itself be part of your life, a resolve that is itself a deed within you, that endures there and continues to hold sway without being moved or shaken, a resolve that never grows cold, until it has obtained its object (*und jedweder, der diese Stimme vernimmt, fasse diesen Entschluss bei sich selbst, und für sich selbst, gleich als ob er allein da sei, und alles allein tun müsse. Wenn recht viele einzelne so denken, so wird bald ein grosses Ganzes dastehen, das in eine einige engverbundene Kraft zusammenfliesse....Eine Entschliessung sollt ihr fassen, die jedweder nur durch sich selbst und in seiner eignen Person ausführen kann....Es wird von euch gefordert ein solcher Entschluss, der zugleich unmittelbar Leben sei, und inwendige Tat, und der da ohne wanken oder Erkältung fortdaure und fortwalte, bis er am Ziele sei*). (14th Address, 229-30/249-50)

And above all this object or *goal* itself is only ever described as a moral and spiritual goal, the (re)constitution of a virtuous community whose specifically "German" character will be founded upon the reciprocal inherence of the German language (the "true" or sincere language *par excellence*) and a culture of morality. At the end of the thirteenth Address, after having stigmatized the Napoleonolatry of some of his compatriots in barely disguised terms, Fichte demands only that they preserve from such "defilement" (*Besudelung*) "our language, which is formed to express the truth (*unsrer zum Ausdrucke des Wahren gebildete Sprache*)" (13th Address, 227/247). His call is a call to *reflection* (*Nachdenken*) (14th Address, 231/251), to the liberation of a spiritual world (*Geisterwelt*) "freed from all sensuous motives (*der Geist allein, rein, und ausgezogen von allen sinnlichen Antrieben, soll an das Ruder der menschlichen Angelegenheiten treten*)" (243/265), the advent of a "realm of justice, reason, and truth (*ein Reich des Rechts, der Vernunft und der Wahrheit*)" (245/267).

Do these formulations mean that all Fichte did was to impose a messianic discourse (clearly theological at bottom) on the conjuncture? And if so, was it to the benefit of religion or politics? Or are these formulations rather to be explained by tactical preoccupations, that is, because Fichte overestimated the power of the Napoleonic empire and did not believe that political liberation could be accomplished by the present generation, or because he had to use a duplicitous language to get around censorship? One might think so, hearing him explain to his listeners from the first Address on that his theses will present no *danger*, or that the formation of a national consciousness by education is a long-term, multi-generational project.

But other developments show that this retreat from or of the political (*retrait du politique*) has a more essential meaning and is itself part of the final goal. Thus military glory is denounced as foreign to the purity of the German spirit. It indeed seems that, even if he describes dying for one's country as the supreme sacrifice, *nonviolence* is the principal characteristic of the "patriotism" called for by Fichte as the means of a true liberation. This would explain why he presents the political fragmentation of Germany, the apparent cause of its military weakness, not as a misfortune, but quite to the contrary—adopting with insistence the romantic model of ancient Hellenism—as the historical fortune to which the Germans owe the preservation of the originality of their culture and the development of the "human as such" (*das rein Menschliche*) in their popular consciousness. For the political effect of this fragmentation was to *dissociate the state and the nation* (8th Address, 139/147). This would even explain how he can present German national independence, in the sense defined here, as a requirement for all of humanity, beginning with the *foreign conqueror.*

> A solemn appeal comes to you even from foreign countries, in so far as they still understand themselves even to the slightest extent, and still have an eye for their true advantage (*Es beschwöret euch selbst das Ausland, inwiefern dasselbe nur noch im mindesten sich selbst versteht, und noch ein Auge hat für seinen wahren Vorteil*) (14th Address, 244/266-67).

From this point of view, the *internal* aspiration of peoples to universal peace (distinct from the interests of their governments) and the equally *internal* aspiration of Germans to freedom do not constitute two facts that are different in nature: they are only the two faces of a single spiritual event in which the meaning of present history is made manifest.

But is not the *positive* condition (in a mystic and apocalyptic mode) of this profound unity *the annihilation of all external forms of German identity*, which is only the concentrated form of the "fundamental traits" of the epoch insofar as it presents itself as the "end of a world"? The key to the problem manifestly lies in the signification taken on by the "universal mission" of the German nation, or yet in the way in which, in the perspective of this *singular* historical election, the particularity of the German people turns out to be negated and sublated by its universality. The signs of this election had previously been sought in various historical events (the resistance of the Germanic tribes to romanization, the civic liberties of German cities, the Lutheran Reformation, the *Gründlichkeit* of German philosophy), but they only take on their true meaning retrospectively, with the present moment of radical crisis. What characterizes this crisis *politically* in Fichte's eyes is that, out of a secular confrontation between two different principles of government and organization of Europe, imperialism and European equilibrium, for the first time there appears the possibility of another order, one that would be intrinsically or *naturally pacific*. What characterizes it morally is that it gives birth to an entirely new spirit (*das Beginnen eines ganz neuen Geistes*) through a revolution that "recreates" the whole human being (*eine gänzliche Umschaffung*) (13th Address, 223/243). This morality and this politics are tied together by a philosophy of history, which we must now examine briefly.

Two "dialectics" are interwoven in the historical tableau drawn up by Fichte: a temporal dialectic and a dialectic of territory. They fall under the domain of empirical realism, that is, they characterize the world of phenomena (*Erscheinungen*)—phenomena behind which, in conformity with Fichte's constant critique, it is useless to seek a "thing in itself." But they are only connected by means of a moral category, *egoism*. In fact both are only dialectics of its unfolding and its self-destruction.

The temporal dialectic of the forms of domination in European history can be easily summarized. It begins with Roman imperialism, and is prolonged into the Middle Ages by the dream of a "universal monarchy" fusing the Roman conception of the state with ecclesiastical authority, that is, with external religion, the incorporation of individuals into the structures of the visible church, the "Latin" negation of national particularities. This domination (*Herrschaft*) from the beginning encountered its limit in the resistance of the Germanic tribes, reported by Tacitus in a famous sentence. Above all it was broken when confronted by the affirmation of individuals who want "to remain like themselves (*sich selbst gleich bleiben*)" (13th Address, 219/238). From natural independence they pass to *self-consciousness*, that is to consciousness *of the self* in culture and education (*ibid.*). Against the uniformity imposed by church and state, one can then see new historical subjects, the princes and the peoples—the former ruling but moved above all by particular interests; the latter subordinate but representing universal interests and thus truly *active*. When these interests fuse, for example in the Lutheran Reformation (cf. the 6th Address), humanity as such progresses.

Then opens a new period, which can be characterized as that of *alienation* (*Entfremdung*) properly speaking: the era of competing individualities, or of the war of all against all, in which the peoples are driven (*Trieb*) to affirm

71

themselves at each other's expense, and become the instruments of dynastic ambitions. This situation takes on the figure of "European equilibrium," officially instituted by the treaties of Westphalia and theorized by the classical understanding's "art of politics." The politics of *Verstand* treats individuals and peoples, both at home and abroad, as cogs in a complex mechanism and not as autonomous citizens: it thus goes hand in hand with absolute monarchy, "enlightened" despotism, etc.

European equilibrium is a balance of powers that one hopes to submit to calculation and stabilize. Peace is certainly its official goal, but it does not attain it, for two reasons. The first reason is theoretical: the artifice itself, the permanent contradiction between its motivations and its means. It is sufficient to read Machiavelli to be convinced that there are no natural limits to human avidity (*natürliche Beschränkung der menschlichen Habsucht*) (13th Address, 209). The other reason is practical, historically singular: the system of European equilibrium from the beginning rests on the presence, in the center of Europe (*im Mittelpunkte von Europa*), of a *nonstate* (Germany), which does not take part in the pillage (*Beute*), which is left out of the balance of powers and therefore can balance it by holding all forces at a distance. Unfortunately this situation turns around into its opposite: instead of holding the adversaries in respect, like a wall or screen of dissuasion (*ein fester Wall*) (13th Address, 210)—that is as an uncrossable human border—the land of Germany has only ever been their common prey, the closed field of their political interests into which the divisions of Europe are projected (in the form of small, splintered states—*Kleinstaaterei*—of alliances made and broken, of dynastic rivalries). Germany foreign to itself is the image of alienated Europe, and the permanent cause of its instability (*Unruhe*).[5] European equilibrium is thus a murderous "dream" (*Traum*), a "nothingness" (*Nichtigkeit*) that returns to nothingness.

This is the picture presented by the current situation. By definitively destroying the shadow of German autonomy, the Napoleonic conquest resuscitates the project of universal monarchy, along with the cult of the state and the development of the administrative machine as an end in itself. Nevertheless this return to the beginnings—to the "Roman" conception of the social bond—is in total contradiction with the current aspiration to civic liberty, as well, doubtless, as with the "economic" fact of the universal expansion of commerce. This is another figure of "egoism" to which we should now turn our attention.

In the *Addresses*, Fichte refers back to his own analysis of *The Closed Commercial State*.[6] This controversial text—the privileged target of Hegel's irony and of the irony of the liberal current more generally—generated uneasiness from the beginning, and has been presented in turn as an egalitarian utopia (Rousseauist or Babouvist), as the expression of an archaic "mercantilism," as an anticipation of socialist planning or "economic nationalism" (from List to Schacht, or to Keynes…). I will point out only a few themes here.

The declared objective of *The Closed Commercial State* is twofold: social peace at home and universal peace abroad. But these two objectives both run into the same obstacle: the power of *money*, the hidden cause behind which is the indefinite expansion of commerce, and particularly of international commerce. This is another form of *imperialism*. The well-known "excesses" of *The Closed Commercial State*—the suppression of the right to landed property in the name of the right to work, guaranteed by strict state regulation, the "closing" of borders to all circulation of goods and persons, with the exception of a few scholars and artists charged with organizing cultural exchanges—can doubtless be traced back to various ideological sources. But in the final analysis they are to be explained by the logical consistency with which Fichte attacks the common principle of inequality and war. On the one hand the division of labor is subordinated to commercial property, leading to the antagonism of social conditions; on the other, one finds the economic antagonism between states that have become "open commercial states," of which colonialism (violently criticized by Fichte) is an essential moment. The "secret war" culminates in open war. The authoritarian closing of borders called for by Fichte, a means of doing away with money (or at least of separating money within the country from international money and thus of getting rid of the "worldwide" space of capitalist accumulation) should resolve this double problem, so to speak, with a single stone.

We can draw a very interesting lesson from this confrontation between *The Closed Commercial State* and the *Addresses to the German Nation* with respect to the reasons underlying his critique of "cosmopolitanism," which we will encounter again with respect to his plans for national education. Cosmopolitanism presents itself as a universalism (going beyond historical borders) and as a humanism (going beyond differences of social status, of "majorities" and "minorities"). In reality it can be neither the one nor the other. "Cosmopolitanism"—as it appeared in the eighteenth century in the "Republic of Letters," for which it was a point of honor—is only the *alienated* figure of humanism and universality.[7] Far from announcing the overcoming of national rivalries, it is their ideological manifestation, whose truth lies in what is *done* in its name and not in what is *said*. Now what is done is, on the one hand, the imposition of French as a "universal language" on the philosophy and science of all peoples, and on the other hand the institution of a split between the lower classes, the masses, and the "cultivated class" of all nations, the two processes being obviously related.[8] A double alienation, both for the intellectuals (*Gelehrten*) and for the people: the former feel nothing of what they express in a foreign language (their concepts are empty), the latter have no rational knowledge of what they feel (their intuitions are blind) and thus become foreign to their own thought (we will encounter this problem of the sensible side and the intellectual side of language again).

Contrary to appearances, *modern* (Napoleonic) *imperialism* and *economic liberalism*, or the "French" and "English" versions of cosmopolitanism, two forms of the decomposition of "European equilibrium" whose mutual incompatibility characterizes the current crisis and provides a continual cause of war, are thus not phenomena of a different nature. Both are forms of *exteriorization* of the social bond (*Band*), in which the self (*Selbst*) becomes lost and vainly seeks itself (despite the fact that the etymology is false, how can we not be tempted by the play on words with *Selbstsucht*, egotism) outside itself (*das Fremde, das Ausland*). This alienation begins with the fetishism of property (*Habsucht*), whether in the form of the territorial expansion of a state or of the individual possession of the earth, that is the substitution of *being what one has* for *being what one does*, or of *being for things* (*Dinge*)—things in the world of things—for *being by action* (*Tat, Tätigkeit*).

It is this configuration that gives Germany a universal mission: not by virtue of a predestination, but by virtue of a historical situation, although it is one in which the empirical fact runs into its own internal limits. In short, this is a situation of all or nothing: for Germany, disappearance or regeneration *on another level*; for Europe, generalized war continuing indefinitely, or beginning history over again *on other principles*. If only Germany effectively *wills* what necessity has imposed on it—to form a nation of minds united around a moral principle, intrinsically pacific—the example it gives will become irresistible and a new era can begin. Its own independence will come as a bonus.

Nevertheless, is not such an explanation contradicted by the way that, before the fact, Fichte had given "Germanness" (*Deutschheit*) a *natural* privilege by making the German people the *Urvolk* of European history: at once origin of the other peoples, the originary people, people in itself and people *par excellence....* And did not this characteristic also imply granting it a political primacy?

Now, the definition of the Germanic *Urvolk* is inseparable from that which makes German the *Ursprache*, the originary language or first language. It is even on the basis of this conjunction (in the fourth, fifth, and sixth Addresses) that Fichte had tied together the themes of identity and national purity that later (throughout the nineteenth and twentieth centuries) were put into action by the "linguistic policy" of national states or inversely were claimed by movements seeking nationhood, and which on this account would seem to be the truth of nationalism stated in its own language. Let us examine them more closely by setting out, as Fichte does, from the notion of border. The very rigorous order of its development will clarify the singular meaning finally taken up by the constantly repeated formula that the original people (*das ursprüngliche Volk*) or originary people (*das Urvolk*) is "the people of an originary language (*das Volk einer Ursprache*)" (6th Address, 91/91).

First of all, Fichte submits the notion of "natural border" to a polemical displacement. We have already cited the key passage of the thirteenth Address. The same theme had already been put forward in the fourth Address: there is no geographical or geopolitical determinism; what constitutes the difference in meaning (and in value) between German history and that of other peoples who come from a Teutonic "stock" or "lineage" (*Stamm*) is not the autochthony of the former in opposition to the migrations of the latter, but only the relation to the linguistic origin. It should be recalled here that a few years earlier, in a style quite characteristic of romantic "primitivism," Ernst Moritz Arndt had written:

> The first natural border is that which every land receives from its own sea; the second is a language....The land now called Germany should be the sole possessor of the Rhine and of the sea on both sides of the Rhine as its natural borders (*Die erste Naturgrenze ist, dass jedes Land sein Meer bekomme, die zweite die Sprache....das Land, das jetzt Teutschland heisst, muss den Rhein allein besitzen, und das Meer zu Beiden Seiten des Rheins als seine Naturgrenze*).[9]

Fichte reverses the order of determination: what constitutes a people is not territory but language, which men carry with them; national unity is anthropological, not ecological, for it resides solely in the quality of lived relations between men. But we must go back still further, if not to the (nebulous) origins of the notion of "natural borders," at least to its use in the eighteenth century. The *Encyclopédie* defined *nation* as "a collective word used to express a considerable quantity of people, which lives in a particular stretch of country, enclosed within definite limits, and which obeys a single government."[10] The notions of territory and border here are strictly tied to that of sovereignty, even if still in the perspective of a subjection, of a unity given "from above." In demanding for the armies of the French revolution the conquest of "natural borders," a prelude to the expansion of the "Grande Nation" over ever more vast territories, Danton in practice gave this version of "natural right" its true figure. Fichte, it might be said, draws its consequences: the only "natural" borders are the human borders of a spontaneous linguistic community; territorial borders are always political (that is, based in the state) and are only institutions, the marks of an appropriation of things and not the expressions of the subject itself. They refer to force, not freedom. These analyses thereby *rectify* the thesis of *The Closed Commercial State*, which claimed for the historical state on the way to becoming the "state of reason" the establishment of natural (geographical) borders. Or rather, they relativize its meaning, which remains merely external.

But this is only the first displacement. What does the collective unity, the anthropological community, consist of? Here a second polemical element intervenes:

> Moreover, the variety of natural influences in the region inhabited by the Teutons is not very great. Just as little importance would be attached to the fact that the Teutonic stock (*die germanische Abstammung*) has intermingled with the former inhabitants of the countries it has conquered; for, after all, the victors and masters of the new people that arose from this intermingling were none but Teutons (*denn Sieger, und Herrscher, und Bildner des aus der Vermischung entstehenden neuen Volks waren doch nur die Germanen*). Moreover, in the mother-country (*im Mutterland*) there was an intermingling with Slavs similar to that which took place abroad with Gauls, Cantabrians, etc., and perhaps of no less extent; so that it would not be easy at the present day for any of the peoples descended from the Teutons to demonstrate a greater purity of descent than the others (*eine grössere Reinheit seiner Abstammung vor den übrigen darzutun*). (4th Address, 60-61/54-55)

In other words the anthropological unity is not genealogical. Even as Fichte places himself in opposition to Kant by granting an ethical importance to language and linguistic unity, he follows him in completely dissociating the notions of stock and people, and opposes the idea that there would be a historical link between linguistic continuity and biological continuity. The inheritors of the language and culture that represent the temporal unity of a nation (and in particular of Germanness) have nothing to do with the "blood" descendants of Teutons, Slavs, or Celts. Whence is derived the fundamental thesis:

> More important, however, and in my opinion the cause of a complete contrast between the Germans and the other peoples of Teutonic descent is the second change, the change of language....It is not a question of the previous ancestry (*die vorige Abstammung*) of those who continue to speak an original language without interruption (*derer, die eine ursprüngliche Sprache ohne Unterbrechung fortsprechen*); on the contrary, the importance lies solely in the fact that this language continues to be spoken without interruption (*dass diese Sprache ohne Unterbrechung fortgesprochen werde*), for men are formed by language far more than language is formed by men (*indem weitmehr die Menschen von der Sprache gebildet werden, denn die Sprache von den Menschen*). (*ibid.*)

This thesis reverses the use of the notion of origin, and with it the meaning of the notion of *Urvolk* as applied to the Germans. It allows us to understand how Fichte, in reality, applies a theoretical strategy whose goal is to turn this notion away from its contemporary use. One might fear dangerous political consequences from this strategy, since it permits the substitution of one *Urvolk* (the Germans) or perhaps two (the Germans and the Greeks) for the "egalitarian" multiplicity of national-popular cultural sources defended by Herder. But things are less simple than that since, simultaneously, it is the myth of descendance which is challenged. In what makes a people *a* people there is indeed an essential link to something originary, but this something originary is not the empirical *being* of the people; it is only the *effect* of its practical relation to the linguistic origin. There is indeed an essential continuity, but this continuity is not the "natural" result of the succession of generations; on the contrary, its task is to confer an intelligible, properly historical meaning on this succession.

What then is the originary language, or rather what is originary in language (*Ursprache*)? In the end everything hangs on this question. But it holds a final surprise for us, which is the third displacement of the problem.

The originary language, Fichte never stops repeating, is "living" language (*die lebendige Sprache* in opposition to *die tote Sprache*).

But Fichte here is playing on words: both on the word "language" and on the word "life." The romantic linguists,[11] substituting for the classical rationalist question of the origin of languages (and of primitive language) the "historical" question of the *Ursprache* or the "mother language" of all the others, had concluded on the priority of German, or rather Indo-Germanic, basing themselves on the nascent techniques of comparative grammar. Fichte totally ignores this genetic point of view, just as he ignores linguistic reality and in particular grammar, which has nothing to do with his problem. The opposition he draws between the Germans and the other people of Teutonic origin does not concern the "special quality" (*Beschaffenheit*) of their respective languages, but "solely the fact that in the one case something native is retained, while in the other case something foreign is adopted (*sondern allein darauf, dass es dort Eigenes behalten, hier Fremdes angenommen wird*)" (4th Address, 61/55), that is, the fact of "purity" or "mingling." Independently of the secondary question of how old it is, a living language is a language kept pure of influences, subtracted by its very nature from cosmopolitanism, and more profoundly from what it is tempting to call here—to borrow a recently proposed terminology—European "colinguism"[12] (which is why Greek and German are equally considered "living" languages). But this, with the exception of a few elements that are indexes rather than essential characteristics (borrowings of Latin vocabulary among the literati of the *Aufklärung*), refers less to the *objectivity of the language* than to the *subjectivity of speech*: it is a way of "living" a language and of living "in" the element of a language, an ethical attitude. This is why in the end Fichte characterizes living, originary, or authentic language by the unity of three phenomena: it is practiced in a continuous way, which allows it to gather its own history within itself and ceaselessly transform itself; it rests upon direct communication among the various classes of the people, which allows the people to be educated by *its own* intellectuals and allows these intellectuals to understand themselves; it has a "symbolical" (*sinnbildlich*) character, which means, in opposition to the arbitrariness of the borrowed sign and to the conventionality that is part of any mixed language, that each "act of language" makes real the necessary unity of the sensible and the spiritual.

Let us stop here to examine the effects of these successive displacements. It is first of all clear that Fichte has progressively emptied the notions of *Urvolk* and *Ursprache* of all "naturalist" content, but also of all "historicist" content. Thus the Germanness he seeks to define has nothing essential in common with a *past*, except insofar as the past inspires a project for the future (in the final analysis, spiritual and moral regeneration), insofar as the contingency of the past is sublimated in the production of the *future*. The "original life" of the people, and first of all of the language that weaves the fabric of the community, is essentially the movement of a continuous formation (*Bildung*), of a practical activity (*Tätigkeit*), of a transcendence of everything that is given, and determined as given ("*Etwas*"). It is a permanent inner revolution. The originary does not designate *whence a people comes*, but *what it is moving toward*, or still more precisely the moral destiny that it actively gives itself, and whose proof Fichte thinks he can locate in a particular "German" disposition to *take seriously* the words of the language: to "live as one speaks" and to "speak as one acts." The originary, authentic language is not only the language of action, it is moral action in language; it is not a language that has a history, but a "live speech" that makes history, and that must be seized in the moment of its making.

It is no less clear, in these conditions, that Fichte's "definition" is circular. But it is precisely this circle that is important to him. The circle of a language and a people, of their reciprocal belonging: a people which is itself living makes a living language, a living speech gives life to the language of a people and thus makes the people itself live. The circle of "life" (*Leben*) and of "mental formation" (*geistige Bildung*): "Where the people has a living language, mental formation influences life; where the contrary is the case, mental formation and life go their way independently of each other (*Beim Volke der lebendigen Sprache greift die Geistesbildung ein ins Leben; beim Gegenteile geht geistige Bildung, und Leben jedes seinen Gang für sich fort)*" (4th Address, 74/70). In the final analysis this circle is the form taken on in the *Addresses*, thus in a "popular" style (which doubtless was what allowed Fichte to find the *theoretical* solution he had sought through the incessant reworkings of the *Wissenschaftslehre*), by the notion of the *transcendental*.

In fact it is necessary to say both that "men are formed by the language" *and* that "men make themselves," in that they make the life of their language: but *not in the same sense*. Inasmuch as men are empirical individuals, that is, that they belong to the world of reciprocally determined "things" (that they are *etwas*), it can be said that they are "made" above all by the language, that is, that the language fixes the limits or conditions of possibility of their understanding, of their knowledge. It can even be said, depending on whether the language is pure or perverted, that this understanding is true or illusory and inauthentic. Were it not for the *form* of the language, it would not be comprehensible why Fichte can write:

I must invite you to a consideration of the nature of language in general (*das Wesen der Sprache überhaupt*). Language in general, and especially the designation of objects in language by sounds from the organs of speech (*besonders die Bezeichnung der Gegenstände in derselben durch das Lautwerden der Sprachwerkzeuge*), is in no way dependent on arbitrary decisions and agreements. On the contrary there is, to begin with, a fundamental law, in accordance with which every idea becomes in the human organs of speech one particular sound and no other (*es gibt zuvörderst ein Grundgesetz, nach welchem jedweder Begriff in den menschlichen Sprachwerkzeugen zu diesem, und keinem andern Laute wird*)....It is not really man that speaks, but human nature speaks in him and announces itself to others of his kind (*Nicht eigentlich redet der Mensch, sondern in ihm redet die menschliche Natur, und verkündiget sich andern seinesgleichen*). Hence one should say: there is and can be but one single language (*Und so müsste man sagen: die Sprache ist eine einzige, und durchaus notwendige*). (4th Address, 61/56)

And further along:

If we give the name of "people" to men whose organs of speech are influenced by the same external conditions, who live together, and who develop their language in continuous communication with each other (*und in fortgesetzter Mitteilung ihre Sprache fortbildenden*), then we must say: the language of this people is necessarily just what it is, and in reality this people does not express its knowledge, but its knowledge expresses itself out of the mouth of the people (*nicht eigentlich dieses Volk spricht seine Erkenntnis aus, sondern seine Erkenntnis selbst spricht sich aus demselben*). (4th Address, 62/56)

But inversely it must be said:

For him (i.e., for he who thinks like a German: *der deutsch Denkende*) history, and with it the human race, does not unfold itself according to some mysterious hidden law, like a round dance (*nach dem verborgenen und wunderlichen Gesetze eines Kreistanzes*); on the contrary, in his opinion a true and proper man himself makes himself (*macht der eigentliche und rechte Mensch sich selbst*), not merely repeating what has existed already, but throughout all time creating what is entirely new (*nicht etwa nur wiederholend das schon Dagewesene, sondern in die Zeit hinein erschaffend das durchaus Neue).* (7th Address, 115/119)

The "man" in question here is no longer empirical man, but essential man or inner man, the one who *decides* in conformity with his vision of the absolute, of eternal life, and thus at the same time practical man, the man who is nothing other than his own constitutive *act*. That man is not "made" by language, but, by speaking in an originary or authentic way, thus by transforming language to infinity, by always posing its limits *beyond* what exists, he makes the idea penetrate into life. The transcendental of language is thus not a *given* transcendental, in which thought is enclosed by categories or "means of expression," but a transcendental speech, which is at the same time the act of auto-constitution of thought. To these two indissociable (at least originarily) faces correspond the two sides of the symbol, the sensible side and the spiritual side, or yet the side of the *image* (*Bild*) and the *invisible* side of the language. It is not impossible to consider that this conception supports itself by means of a permanent self-reference: the model for con- stitutive speech is Fichte's own speech, in the course of recreating the unity (the self-comprehension) of the German nation by his preaching (just like in the past Luther, "*der deutsche Mann*"). It is thus the originary meaning that he is restituting to German words, by giving a sensible (imaged) body to the people to come, by thereby opening the possibility of a new history. By this conception, the notion of an "internal border" acquires its most pro- found import: it is the point at which it speaks (*ça parle*). Better: it is the point at which *I* speak by identifying myself to it (*cela*) (let us remember here the insistent *Es* in the text that we cited at the beginning); the point at which *I* incessantly transform the historical past fixed in institutional "space" into a future, that is, into real historicity. But also the point at which "it"—the language, essence of the social bond ("*die Sprache, die niemals* ist, *sondern ewigfort* wird": the language/speech, which never is, but eternally is becoming) (5th Address, 86/86)—speaks in the first person. Now, this self- reference is supported by a *name*, both "proper" and "common" (*der Deutsche, die Deutschheit*): without it speech would not proceed from any determinate language, the language would be *no one's* act. But this name covers over an equivocation, an internal scission: I, Fichte, new "German man," I am speaking to the Germans because they are other than what they believe, I give a pure sense to the words of their "tribe" (*Stamm*) in order that they might become new (German) men. It is then necessary to go so far as to say that this "border" does not separate *spaces*, (whether it is a matter of territorial spaces or, metaphorically, of cultural universes), but rather represents the point or moment of conversion from constituted space to constituting *time*, which is the time of projection, of decision, of action, of the future, the spiritual future.

Let us conclude provisionally. The passage, through the symbol of language, from immobile space to the invisible mobility of time, implies posing the question of *progress* (*Fortgang, Fortschreiten*), of *perfectibility* (*Verbesserlichkeit*), of *formation* (*Ausbildung*). Fichte does not expose this question in a purely speculative way, but in a very concrete one: he makes it the field *par excellence* of the realization of his politics, inasmuch as it is a politics by and for moral education (*Erziehung*).

On this point I will be content to extract a few significant features from the long developments of the second, third, ninth, tenth, and eleventh Addresses. New figures of the "border," that is, of division and unity, of closure and opening, of the displacement of limits. Three principal theses are involved:

a) the constitution of a new system of education is the condition, or better, the very form that the regeneration of Germany must take: in fact, since this regeneration represents the actualization of an originary character (*Ursprünglichkeit*) that *has not yet begun* to exist in history, what must be said is that it is the form that the birth of Germany must take. It is a matter of a means, but one that contains in itself the actualization of its own end, which is activity (*Tätigkeit*) *par excellence*;

b) this is possible to the extent that education is conceived of as *national* education (*Nationalerziehung*), and not as a literary and cosmopolitan formation reserved for the "cultivated classes" or as a simple popular school destined for the children of inferior social conditions (*Volksbildung*);

c) finally, national education must be organized by the state, which means both that it must be withdrawn from the authority of the family and the church, and that it must immediately be a civic education (Fichte indicates that, by this characteristic, it will rediscover the Greek unity of education and citizenship). Nonetheless this does not mean that national education is a "lay" education, either in the sense of an opposition between religious education and civic education, or in the sense of a separation between collective morality and individual faith. On the contrary, national education is that of the "whole man" (*der vollendete Mensch*), sensible and spiritual, physical and intellectual, in the perspective of an identification of patriotism with pure morality, or of each individual's interiorization of the patriotic community as the community of human freedoms, the site of the moral progress of the generations. In particular the eleventh Address emphasizes this theme. Correlatively, the educational function appears as the principal function of the state, the one that defines it as rational: it commands the military, economic, and juridical functions, and at the limit can be substituted for them. Historically, it allows us to compare the *real* (empirical) *state* to the *state of reason* which it must try to approximate, which is an *educational state*. In its ultimate aim, it prepares the "end of the state," its withering away in the accomplishment of its essence.

The exposition of these theses, taken up over and over again and made concrete in a plan of national education, is traversed by a movement that can be resumed in these terms: national education creates the national community by suppressing the differences between conditions, which constitute another, artificial kind of internal border, and install the reign of egotism under the appearance of nature. But by suppressing these differences it *adds* a spiritual element to nature (a "surplus" or "supplement": *ein Mehr*) without which nature is not properly human, and which is precisely morality. The question which then poses itself is the following: morality means individual freedom, equality of citizens whatever their condition might be, and universal human fraternity. But morality also means an entirely autonomous spiritual *decision* on the part of those who are capable of love and of hope in human perfectibility. Education prepares this decision, in particular, in that it organizes itself in the form of a *closure*, of a quasi-monastic pedagogical cloistering, which should make possible, at least for the majority of men, the expression of their original goodness (tenth Address). But education does not *determine* it. It can thus be asked whether the whole educational process does not tend to substitute, for the historical division of social conditions, another division between the good and the wicked, an invisible border between two species of men: those who live in egotism and those who live in the realm of the spirit.

This then culminates in one final figure of ambivalence. The "true Germans," subjects and products of this national education, are none other than those among the empirical, historical Germans, who are *true* Germans, or better, Germans realizing in action the spiritual destiny of Germany, that is, of eternal humanity (whose fatherland is "heaven on earth"); or yet, Germans as they ought to be rather than Germans as they are; better yet, the *Germans of the future*, empirically mixed up in the present, in the passing crisis, with the Germans of the past. But this means that the German nation can *never* coincide with a German state, even if this state were a unitary and independent state, an educational and egalitarian state, a "republic." Or rather, this means that the concept of the nation, once again, like that of man in his relation to language a moment ago, is divided into an empirical nation and a transcendental nation (which is also the spiritual nation): the empirical nation is produced by the state (and every production—*Erzeugung*—of man is fundamentally an education—*Erziehung*), but the state can produce the nation as a real community only by submitting to the primacy of the ideal nation, of which it is only an instrument. Or yet, if we synthesize the "internal" and "external" determinations of freedom: the state can produce the external independence of the nation, the material condition of its culture, of the autonomous development of its "self" (*Selbst*), of the life of its language and its literature, etc., only by making itself the organizer of education *according to* the ideal model of the inner nation, the invisible nation of minds, and on the condition that this model "live" in it as an *Urbild*, as a constant moral resolution.

This is why Fichte's "patriotism" finally appears as conditional, even though it proclaims itself to be "unconditioned" (and proclaims patriotic duty to be each individual's unconditional duty). Fichte's activity between 1808 and 1813 translates this fact: his projects of organizing the university *against* calls for "academic freedom" but in the name of the superior freedom of the mind, or again his permanent hesitation between public speech and private speech about the patriotic war when it was finally to break out: as if he never was able to reach a determination of whether or not it was in conformity with the concept of national liberation, and thus himself to decide.[13]

But naturally this personal uncertainty on Fichte's part—the empirical Fichte—leaves wide open the possibility for others, speaking *from within* the state apparatus, or in *confrontation* with it, to decide on the conjunctural meaning of his interpellation. The controversy begins right away after his death, and it shows that in practice the national *idea*, thus formulated, is infinitely plastic.

PART TWO

ANTINOMIES OF MARXIAN POLITICS

Materialism, History, and Teleology

4

THE VACILLATION OF IDEOLOGY IN MARXISM

C'est dans le détail même des notions que s'établit un relativisme du rationnel et de l'empirique. La science éprouve alors ce que Nietzsche appelle "un tremblement de concepts," comme si la Terre, le Monde, les choses prenaient une autre structure du fait qu'on pose l'explication sur de nouvelles bases. Toute l'organisation rationnelle "tremble" quand les concepts fondamentaux sont dialectisés.

—Gaston Bachelard, "La dialectique philosophique des notions de la relativité," in *L'engagement rationaliste* (Paris: P.U.F., 1972), 120-21

I

The political and ideological uses of Marxist theory are no more logically implied in its original formulations than they are exterior to its meaning (or to its truth). In fact, the political and ideological uses of Marxism maintain the historical process of its production, which already includes the texts of Marx, Engels, and their immediate successors. From this point of view, Marxist discourse presents from the beginning an acute internal contradiction between the old and the new, materialism and idealism, the effect of a revolutionary irruption and a conservative recuperation, if not a counter-revolutionary one in the strictest sense of the term.

Because the Marxist contradiction cannot be simply located between this or that part of the system but cuts across each of its fundamental theses or concepts, because it keeps displacing its point of application, it is perfectly vain to imagine that one could get rid of that contradiction either by *purifying* Marxism of its bad side, in order to make it entirely positive, or by *refuting* it, in order to consign it to the trash can of history. Whether in the name of Marx, or of Marxism-Leninism, or of scientific socialism, the contradictions at stake here are, at present, strictly insurmountable; they never stop being at work in our everyday existence, just as that existence never stops working on them. On this point at least I agree with Alain Badiou: we have no other way, today, to think philosophically and politically than to stay within the immediate vicinity of this internal/external crisis, closest to its sensitive points.[1]

The initial political and epistemological "break" in Marxism occurs when the terms of this contradiction are bound up—with the double positioning of the concepts of a science of history and the watchwords of a proletarian politics—within the unity of a "class point of view in theory." Nonetheless the contradiction within Marxism only exists within a history. To grasp it we must embark upon a detailed examination of this history, by addressing, simultaneously, the formulation of problems, the application of concepts, and mass social practice. Such an analysis is neither ready-made nor well known; it can no longer be got at simply by destroying traditional illusions about the meaning and internal coherence of Marxism as a "scientific world-view." However, it involves nothing unknowable or mysterious *a priori*. I am offering only a small part of such an analysis, an account of the history of theory. I will speak of the place occupied by the concept of ideology in the Marxism of Marx and Engels, which was to have a decisive historical importance. This place is highly paradoxical. I will express it in terms of the *theoretical vacillation* that characterizes the concept of ideology, a vacillation that consistently manifests itself in terms of eclipses, antithetical deviations, or displacements of problematics.

A Double Birth for a Single Concept

Our starting point is marked by the odd distribution of the term "ideology" in Marx's and Engels's texts themselves. Omnipresent in the writings of 1845–1846, reduced to a few peripheral appearances in the period 1847–1852, ideology is almost nowhere to be found after that until its full-blown restoration in the 1870s, chiefly from the *Anti-Dühring* on. In a sense, this is simply a "well-known" philological fact; but if we look more closely, it can also be seen as the source of a *fausse reconnaissance* played out in all contemporary discourse about Marxism, starting with its own discourse about itself.

The concept of ideology is clearly a decisive innovation and ensures Marxism's theoretical specificity.[2] To use Althusser's terms, its formulation is a mark of the "break" that engenders historical materialism. Yet it has actually been formulated *twice*, in disparate historical contexts and within problematics that preclude any immediate conflation; *first*, in *The German Ideology* by Marx and Engels (mostly Marx), an unpublished text whose uneven yet insistent influence, brought to light by various rereadings and rediscoveries, can be traced throughout the entire history of Marxism; and *second*, in the group of historical and philosophical texts, mostly by Engels, designed to provide Marxism, for the first time, with the appearance of a system. Writing these texts over two decades, Engels at once gave historical materialism its name, rediscovered the term "ideology," and (temporarily) covered over the problems it posed in the guise of an entirely coherent, indeed even positivistic, definition.

How can we fail to assign some symptomatic value to this twenty-year eclipse of the crucial term "ideology" following its massive use in *The German Ideology*? Ideology almost vanished from the discourse of Marx and Engels. There are a few furtive appearances from 1846 to 1852, primarily as polemical references to the "ideologists" of the bourgeoisie and the petty bourgeoisie (Proudhon *et al.*), then nothing more. There is no mention of ideology in the great analyses of the conjuncture and the balance of power such as *The Eighteenth Brumaire*, which Engels nonetheless took as the model of a materialist account of historical events. What is at stake in this subtle analysis of the political representation of social forces is the question of "class in itself" and "class for itself." Ideology does not appear in the preliminary work of *Capital* (notably the *Grundrisse*), nor even in the detailed critique of the economists (*Theories of Surplus Value*). Here again, it is simply a matter of the difference between classical economics and vulgar or apologetic economics.[3]

Above all, there is nothing about ideology in *Capital*, which, whether one likes it or not, is the cornerstone on which the Marxist edifice rests. It can no doubt be argued that a good number of the theoretical models that figure in the classical analyses of ideology are well and truly present in *Capital*: those pertaining to commodity and money fetishism and, more generally, to the inverted relation between the deep sphere of production and the superficial sphere of exchange. Clearly these analyses, by dint of their object, ought to be part of the field of a theory of ideology (or of bourgeois ideology), either to explain the specific effects of ideology or to give an account of its genesis. That only makes more conspicuous the absence of ideology in the theoretical space of *Capital* and generally within what can be called the moment of *Capital* in the history of Marxism. Far from signifying the absence of any corresponding questions, this suggests a recognition that the question is not so simple that it can be inscribed, unequivocally, within any one theoretical statement.

I think it is worth considering this eclipse, not as an accident or an irrelevant terminological quirk, but as the sign of a fundamental difficulty. This hypothesis would be confirmed if we could find one or more instances where the definition of ideology is incompatible with the critique of political economy and where the description of fetishism can be inserted. Our hypothesis already has its counterproof: after *Capital*, the term "fetishism" *disappears in turn* from the texts of Marx and Engels, in spite of its conceptual precision and the organic place it occupies at the core of the development of the "value-form" or of the relation between the essence and appearance of capitalist production, hence of the relation between wage exploitation, the consciousness assumed by the laborers themselves, and the discourse of the economists. In place of fetishism (but is it really in the same place?) a new term appears, one that Engels salvaged from a forgotten manuscript and whose meaning he transformed: "ideology." This extraordinary shuffling of identities suggests that if the question of ideology is constitutive for historical materialism, then several relatively incompatible approaches are involved, each of which has to be pursued in its turn. The study of these differences then becomes a privileged means of access to the internal contradictions of the Marxist problematic.

Materialism and Criticism

Without going into the details of the text of *The German Ideology*, I would like to point out a few of its noteworthy features in a way that will throw some light on the paradoxical nature of the concept of ideology. We can start with a double question: what makes Marx's materialism historical? and, what makes his concept of history materialist?

Marx's history is obviously not materialist simply because it purports to eliminate the speculative in order to constitute itself on an empirically verifiable causality. In principle, this elimination entails snatching history from the clutches of teleology, both in its religious forms (providence, the meaning of history, origins and last things) and in its philosophical forms (a periodization, governed by a principle of human progress—moral, legal, spiritual, or logical); in short, this entails eliminating any identification of a subject of history. This critique coincides with the denunciation of an illusion that makes the *state* the universal component of the historical process, and *man*, as a universal abstraction, its proper subject. Yet this critique of speculation cannot be reduced to an empiricism or positivism. Nor does it consist in a simple clarification of the economic process, of social labor, and of the needs and material interests of classes. By itself such an analysis (of the "real bases" of history) can only return to the presuppositions common to both political economy and classical philosophical utilitarianism, whose individualist materialism itself also rests on an abstract hypothesis of human nature.

Despite what the term traditionally suggests, Marx's materialism can be contained neither within the definition of the matter of history nor within the application of a historical point of view (evolutionary, progressive, dialectical) to matter. It is presented as an essentially derivative position, as a critique of idealist (abstract, speculative, etc.) representations or illusions which mask, mystify, and repress the determining reality of the labor of individuals and social production. Only this critique, by virtue of its own "labor," can provide materialism with its specific content.

Historical materialism is primarily a program of analysis of the process of the formation and real production of idealist representations of history and politics—in short, of the process of idealization. In *The German Ideology* this is the professed objective of a complex and incomplete construction centered on the role of the "division of manual and intellectual labor." In other words, historical materialism is constituted to the extent to which it can prove that the idealization of history is itself the necessary result of a specific history. We can then see how the idea of a scientific critique (along with the equation, science = history) might be justified: because the movement of criticism that opens the analysis of these questions is itself just as much the result of "real historical relations" as are the idealities it addresses.

Yet this is still not enough. We must come to terms with the *force* or forces that allow the idealization of history to impose itself, not only on those who have an interest in it, but also on those whose real conditions it mystifies and whose "movement" for liberation it prohibits. On this point, someone like Stirner can only offer a tautology: the domination of ideas is the reign of ideas of domination (order, hierarchy, the sacred, etc.). What then becomes of ideas of democratic liberation (individual rights, political equality) when they are incarnated, in their turn, in the order of a state, albeit a profane, nonhierarchical one, that of the postrevolutionary bourgeoisie? In suggesting that every state makes use of religion and morality to impose its power, and that every discourse, when it begins to conflict with their interests, divides individuals, Machiavelli and Hobbes do nothing to break out of this vicious circle; they only translate it into the language of a functionalist philosophy of power (the dominant ideas, whatever they are, are those serving the interests of the powerful; at best the powerful must believe in these ideas so that those they dominate will do likewise). It is necessary to determine the question historically, to examine the nature of the "ideas of the ruling class" and the way they become the dominant ideas. Thus, the concept of ideology adds a third question to the preceding two. With respect to the other critiques of the speculative illusion (Kant, Feuerbach) or of the necessity of appearances (Hegel), whether anthropological or dialectical, Marx's originality lies in his overdetermining the question of the cause or necessity of idealities by questioning their mode of action, their power, and their subjugating effects.[4]

Considered in the light of this triple determination (the critique of teleology and speculative theory, the materialist origin of idealization, and the analysis of effects of domination), the concept of ideology seems to be the corollary of a definition of the *real relations* that determine the historical process. In traditional philosophy such an invocation of the real and the empirical could only correspond to a denunciation of error or illusion, an antithesis between idealism and realism. The materialist critique of ideology, for its part, corresponds to the analysis of *the real as relation*, as a structure of practical relations. It corresponds to the discovery that the reality of the real is not a "being" immediately identical to itself but is, in a sense, a specific abstraction the individual can only at first perceive as an abstraction twice-removed—speculative or, as Marx puts it, inverted and rendered autonomous. It is not individuals who create this abstraction, for they are themselves only relations or the product of relations. The whole science of history is virtually the distinction between these two antithetical abstractions, which is to say that it deconstructs their identification. It is thus that the science of history is "concrete."

The Purely Proletarian Act

In rereading Marx's argument, however, it seems to be dominated by a frighteningly fragile theoretical *coup de force* which posits against ideology, in the form of an antithetical force or instance, the very being of the proletariat, or, more precisely, the prophetic establishment—in the very place occupied by the revolutionary proletariat—of the discourse that critiques ideology. Thus, it is from this site, the veritable site of truth as well as the place from which the world is changed, that one can grasp the equivalence between the different types of idealization that constitute ideology:

"consciousness" produced at a distance from the real, "abstraction" from the conditions of existence, inversion of their limitation (or their particularity) in a fictional universality, autonomization of "intellectual labor," political idealism, and philosophico-religious speculation (of which German Hegelianism is the quintessential example). It is only from this site that we can *see* the fundamental equivalence between *ideology* and *idealism*, a correspondence that makes the idea of a materialist ideology or a materialist philosophy a contradiction in terms.

By the same token, however, materialism is defined as an absolutely positive term that gathers within itself all the antitheses of ideology/idealism: (real) life, (real) individuality, production (of the conditions of existence), history, practice, and finally, the revolutionary practice of the proletariat (or communism, not as the ideal future, but as the "real movement which abolishes the present state of things"[5] without ever losing touch with production, its initial condition). The real movement of history is a becoming-labor of production ("estrangement, to use a term which will be comprehensible to the philosophers," Marx tells us [*CW* 5:48]), followed by a becoming-production (or better still, a becoming-productivity) of labor. The proletariat is thus a self-affirmation of production and a self-negation of labor. But it must be said that the materialist instance is only seen to be a revolutionary practice when ideology in general can be identified with idealism. And this identification is only possible from the point of view of the proletariat.

Marx's argument thus comes full circle, and it is a strictly *philosophical* circle. Although his thesis—completely identifying material *being* with *practice* and formally bound up within what he calls the "totality of productive forces"—is powerful and profound (if not wholly original), it nonetheless reconstitutes itself as philosophical at the very moment Marx claims to have abolished philosophy (or to have definitively "left" the element of philosophy).

This circle is actually the result of a *coup de force* (which radically divorces practice from theoretical abstraction) followed by a denial. The theoretical discourse announcing this divorce, we are told, is not a true "discourse"; it does not speak from a theoretical position but from the site of practice itself—practice speaking itself about itself (which presupposes, among other things, a notion of the absolute transparency of language—"the language of real life" [*CW* 5:36]). Moreover, it should be the only discourse that, because of its obviousness, is held not by intellectuals but by the proletariat itself, or at least in the very *site* of the proletariat—the discourse of communism.

This initial circle presents a major difficulty which *The German Ideology* copes with only by way of new denials, precisely in reproducing the same circle for the proletariat itself. Consider two of its forms.

1. The self-consciousness of the proletariat is opposed to ideological illusion or inversion, but this consciousness must be both *immediate* (consciousness of its being, that is, its conditions of existence) and *produced* as a practical negation of immediacy; to coincide with its concept, the proletariat must transform and revolutionize itself. The proletariat is the prerequisite condition and the end result of its own revolutionary practice. Marx writes: "In revolutionary activity the changing of oneself coincides with the changing of conditions (of existence)" (*CW* 5:214).

2. The proletariat is first and foremost a class, the class antagonist of the bourgeoisie, and hence places its own interests above theirs. Put like this, however, the proletariat would, by definition, lack universality, or, more precisely, it would in turn be caught up within the mystifying process that abstractly erects a "particular interest" as a "general interest." For the interests of the proletariat to tally with a real universality, with practice as such, those interests must cease to be class interests, and for that to happen, the proletariat itself must *cease to be a class*, must be a class/nonclass. Marx writes of "a class which has really rid itself of the old world, and that stands in opposition to it at the same time." This is the surprising distinction made between *the proletariat as a class and the proletariat as the masses*, analogous in many respects to Rousseau's distinction between the "will of all" and the "general will" (we will encounter Rousseau again further on). Only the masses are revolutionary, because they are *the actual dissolution of society* as it exists, at the point when extreme exploitation has completely stripped the workers of all property and all inherited historical specificity, leaving them effectively naked. Marx presents us with this radical loss of individuality in the shape of a radical individualization. Revolution is nothing but the deed of this act, or the way that history records this dissolution which is its own product. But by the same rigorous logic, this means that there is no—or, at this point, no longer any—class struggle. Properly speaking, *the bourgeoisie is the only class in history*; before it there were only castes, orders, and estates (*Stände*), which were not yet real classes. As for the proletariat, once it matches its definition, it is no longer simply a class but the masses.

I will not discuss here the historical analyses that Marx uses to support this thesis; they are primarily a generalization, a hyperbolic extension of Adam Smith's ideas about the division of labor. In fact, they are derived from the politico-philosophical assumptions that define the proletariat. Yet we must emphasize the disastrous logical consequences of these analyses in the case of the relation between the (communist) proletariat and politics: these two terms are simply incompatible. The proletariat, by definition, is the negation of all politics, identified with an ideological illusion/abstraction. Similarly, communism is the nonstate (*Staat*), it is a state of things (*Zustand*) in which all political mediation has, by definition, disappeared.

Because the proletariat is the act of practical negation of all ideology, there is no such thing as a proletarian ideology, or an ideology of the proletariat, just as we have seen that it would be absurd to talk about a materialist ideology. The proletariat is precisely the mass of concrete individuals, inasmuch as, and under the effect of their conditions of existence, these individuals destroy all ideological consciousness. That is why, as the *Manifesto* will continue to say, the proletariat has no nationality or religion, no family or morality, no politico-juridical illusions: the absolute "*Illusionslosigkeit*" of the proletariat as such. This leads us, of course, to ask about the empirical working class *hic et nunc*: is it really so devoid of all ideological consciousness? The answer suggested by the text of *The German Ideology* is simple but completely tautological: such a working class would not (or not yet) be the revolutionary proletariat.[6]

We should not, however, hasten to pass judgment on this construction, doing no more than condemning it for its idealist or speculative, if not mystical, character and thereby repeating Marx's attack on Hegelian and post-Hegelian philosophy.

On the one hand, this construction includes concepts that will be shown to be susceptible to a series of modifications, ending with its very opposite: a historical analysis of proletarian class struggles as they are determined by the successive configurations, created by capitalism, of the working class and the bourgeoisie.

On the other hand, and most important in virtue of its critical radicality, these formulations are likely, in a different context, to take on a new function and hence a new meaning. They will come to stand for something all the more pertinent to our reading of them, something more than a separation: an inevitable *contradiction* between the ideologies of the proletariat (whether spontaneous or imported) and revolutionary practice. The corollary is that there always comes a time when "revolutionary ideologies" prove to be counterrevolutionary in practice, a time when revolutions occur *against* revolutionary ideologies or ideologies of the proletariat and effectively destroy them. In other words, what Marx does not "think" but what we can think, by no means arbitrarily, in some of the concepts of *The German Ideology*, what these concepts *can think* today, is this intrinsically contradictory relation between revolution and ideology. Though this is not what Marx says in *The German Ideology*, it is a use we can make of his most radical philosophical theses, turned back on themselves and against the "dogmatic sleep" of Marxism.

Domination without the Dominated?

Almost immediately the theses of *The German Ideology* must have raised insoluble contradictions for Marx himself. One therefore understands why he had to do away with this concept of ideology even if he could not do away with the problems it harbored.

The first difficulty lay in the impossibility of inserting the discourse of political economy into the theoretical space thus defined. It would not, in fact, fit into either the category of ideological abstraction (since its specific object was productive labor, analyzed as a social relation: division of labor and exchange) or into that of historical materialism or the science of history (because, expressing the point of view of the bourgeoisie—Marx calls economists their "scientific representatives"—the discourse of political economy always erects a specific interest, that of private property, into the realization of human nature in general). This difficulty lies at the heart of *The German Ideology*. Indeed, it is from Adam Smith, Ferguson, and the Saint-Simonians that Marx draws the "materialist" categories of a periodization of civil society, a correspondence between the forms of property and the forms of the division of labor. All this becomes untenable when Marx, progressing from Smith to Ricardo, comes to grips with the Ricardian definition of value in order to extract socialist conclusions from it, in *The Poverty of Philosophy* and, implicitly, in the *Manifesto*.

Far from clearing up this difficulty, Marx's extension of this critique to Ricardian economic principles (the definition of labor and value) only makes things worse, The critique of economic categories can no longer consist in the prior separation of the domain of the real from that of illusion but rather consists in the work of internally deconstructing each theoretical category. Such a critique involves separating the contradictory elements imbricated within the economic concepts in order to confront them with a practice that is not directly the revolutionary practice of the proletariat but is, rather, *the practice of capital* (with its own contradictions). Thus, one would have to be able to think both the objectivity of economic discourse and its bourgeois class character simultaneously; or even, contrary to the original definition, to think both *the real and the imaginary* within ideology. This is precisely what Marx tries to do in his analysis of fetishism, in attempting to demonstrate how the simultaneous birth of the "form of value" and the necessary illusions of commodity production are brought about, though he returns to a problematic of illusion inspired by Kant and Feuerbach.

A second difficulty, however, may be more directly decisive. It arises from the radical antithesis between the autonomous action of the proletariat (absolutely creative because it is absolutely determined by its conditions of existence) and the abstract world of politics. One would think that by the time Marx (and Engels) wrote *The German Ideology* this difficulty could no longer be ignored, since at that very moment Marx was doing his utmost to bring the communists of several countries together within a single international organization, soon to become the Communist League. If that is not *practicing politics* (against the politics of states and their ruling classes), one wonders what is.

The evidence of this difficulty in the text itself is a symptomatic lack of coherence, political theses that seem to be totally out of place, or equivocal statements for which several contradictory readings are possible.

For instance, we may recall those sentences which no longer have anything to do with communism as a real movement of universal history but rather with real, living communists of the sort one meets *hic et nunc* (in Paris, for instance), communists we have to call to mind in order to explain this name we give to the real movement: "The few non-revolutionary communist bourgeois who made their appearance since the time of Babeuf were a rare occurrence; the vast majority of the communists in all countries are revolutionary" (*CW* 5:226).

We may also recall how Marx emphasizes the difference between French (political) ideology and German (philosophical) ideology: the former is to the latter what history or practice in general is to ideology in general, namely, its antithesis, and thus its real criterion. Here, again, Marx takes up the old nostalgic notions of the young German radicals going back at least to Fichte: "in Germany it is impossible to write this sort of history…since there history has stopped happening" (*CW* 5:43). History happens in France; it happens politically. And it is because this political element is not purely illusory, or rather because all illusions are not equal, that the real differences between these ideologies offer as important a base for the concept of the revolutionary proletariat, perhaps, as the bedrock assumption of material existence or production. Above all, these differences are the effect of a different relation *to the state*. They do not refer to an absolute action, with neither past nor future, but to a specific historical memory: the French had Danton and Robespierre, the mass levy of 1793, Babeuf, Bonaparte; the Germans had only Metternich and Wilhelm-Friedrich—at best they watched history pass by on horseback in the streets below.

The problem becomes more sharply defined in Marx's paradoxical formula of the "*dominant ideology*," whose importance we have noted. What does "ideology of the ruling class" mean? From one paragraph to the next, Marx gives us two answers, and it is from these that we can infer, not without ambiguity, the meaning of the question posed. This ambiguity is clearly reflected in the double semantic value of the term "*herrschend*": is it the *dominance* of a body of representations or a discursive paradigm that typifies the epoch of its own, more or less undivided, "rule,"[7] or else the *domination* exercised (in a "repressive" manner, overtly or not) by one body of representations over another, and, through this mediation, by one practice over another, by one way of life or thought over another? Both are correct, but to understand the causality at work we must look to another, more tricky ambiguity.

We can construe the dominant ideology as a kind of "symbolic capital" of the ruling class itself, as the body of representations that expresses its relation to its *own* conditions and means of existence (for the bourgeoisie, for instance, commodity ownership, legal equality, and political freedom), or to put it another way, as the expression of the relation of the average members of the ruling class to the conditions of rule common to their class (hence, the kind of universal values this rule assumes for each of them). But how does this representation impose itself on individuals who do not have the same relation to the conditions of existence of the ruling class ("manual" workers, for example)? Apparently it can only be because it is forced on them by the "material" means (which include the press and intellectual production in general) monopolized by the ruling class (a monopoly acquired through the mediation of their ideological servants—scribes and scholars of every ilk).

Such a domination, however, remains necessarily exterior to the consciousness of the oppressed (without bringing in, as Marx did not, the irrationalist hypothesis of a "desire for submission"). This is why Marx writes that, for the proletariat, the representations of the dominant ideology—whether legal, moral, patriotic, or otherwise—ultimately "do not exist" (*CW* 5:56), or are purely fictional. But then the concept of ideology disintegrates, surviving only as a variation on the conspiracy theories of the "useful fictions" of power ("if God did not exist, they would have to invent him") of the sort put forward by the mechanistic rationalists of the eighteenth century.

Alternatively, we can construe ideological domination as the result (always already present, which is not to say eternally assured) of a true ideological struggle, that is, as the domination of one ideological consciousness over another. From this point of view, what always corresponds to the constitution of a *dominant* ideology, in tendency at least, is the constitution of a *dominated* ideology, yoked to a process of repression but capable of subverting it. How do we interpret this conflicted birth? Should we posit the reciprocal confrontation, for example, of the representations of the relations members of the antagonistic classes have with their *respective* conditions of existence? Probably not. Rather, we should posit against each other the representations of the relations individuals of antagonistic classes have *to the antagonism itself*, that is, to the social relation that unites them while opposing them and to its derivative forms (property, division of labor, the state, etc.)—a relation they cannot, of course, "live" in the same manner but one that necessarily represents, for them as for others, what is universal in a given epoch, "their" epoch, or the epoch of their antagonism.

This second interpretation is much more profound than the first. It is in fact the one toward which Marx's text is heading. At any rate, we find its deferred trace in the résumé of 1859 (the preface to *A Contribution to the Critique of Political Economy*) in a reference to the "ideological forms in which men become conscious of this conflict and fight it out."[8]

If we ourselves are to fight out an understanding of the logic brought into play here, we will obviously find ourselves opposed to any thesis imputing an absolute lack of reality to the ideological world, and we will no longer understand the sense in which this world "lacks history," or the sense in which it "cannot exist" for the proletariat. We will conclude that there are not only real differences in the ideological world but also contradictions, and that they clash with the contradictions of practice, contributing, in themselves, to "real life."

At this stage of Marx's problematic, however, this interpretation is no less aporetic than the one before; and in order to be able to bring it to conclusion, a dominated ideology would have to be placed in opposition to the dominant ideology—*which is exactly what Marx does not do*, except implicitly, in the emptiness or vacillation of his first expression. The whole of *The German Ideology* is precariously balanced on this concept of "dominant" ideology, for which there is no corresponding "dominated" ideology. It would be impossible to take this term literally without giving credence, finally, to the concept of a proletarian ideology and thus without questioning, again, the divorce of the proletariat from all ideology. And this means breaking up the whole constituent structure of materialism, the layers of correspondence between materiality, production, practice, history, and revolution.

Historical Materialism or Political Materialism

It is obvious that Marx has no solution to the problem. But he is hardly able to ignore it, since it is the essence of revolutionary politics. Ample confirmation of this is provided in the *Communist Manifesto*, written two years after *The German Ideology*. The *Manifesto* presents more than ever the radical antithesis between revolutionary consciousness and all the forms of social consciousness that actually reflect the *past* history of former class oppressions: "The communist revolution is the most radical rupture with traditional property relations; no wonder that its development involves the most radical rupture with traditional ideas."[9] These ideas are none other than those of nationality, religion, family, freedom, culture, law, and so on, which made up the content of what Marx used to call "ideology."

If the *Manifesto* refutes accusations of immorality and barbarism leveled at communism—the "specter that is haunting Europe"—it is clearly not to paint a better picture of proletarian morality, nor even proletarian culture, but rather to establish that the bases of morality and culture have already been destroyed by the rule of bourgeois property.[10] This essential de-ideologization, or, if you like, this anti-ideological tendency of the proletariat, is consistent with the catastrophism of the *Manifesto*'s theses on class antagonism (the idea of "absolute impoverishment," the bourgeoisie can no longer feed those who feed it), and with its universalism (the ideal of crisis and world revolution). It is consistent with the description of socialist and communist literature put forward in chapter 3, a remarkable outline for a class analysis of anticapitalist ideologies but one strictly limited to the range of *nonproletarian* discourse, or discourse that expresses not the proletariat itself but rather the figure it cuts in the imaginary of other classes.

Confronted with this imaginary, the discourse of the *Manifesto* is positioned by both the critical relation it maintains with this imaginary and another radically different relation, since it looks not to the past but to the future of the movement, to the way this future is already at work in the present: toward what, in the whirlwind of the revolutions of 1848, Marx was soon to call—fleetingly—the "permanent revolution."[11] It is nonetheless necessary to give a name and an empirical proof of existence to this other-than-ideological discourse, if only in order to conjure away the vicious circle that would appear immediately if the "proletarian" character of Marx's and Engels's theses "only drew their authority from themselves," if communism had no other existence than the publication of its "manifesto." The name and the proof are combined in one phrase: "We do not refer to that literature which, in every great modern revolution, has always given voice to the demands of the proletariat, such as the writings of Babeuf and others" (*Manifesto*, 94). Perhaps the whole trouble lies in the interpretation of "and others." What irreducible *tendency* do the writings of Babeuf represent? And how is this tendency less ideological than that of the "systems of Saint-Simon, Fourier, Owen, *etc.*"?

The context of this question is quite clear. What distinguishes Babeuf's communism (and that of the Blanquistes) is simply that it is purely political, that it identifies itself with the practical revolutionary will against the various systems, themselves identified with reformism. In this, however, we have the full-blown contradiction of the *Manifesto*: how do we think a politics without a political ideology, without a discourse on the state, or the future state, or the future of the state (were this future its disappearance)?

On this question the *Manifesto* strikes a markedly different note than *The German Ideology*. It uncovers, or recovers, a materialism other than that of history or even practice: *a materialism of politics*. Its analysis of the class struggle is articulated with the definition of a strategy.[12] The principal ideal, with respect to the revolution, is no longer that of an act at once complete and instantaneous, although this image always haunts its catastrophic vision of the crisis of capitalism. Rather, it is a process, or a transition, that will bring about the change from a class society to a classless society, starting from social contradictions in their actual configurations. Henceforth, the very concept of practice changes its meaning; it has to include the moment of a direction, in the dual sense of the term—orientation and program. The real movement of the revolution is no longer a radical *breakup* of bourgeois society, liberating the totality of the productive forces—or at least this is only its negative condition. Rather, it is a progressive construction, or *composition*, of forces, capable of joining together "the interests and immediate goals of the working class" with "the future of the movement," and capable of severing the constraints common to all of the "already established workers' parties," transcending their national divisions and the limitations of their respective "class points of view."

It is clearly no longer a case of representing the revolutionary proletariat as situated *beyond* any existence as a class, in a mass of de-individualized individuals, as *The German Ideology* would have it. On the contrary, the concept of a class struggle must be extended to the revolutionary process itself in order to *think the revolution within the class struggle* (and not the class struggle within the imminence of revolution). Within the revolution, far from distinguishing itself from the bourgeoisie by ceasing to be a true class, the proletariat actually "constitutes itself as the ruling class" (by way of "winning the battle of democracy"), which must lead dialectically to its own negation and the destruction of all class rule, including its own. It is hardly credible that the proletariat, acting in this process as a specific class, would not be both the bearer of an ideology of its own and driven by the representations borne by that ideology. Thus, the proletariat is ultimately determined in its action, or in the strategic vicissitudes of its action, by these representations.

Does Marx pose this problem? Yes, he does, if you take into account his reflection on the historical conditions in which the *bourgeois* class struggle inevitably had to provide a political education for the *proletarian* class struggle. And no, he does not, in the sense that none of the theses of the *Manifesto* correct, however modestly, the myth of a class consciousness as radically exterior to ideology, nor do they give any idea of what a proletarian ideology might be. Thenceforth, theoretical conflict could only be resolved (apparently) by breaking up the concept of ideology and even abandoning its very use. Exit ideology, German or otherwise.

II

I shall now take the liberty of jumping over twenty years of history in order to consider the conditions of the revival of the concept of ideology in Marxism in the form given it by Engels. Again, we should speak of a vacillation, but in a different way, for it is no longer the case of a possible double reading of a single term. Rather, there is an unresolved theoretical conflict signaled by the recourse to *two* competing terms, each of them assured of a long life: "ideology" and "worldview." What does this conflict consist of? And what can it teach us about the contradictory articulations of theory and politics?

Two Concepts for One Problem?

These two terms make their debut in Engels's writing at the same time; the formulations of the *Anti-Dühring* can be used as a point of reference. At the beginning of chapter 10, part 1, "Morality and Law: Equality," is the first definition of ideology: it comes from the opposition between the methodology of materialist thinking, which proceeds from the real to the conceptual, and that of idealist thought ("apriorist" and "axiomatic"), which inverts this process in order to pass (fictitiously) from the concept, or the abstraction, to the real which it spuriously purports to engender.[13] The definition, then, is purely epistemological. It implies, however, that if the effect of ideological discourse belongs to the order of knowledge (and of misunderstanding), its object, and its raison d'être, is social and political: ideological systems always result from the combination of a completely arbitrary element, which according to Engels would be a result of the individual imagination, and an objective element constituted by pre-existing social perspectives or conceptions (*Anschauungen*), which express real social relations. These perspectives are always already invested in a side chosen or a position taken (*"positiv oder negativ, bestätigend oder bekämpfend"*). We are thus led to believe that if the specific modality of the ideas of ideology is to appear in the form of "eternal truths," universal and ahistorical, then it is precisely because they represent a political value judgment, a sanctioning of the existing order, which goes forth masked.[14]

This interpretation is strengthened by the fact that the model for ideological discourse is the juridical discourse that turns on freedom, equality, justice, the rights and duties of man, contractual relations, relations of violence, and so on. Engels returns here to a habitual theme of Marx's critique, one that joins the economic critique and the political critique in making legal ideology the kernel of all bourgeois philosophical ideology.[15] Within this arrangement, the term "ideology" stands only for the misunderstanding, or the illusion, implied by these additional elaborations. Ideology, by definition, does not admit of any historical efficacy, apart from its blocking knowledge and consciousness of the real movement: ideology is "pure" ideas.

Another term surfaces, however, alongside this critique: "worldview" (*Weltanschauungen*). It is remarkable that Engels never gives it a general definition. Clearly it has been borrowed: even more than "ideology"—a word riddled with allusions to the philosophical issues of Franco-German history,[16] but which, before the diffusion of Marxism (with an exception made for the brief career of the French "Ideologues," such as Destutt de Tracy), had never figured as a systematic concept—"worldview" is an imported term. In the *Anti-Dühring*, and simultaneously in a series of other texts, published or otherwise (particularly those exhumed under the title *Dialectics of Nature*), there is not only an attempt to counteract "ideology" (and idealism) with a "scientific" and "materialist worldview," but also an attempt to expose in its own right "the communist worldview championed by Marx and myself…covering a fairly comprehensive range of subjects" (*CW* 25:8) (which, taken literally, implies that *others* could champion it, too, in their own way, with respect to other subjects).

The goal of this project poses an immediate problem. In opposition to the idealism of bourgeois ideology which vindicates the existing order, the idea of a communist *and* materialist worldview constitutes itself as a result of Marx's theoretical "discovery," the theory of exploitation and the state. It is the fact of this theory, or this "discovery," that sustains it. From then on, we find ourselves running counter to the theses of *The German Ideology*. Even when its terms and propositions are taken up again (or rediscovered), the point of reference (and the perspective on the structure and functions of ideology) has clearly been radically displaced—to the other end of the philosophical spectrum—*from practice* (and pure practice at that) *to theory*, or to historical materialism as a science of social production and class struggle.

One insistent theme, developed specifically in the fragments of the *Dialectics of Nature*, conveniently maps out this reversal of perspective: a history of thought (*des Denkens*), the trajectory and principal stages of which Engels tries to chart. Whereas in *The German Ideology* thought had no history of its own, now the logic of this history gives the materialist-communist worldview its content and allows the historical necessity of the idealizations of ideology to be understood. In an ultrapositivist way, the Marx of *The German Ideology* denies philosophy any knowledge value and any historical positivity. Engels now takes the opposite position. If he is hesitant to qualify as philosophy (or materialist philosophy) the communist worldview, whose kernel is the theory of history "discovered" by Marx,[17] he nonetheless sees philosophy as having a legitimate domain ("the laws and operations of thought"), and, above all, he describes the birth of the theory of history in terms of an essential relation to philosophy and its own history. The materialist worldview is not, in this respect, a radical shift of ground, an absolute antithesis of all philosophy. If it succeeds in going beyond the categories of philosophical thought, then it is because *it comes out of them*, or rather because it comes out of their contradictions. So there are contradictions in philosophy. Consequently, in good dialectical reasoning, even if philosophy is not itself *the real*, there is *a reality* to philosophy: for, as Engels will more or less say later, in his best reading of Hegel, all that is contradictory is real.

To put it another way, materialism, or *some* materialism (even in the form of its inversion and its denial), is present within this history of thought in the form of an element always already constitutive of philosophy. The history of thought, of which philosophy is a kind of distillation, is the struggle for and against materialism. In contrast to *The German Ideology*, for which only practice is materialist in the true sense, it is now necessary to posit that there is a *theoretical materialism* (well prior to historical materialism).

Let us not join those who have hastened to label this new discourse of Engels's regressive. Such a way of posing the problem of materialism, regardless of its own difficulties, is much less speculative than a direct identification of practice with reality that makes it equivalent to the purely revolutionary act and establishes ideology (if not all theory) on the level of illusion or nonbeing. At least in this new arrangement a *site* (that of discourse?) is set aside for the confrontation between revolutionary practice and ideological domination, across the opposition of worldviews and the interference between the history of thought and the history of class struggle. If materialism is a specific relation between theory and practice, it ought to be legible in theory itself.

As we will see, this modification is linked to new political conditions within the working-class movement. But it is also clear that it is ordained by the incontrovertible intellectual "fact" of Marx's production of a theory of class struggle. The first concept of ideology ran up against the difficulty of thinking of the classical economic theory targeted by Marx's critical project at the beginning of the 1850s as a science, or even as a nonscience. The second concept of ideology and its antithesis, the worldview, constitutes an initial attempt to come to terms with the scientific result of this critique, as much in the field of theory (the identification of the juridical and anthropological presuppositions of bourgeois economics) as in the practical field of proletarian revolution (the passage from the moral idealism of utopian socialism to the mass politics of scientific socialism, transcending the abstract alternatives of law and violence, or anarchism and "state socialism," etc.).

A well-known term sums up this recasting of the Marxist problematic: "dialectical materialism" (or "dialectical method"). But does this ambivalent term (as the later history of Marxism was to prove) not serve, again, to camouflage a simple *coup de force*? Is the idea of a "history of thought," supporting this recourse to the dialectic, anything more than the confused designation of two separate processes that cannot be completely unified, and inevitably tend to drift apart—namely, a history of ideologies (political history) and a history of worldviews (theoretical history)? In Engels himself the immediate breakup of this false identity is quite evident. The formulations I have just referred to are only the beginning of a contradictory development.

We must recall here the conditions that provided a proper time and space (over twenty years) for Engels's theoretical reflections. At the outset, following the Commune and the dissolution of the First International, the formation of workers' parties was on the agenda. These parties developed within the struggle between tendencies, against the "deviations" represented by anarchism, ("apolitical") trade unionism, and state socialism both national (Lassalle) and liberal (for example the "lawyer's socialism" about which we will hear more; or "possibilism" in France). The struggles for a revolutionary socialism and for the hegemony of Marxist theory—indeed, for the control of the Social Democratic Party—are effectively bound together. However, from the 1880s on (after Marx's death), the situation is reversed: already within German social democracy this hegemony has been officially attained (and sanctioned by the Erfurt Program). Book I of *Capital*, resituated by Engels himself in the more general historical framework set forth in the *Manifesto*, is recognized as the theory of the party, along with the interpretation of it put forward by the *Anti-Dühring*. While the first texts by Engels (and the last by Marx) are written to inaugurate and enforce "Marxism," Engels's last texts are also written against it, and take a distance from it, because its mission, even though incomplete, has been too successful. They are written as an attempt to rectify what, in the process of constituting a Marxist orthodoxy, appears from the start to be an idealization and an ideologization of theory, as disturbing in its critical form (neo-Kantian: Bernstein) as in its materialist form (Darwinian: Kautsky).[18]

As part of this realignment, could there not also be an element of self-criticism, more or less avowed, directed not only at Engels's own texts (since Bernstein and Kautsky insist they became Marxists by reading the *Anti-Dühring*) but also at the "perverse" effects of the (available) texts of Marx, along with their omissions or excesses? These reflections also anticipate the character of the "crisis of Marxism" openly proclaimed in the years following Engels's death. They are inscribed, moreover, within the compass of the same practical contradictions, the same historical dislocations. The same contradictions arise: on the one hand, the growth of the Socialist party, the strengthening of its organization, and its trade union ties; on the other, its tendency to subordinate itself to the "rules of the game" of bourgeois politics, drawn up by the state, such that Engels feared Germany would repeat the English counterexample (an "*embourgeoisement*" of the proletariat, which the concept of a "workers' aristocracy" does not suffice to explain). The same dislocations emerge: between the theses freshly culled from *Capital* concerning the development of class relations in capitalist society and the actual results of the Great Depression of the 1870s (the emergence of finance capital and the first signs of a "social policy" from the bourgeoisie, not easily reducible to the simple schema of the bourgeoisie having become a "superfluous class").[19]

This displacement (Engels literally changes his position toward "Marxism," or if you prefer, "Marxism" escapes him) is translated by conceptual reworkings. The drift of the pair ideology/worldview can be taken as a symptom of the crisis. Tendentially, these concepts change ground: having arisen out of an essentially epistemological problematic, they end up, in the 1890s, being formulated in an essentially historical and political way (it is tempting to say that they are now back where the whole thing started). Their symmetry falls apart; they become partly interchangeable and, at the same time, partly incompatible.

The Failure of Engels's Epistemological Project

If Engels's first formulations are so heavily drawn toward epistemology, this is not only a result of the theoretical "fact" represented by *Capital* (and the use to which he is trying to put it in the construction of a party); it is also the effect of the intellectual environment. "*Erkenntnistheoretisch*," the adjective Engels uses, is the very word that for the neo-Kantians qualifies the problem of knowledge, which is not the case for *Weltanschauung* (or at least not yet).[20]

In the *Anti-Dühring*, Engels sets out by opposing to philosophy a simple *Anschauung der Welt*; he then graduates to the idea of a *Weltanschauung* (or *Weltauffassung*), which takes into account the materialist aspect of philosophy, basing itself on a history of nature, of society, and of thought—a "worldview" that must be "scientific" as much in its form as in its content. This brings us back to the question of "method," to a traditional opposition between a "system of knowledge," fantasmally constructed, and "systematic knowledge," proceeding indefinitely, beyond any closure. As for the content, it leads us back to the laws of "internal connection" between things, discovered by science, and to the general "law of evolution," which it eventually articulates for each specific domain (the examples of Laplace in cosmology,

Helmholtz in physics, Darwin in biology, and Marx in economics). If philosophy as Engels practices it does not claim to "found" these laws, it does reflect their common opposition to metaphysics and their analogy with each other (in this, Engels is clearly more Aristotelian than Kantian). The idea of the history of thought is thus established; it stands for the claim that, in history, "materialism" and "dialectic" reciprocally imply each other. Each is a means of developing the other.[21]

Engels's argument is obviously neither conclusive nor free of vacillation (particularly over the definition of philosophy). However, it is plainly not vulgar, and certainly not scientistic according to the criteria of contemporary discourse.[22]

Its basic features would have to be confronted with positivism properly speaking, whereby it could be seen that any significant agreement between them points, nonetheless, to an entirely different attitude toward historical "tendencies." Engels indeed clearly disavows a conception of the relation between theory and practice (and, consequently, the status of a "political science") in the positivist mode of a simple exteriority as a prediction or application, implying the primacy of theory.

A more delicate question is that of the relation between Engels's epistemological project and post-Darwinian "evolutionist" ideology. Whenever he characterizes the dialectical element of the "worldview," Engels always hearkens back to the Darwinian example, the analogy between the discovery of a "historical law of nature" and Marx's own "natural law of history," as well as the analogy between these two discoveries, on the one hand, and the historicism of Hegel, on the other. (They share, Engels tells us, the same basic idea of process.) More seriously, this same Engels, who openly challenges social Darwinism (in the often cited letter to Lavrov, for example, dated November 12, 1875), does not think twice about applying pseudo-Darwinian models of the "natural selection of ideas" to the history of Christianity and socialism (he was neither the first nor the last—think of Sir Karl Popper!—to take this path so well worn today).[23]

We can observe in this the undeniable effects of the attraction exercised on Engels's thought by that of Haeckel, the first, it appears, to have used the phrase "struggle between two worldviews"—one monist, mechanist, even materialist, the other dualist, finalist, spiritualist—in his *History of Creation* (1868). If Engels does not employ the technical principle that Haeckel made the cornerstone of his evolutionism, the "fundamental law of biogenetics," the "theory of the recapitulation of phylogeny by ontogeny"[24] (could it be that he thought it too "mechanistic"?), he nonetheless retains the idea of the principle of evolution as a passage from inferior to superior, in the sense of an increasing complexity, by shifts at levels of organization. Written into this law is the passage from natural to human history and the differentiation therein (from life to work, from work to language and consciousness). Hence, the linking of Darwin with Marx—one a theorist of the descent of humankind, the other a theorist of the necessity of the passage from capitalism to socialism—results in founding the latter upon the increasing mastery over nature (by way of science, social planning). So the proletariat is not only "heir to German classical philosophy" (as he was later to write),[25] it is *heir to the full range of evolution,* in short, the Son of Man (not, of course, theological man, but "natural" Darwinian man).[26]

If we are obliged to take this tendency seriously—one well and truly present in Engels, which will be dominant for a good part of his posterity—it is because it goes hand in hand with a countertendency that is, perhaps paradoxically, manifest in the way he rediscovers Hegel and reverts to his dialectic, itself surely "evolutionist" though irreducible to the model of biological evolutionism. The idea of history conceived as evolutionary law, though heavy with consequences, only temporarily provides Engels with the structure of his materialist dialectic, in opposition to a specific worldview or image: the fixed or mechanistic structure of the natural science, political philosophy, and metaphysics of the seventeenth and eighteenth centuries. This critique, however, very quickly changes its tune. Having used the weapons of evolutionism against the doctrine of immutability, it directs the firepower of its Hegelian references (and occasionally Fourierist ones) against the transformation of evolutionism in its turn into a metaphysics or a system. For Engels, the idea of an "evolutionary law" never works alone; it is always accompanied by its opposite number, which defines the dialectic *through contradiction.* Evolutionism ignores this completely (including Darwin and, most of all, Haeckel). Contradiction, however, is not the "struggle for existence." The importance of Hegel's thought, according to Engels, lies in the fact that, even though it is totally incapable of discovering any determinate scientific laws, it posits the whole world (natural and social) as a process and immediately identifies this process with the immanent interplay or internal concatenation of a set of contradictions. In Engels's sense, a "dialectical law," holding sway within the material conditions that specify it and with which it "interacts" (what Engels calls, more in a Spinozist than in a Kantian sense, *Wechselwirkung* or *Zusammenhang*), does not express the continuity of a developing order or plan (belonging, implicitly, to a subject) but rather the moments of a contradiction or the phases of an antagonism. It is above all here we must grant all its importance to the thesis that calls for the world to be thought of not as a "complex of things" but as a "complex of processes," that is, a complexity without a pre-existing or final identity, without a substantial identity of the elements that make up its reality.

Though the results of this investigation were later to be presented as a "coherent" system, I do not think that it is tenable; quite the contrary. But it must be judged in context. Ultimately, Engels can be seen here *playing one teleology off against another*. Under the circumstances, we should not be surprised by the political and theoretical ambiguity that results when, in the name of his dialectical explanation of the tendency toward socialism—the source for which is Marx's famous phrase about the "expropriation of the expropriators" as a "negation of a negation"[27]—he finds himself cornered once more by the insoluble problem of a nonteleological conception of the "end of the state," or if you will, of an end of the state that would not be the end of history). However, if we want to accept, as a working hypothesis, the general inevitability of evolutionism as a nineteenth-century scientific ideology,[28] we will have to call attention to both the impasse caused by this recourse to Hegel in the constitution of a materialist worldview and the singular place it occupies, historically, between the official bourgeois evolutionism of the nineteenth century (notably, that which will inspire *Kulturkampf*) and the Darwinian Marxism of social democracy. Engels's efforts then take on the air of a *proleptic critique* of the evolutionism at the heart of the working-class movement and of Marxism itself.

This project turns out to be untenable for Engels himself, however, an indication of which is the incompleteness and abandonment of the theoretical project whose fragments are collected in *Dialectics of Nature*. Our understanding of this stems from the paradox inherent in the idea of such a history of thought: indeed, the more Engels adds to his empiricist proclamations (for example, all thought comes from experience, or social experience), the more it appears his history of thought is fundamentally autonomous, with its own pre-existing logic, and consonant with an overall dialectical structure that comes not from experience but from the idealist tradition. As if by chance, this structure always falls back upon the trinitarian model of the familiar adventures of the dialectic and posits materialism, hence the materialist and communist worldview, as the end of the process. And it easily falls under Engels's own critique of Hegel with respect to the system and absolute spirit. Could communism-materialism not be another name for the absolute spirit? How can one not ask this question?

Above all, Engels assumes that the materialist worldview is identical to the communist one. What justifies his identifying them? To say that it is the fulfillment of materialism by Marx in a science of the historical necessity of communism only provides a mirror image of the question. It can be said that the communist worldview will necessarily be materialistic because it bases itself on extending the contemporary scientific method, culminating in the laws of evolution, to history and politics. But it can also be said that "materialism," basically, means nothing other than this *petitio principii*: "communism + science = materialism." What seems to be missing here is a specifically political component, one both internal to the theory and necessarily implicated in its history.

But where do we go to look for this lack—to the materialist side or the communist side? Which of these two terms suggests a class point of view, and which can thus *add* it to science *without* it being an "alien addition" (*CW* 25:479)? In fact, two historical structures, fundamentally at odds with each other, layered on top of one another, are at stake here. The first is that of the adventures of the dialectic, from its Greek origins to its fulfillment in historical materialism. The second is that of the struggle between materialism and idealism throughout the history of thought. Each of these categories, considered alone, can be read in a perfectly idealistic way, as an expression of the *autonomy* of thought. What would authorize another reading would be to understand each of these categories, and each in relation to the other, as representing the very instance of the class struggle.

It would be necessary to be able to say, for example, that materialism in different historical epochs expresses resistance to the established order, the struggle of the oppressed and the exploited, in order to understand how the history of the dialectic, intersected by this struggle, ends up precisely in a theory of exploitation and the advent of communism. Inversely, it would be necessary to be able to show that the first form of the dialectic, the Greek one, is organically linked to the emergence of the class state in the ancient city and that its ultimate form (representing, to some extent, its immanent self-criticism) is aimed at thinking the disintegration of that bond, the end of the state and of classes. Then we would have an explanation of how the relation between materialism and idealism is inverted before our eyes; how, for the first time, the struggle of the exploited ceases to assume the simple form of an endless resistance or rebellion, or of a stepping-stone toward a new order of domination; how, for the first time, the consciousness of the struggling classes ceases to be idealistic (or utopian) and how the theory of this struggle can be identified with materialism, with the thinking of the real movement. However, for this interpretation, or any one like it, to lead us effectively away from any pre-established plan, we would need a complete history of the "class struggle within theory" and its necessary material conditions. The fusion of materialism with the class struggle would no longer seem naturally given or guaranteed (in the way that the philosophy of the Enlightenment figured the identity in nature between the idealism of reason and mankind's struggle for bourgeois freedoms); it would be produced as an encounter, within the determinate conditions on which its modalities depend. But if Engels's assumption implicitly encompasses this historical problem, it also calls an immediate halt to any attempt at concrete analysis.

State, Masses, Ideology

If this analysis is correct, we are in a better position to judge the new definition of ideology that Engels puts forward in *Ludwig Feuerbach and the End of Classical German Philosophy* (1888), and which is clearly inscribed in the phase of rectification of and reaction against the form taken by nascent "Marxism" mentioned above.[29]

This detailed definition begins with the critique of the Hegelian dialectic, showing that the contradiction of materialism and idealism must be thought of as immanent. An idealism can itself be historical; one must, however, distinguish idealism from the "ideological process" in general. The ideological process (a formulation used in *Ludwig Feuerbach*) is more general than idealism, which is a necessary, but derivative, effect of the ideological process:

> Still higher ideologies, that is, such as are still further removed from the material, economic basis, take the form of philosophy and religion. Here the connection between conceptions and their material conditions of existence becomes more and more complicated, more and more obscured by intermediate links. But the connection exists. ...Every ideology, however, once it has arisen, develops in connection with the given concept-material, and develops this material further; otherwise it would not be an ideology, that is, occupation with thought as with independent entities, developing independently and subject only to their own laws. That the material conditions of life of the persons inside whose heads this thought process goes on in the last resort determine the course of this process remains of necessity unknown to these persons, for otherwise all ideology would be finished. (*CW* 26:393-94)

It is clear that ideology is above all a chain of mediations. The opposition of practice to ideology takes the form of a relation (the unconscious last instance) between two histories, one of which (that of secondary ideological elaborations) is inserted into the other (that of economics) by way of a materialist genesis.

None of this would move us beyond a well-worn geneticism and empiricism were it not for the way Engels attaches this definition to a new conception of the state. The birth of ideological forms is mediated essentially by the history of the forms of the state apparatus ("the state (is) the first ideological power" [*CW* 26:392]). What we have again (as in *The German Ideology*, which Engels had just reread in manuscript) is at once a theory of the state and a theory of ideology. Yet their respective articulation has changed. In *The German Ideology*, ideology is formally anterior to the state, since it arises directly out of the division of labor at the base of the development of bourgeois civil society. In substance, however, it is no different from the state itself: they are mirror images of the same critique of political illusion. Strictly speaking, the bourgeois state is itself only an ideological form, its material base being the division of intellectual and manual labor. In *Ludwig Feuerbach*, there is a tendency to recognize a real complexity of the state, not only because it assumes both the general, productive functions of society and the coercive role of a class-state but also because it recapitulates or condenses all the historically anterior forms of domination (whereas the capitalist production relation actually makes the past a *tabula rasa*).

This singular reality of the state apparatus raises the question of a (re)production of ideology by the state, or at least in strict complicity with the existence of the state, by means of those institutions that have a statelike character (like the medieval Church). Only through this sort of mediation is the relation to social antagonisms established, the result being an autonomization of the state as a class apparatus. Only this internal relation to the state explains why the organization of ideology ultimately tends to manufacture dogmas or systems, and to confer upon them the logic that will give them the illusory appearance of absolute truth. In effect, no state is viable that does not repress contradiction, inherent within every difference, beneath the unity of a dominant discourse. This relation, finally, enables the mapping of a topography of ideological regions (religious, legal, moral, philosophical); it shows that in each social formation the articulation and hierarchy of these regions changes. When a new class becomes dominant and the state apparatus changes form, a new ideological form likewise becomes dominant, which means that it imposes on other forms its own logic and, as it were, its illumination (a metaphor inspired by Hegel). Thus every revolt against the state, subject to this determination by the "domi-nant" system, necessarily starts as a heresy.

But his definition of ideological forms is not given for its own sake. It fulfills a well-defined role: to resolve, in a materialist and scientific manner, the question of the historical movement (*geschichtliche Bewegung*) and of its "motor forces" (*Triebkräfte*), otherwise known as the reciprocal problem of the "reduction" of ideology to its "material base." Engels thus comes to terms with what, since Machiavelli and Hegel, was a fundamental question, namely, "the relation between individuality and the mass." Engels tries to solve this by combining two pre-existing theoretical components: first, the construction of the *inverted ideological reflection* as a means of explaining how, "in the minds of men," interests become ideas, then motives, then wills; second, the "statistical" construction of the *composition of individual wills*, which explains why "men" want a determinate outcome but end up with an entirely different result. The conjuncture of these two components makes ideological forms the fundamental explanation of *Rückwirkung*, the "retro-action" that defines the historical movement. What is important here is not so much the fact that ideology "reacts" on its base but, more fundamentally, that ideology is, in its own right, the middle term of the historical process or of *society's reflection upon itself*, which permanently engenders its his-toricity.[30]

Whatever the validity or originality of Engels's constructions, they lead to an incontestable result: the concept of ideology can be both an instrument for the differential analysis of social formations and an organic component of the theory of history. In reality, there was no historical materialism beyond a critique of ideology (*The German Ideology*) and of political econo-my (*Capital*) until the time had come for raising the question of the relation among the economic, political, and ideological "instances." It is crucial that we recognize this problem as that of the historical relation between the masses and the state.

What constitutes historical materialism for Engels is neither the single concept of class struggle, nor even the correspondence of ideology with class relations, but the articulation of a series of concepts: classes, state, masses, ideology. That the class struggle is the "motor of history" and that it is "the masses who make history" still does not represent a solution but, rather, the problem itself. In the conjuncture of what one can analyze as "the classes" (antagonism) and "the masses" (or mass movements), Engels attempts to define what should be understood as ideology: if the masses in their "being" are *nothing other* than the classes—or rather, do not consist in other "real" individuals than the individuals of determinate classes—their mode of historical existence cannot be reduced to the classes.

Just as Rousseau asked himself, "what makes a people a people?" and answered by way of the contract and its distinctive ideality (or its symbolic form), Engels here asks *what constitutes the masses as masses*, and answers by way of ideology and its distinctive unconsciousness, linking it to a materialist genesis in which the state represents the instance of the class struggle. On the political scene, where regimes come and go historically, the classes are not introduced in person, in the abstract, but as masses and mass movements, always already subject to the "retro-action" of ideology. It is this last moment that represents the concrete instance of politics.

In spite of what has just been suggested, however, it would be wrong to believe that the concept of ideology, defined in this way, actually enables Engels to solve the ongoing problem concerning the relation between the scientific theory of historical materialism and proletarian political practice, or the organization of the class struggle in the form of the party. Only this solution would support, *hic et nunc*, a distinction between a revolutionary politics "resulting in a great historical transformation" and the "transient flaring up of a straw-fire which quickly dies down" (*CW* 26:389). This short-coming has to do with the way the theoretical construction of *Ludwig Feuerbach* always comes down to reducing mass ideological formations to the resultant of individual "motives." And it has to do with the fact that, in this problematic, two expressions remain more impossible than ever: on the one hand that of "materialist ideology," on the other that of "proletarian ideology." Both would imply, if not the existence of a proletarian state, then at least the constitutive role played by the existing state in their formation. If there is an ideology of the proletariat, it is either a nonideology, or else it is the dominant ideology itself, surviving in the "lag of consciousness" or miraculously turned against the state. Engels thus, on the one hand, has a principle for explaining the historical movement *in terms of ideology* as a cause; on the other, he has a revolutionary force *devoid of ideology*, which, in this sense, is not a force. How can this circle be broken?[31]

"Neither God, nor Caesar, nor Tribune"?

One would think that it is in order to solve this problem from another angle that Engels embarks on a new attempt to define "worldview." The most interesting text from this point of view is probably the article he co-wrote with Kautsky in 1887, "Lawyer's Socialism," attacking the theses of Anton

Menger. Engels's argument rests on a comparison among the "three great worldviews," medieval, bourgeois, and proletarian:

> The medieval worldview was essentially theological....The unity of the West European world, which comprised a group of nations developing in constant interaction, was constituted by Catholicism. This theological unification (*Zusammenfassung*) was not merely ideal (*ideell*). It actually (*wirklich*) consisted...above all in the feudal and hierarchical organization of the Church....With its feudal land-holdings, the Church was the real (*reale*) link between the different countries, and the Church's feudal organization gave a religious blessing to the secular feudal system of government. Besides, the clergy was the only educated class. It was therefore natural that Church dogma formed the starting-point and basis of all thought. Everything—jurisprudence, science, philosophy—was pursued from the angle of whether or not the contents were in keeping with Church doctrine.

Nevertheless, pursues Engels, the power of the merchant bourgeoisie developed in the bosom of the feudal system. The Reformation,

> theoretically speaking, was nothing more than repeated attempts by the bourgeoisie, the urban plebeians and the peasantry that rose in rebellion together with them, to adapt the old, theological worldview to the changed economic conditions and position of the new class. But this did not work. The religious banner was raised for the last time in England in the seventeenth century, and scarcely fifty years later the new worldview that was to become the classical one of the bourgeoisie emerged undisguised in France: *the legal worldview*. It was a secularization (*Verweltlichung*) of the theological worldview. Dogma, divine right, was supplanted by human rights, the Church by the State. The economic and social relations, which people previously believed to have been created by the Church and its dogma—because sanctioned by the Church—were now believed to be founded on the law and created by the State.[32]

This is explained, Engels argues, by the threefold action exercised by the universalization of exchange (which requires a fixed contractual form in accordance with state norms), free trade (which imposes the watchword of equality for all before the law), and the bourgeoisie's struggles for political power (which, fighting against privileges, had to take the form of demands for civil rights). All that, let us note, is very general but seems incontestable.

Against these two worldviews of the historical ruling classes, Engels posits the proletarian worldview, which is "now spreading throughout the world" through socialism, and the strengthening of the working class movement (Lenin and Gramsci would say that it is tendentially becoming hegemonic).

This idea appears to differ from the outline sketched in *Ludwig Feuerbach* only by way of a substitution of terms. But the substitution is enough to do away with the obstacle that the concept of ideology encounters: it clears a space for the proletariat. We can now speak of a proletarian worldview that would be to the class struggle of the proletariat what the legal worldview had been for the bourgeois class struggle: its weapon and its justification. We thereby move, it seems, away from an schema of the *reproduction* of ideological dominations (in which, to be frank, they are all essentially the same, insofar as they legitimate the existing order) toward a schema of *transformation* in which the relation to the state could be inverted. Thus, the conflict of "worldviews," according to their content and the nature of the classes that hold them, would not be limited to rearranging the various configurations of a game of ideological regions (or discourses of domination, which buttress each other) but would overturn their effects.

Have we really gotten any further? Perhaps not. In describing the "prolonged struggle between the two worldviews," bourgeois-legal and proletarian-communist, as the form of the current class struggle, Engels shows us that the latter has a necessary place in history. It is important that his demonstration is wholly based on the reaffirmation of the *existence of legal ideology*, which is always stubbornly denied, even among the critics of the school of natural right.[33] It is also symptomatic that this demonstration now has as its counterpart the eclipse of the very term "ideology." Engels seems to be in a quandary about defining the proper content of the proletarian "worldview" with a term comparable to "theological" and "legal." He stubbornly agonizes over these difficulties, as is evident in the description he offers for the transition from the bourgeois worldview to the proletarian worldview. He clarifies the analysis of utopian socialism presented in *Anti-Dühring* by identifying two stages. Socialist ideas first appear in a *legal* form by turning against the bourgeoisie its own catchword and ideal of equality. Then they appear in a *humanist* and implicitly moral form that sanctions the critique of legalism but rejects all politics, considered to be bourgeois (this corresponds very nicely to the themes of the early writings of Marx and Engels themselves). We can see that what this transition actually leads to, with the experience of the revolutions and growth of the working-class movement: the recognition of the *political* character of the class struggle, denied by all previous worldviews, for which "politics" is rather the sup-pression of class struggle (but not, of course, of the classes themselves). This implies the recognition of the fact that the field of politics is constituted—in the strong sense of its being the principle of deployment of its forms—not by a substantial community or by an established order, but by the *irrecon-cilable* character of certain antagonisms. Thus, it is not an *a priori* deduction but its very history that would provide us with the key to the original content of the proletarian worldview, namely another theory and another practice of politics.

For all worldviews, it always comes back to an idea of politics (or a polit-ical idea), "for every class struggle is a political struggle," as the *Manifesto* had already posited (*Ludwig Feuerbach*, *CW* 26:391; *Manifesto*, 76) (what was earlier called a "materialism of politics"). However, in the case of feu-dalism and the bourgeoisie, politics appears in different forms and under different names (religious or legal) that translate it or disguise it. In some texts from the same period (preparatory to his work in *The Origin of the Family*), Engels uses a remarkable phrase, speaking of a process of displace-ment toward *tangential* goals or objects (*Nebenzwecke, Nebendinge*), "to the side" of the fundamental problem of the class struggle.[34] This suggests that politics, in its essence, is not juridical, contrary to what is still assumed, if only in order to critique it, by the humanist early writings or *The German Ideology*. The juridical is itself a mask of the political, one of the ways to practice politics by turning it toward real or fictional *Nebenzwecke*. What would characterize the proletarian worldview, to the extent that it tends to remove state compulsion, would be the recognition of politics itself in a directly political form, without any "displacement" or diversion.

This argument only appears to be tautological, for the class struggle, in the last analysis, has a precise stake. Engels enters here into the whole con-sideration of communism, whose blueprint Marx had already provided (particularly in the *Critique of the Gotha Program*): *communism is a politics of labor*, not only as a struggle of workers aspiring to "government by the work-ing class," but, more profoundly, as a recomposition of politics starting from the very activity of labor, as a reciprocal transformation of politics by labor and labor by politics. This is what I elsewhere propose be analyzed as the second concept of the "dictatorship of the proletariat" in Marx and Engels—a new form of politics and not merely a revolutionary strategy for seizing power.[35]

This reading of Engels's historical schema assumes that we put an end to the ambiguity of the term "domination," present as much in the expression "dominant ideology" as in "dominant worldview," not to mention the dominant (ruling) class. Until this point, paradoxically, Engels has always treated the proletarian worldview, that of the *exploited*, in a manner strictly parallel to that of the *exploiters* (apologists for slavery, serfdom, capitalism). In describing this revolutionary worldview, he fictively anticipates the moment when it will, in turn, come to be dominant and "take over the world." Is it not precisely this fictive anticipation that curtails any analysis of the political organization of the class struggle corresponding to a proletarian worldview, precisely by constantly shuttling back and forth between the analogue of the state and its abstract antithesis, from the party-state to the "antistate" party (or movement)? Indeed, according to the logic of Engels's historical account, one would need to have an institution or an organization corresponding, on the part of the proletariat, to what the Church or the state had been for other classes, in order to satisfy this function of theoretically developing the "class point of view" expressed by the worldview. To say that this institution is the "revolutionary party" (which Engels does not) would be to *give a name* to the process it suggests, that of an "affinity" or "correspondence" between what goes on in the mind of proletarians and what Marx's mind produced: a materialist conception of history. But this would be to run the risk, as the anarchists point out, of perpetuating a political form that does not break with the historical succession of forms of domination. God and Caesar are "dead." And the tribunes?

Religion and the "Thought of the Masses"

Engels seeks to bring about this theoretical change by representing the masses not "from above" but "from below," in the light of their own "convictions" or "certainties" (what he designates, in the introduction to the English edition of *Socialism: Utopian and Scientific*, as a "creed" [*CW* 27:290-95]). However, he is only able to do this in an indirect way, through a comparison between the history of socialism and the history of Christianity.

Let us reread, from this standpoint, one of his last texts, "On the History of Early Christianity," dating from 1894-1895. There he expresses satisfaction in discovering in Renan (of whom he has a rather low opinion) a comparison between the groups formed by the first Christians during the decadent Roman Empire and the modern sections of the International Working Men's Association, a comparison he proposes to "set on its feet" in order to explain, inversely, the history of modern socialism by that of

Christianity. It is not enough to identify the base of political class unity with the revolt of the exploited, slaves, or wage laborers; it remains to show how that base is produced out of the multiplicity of groups, sects, and rival organizations, and to describe the way in which, faced with exploitation, they represent to themselves salvation—the hopes and struggles that both unite them and perpetuate their divisions, which are properly the objects to be explained in examining revolutionary mass movements. As opposed to the "Jacobin" model, it is the Church or rather the religious community ("pre Constantinian," egalitarian Christianity, the terrestrial image of the "invisible Church") that, as is so often the case in the German philosophical tradition, stands for the antithesis of the statist *imperium* and the form of autonomous organization of social consciousness. "In fact," writes Engels,

> the struggle against an initially overpowering world, and at the same time among the innovators themselves, is common to the early Christians and the socialists. Neither of these two great movements were made by leaders or prophets—although there are prophets in plenty in both of them—they are mass movements. And mass movements are bound to be confused at the beginning; confused because the thinking of the masses (*Massendenken*) at first moves among contradictions, uncertainties and incoherences (*sich zuerst in Widersprüchen, Unklarheiten, Zusammenhangslosigkeit bewegt*) and also because of the role that prophets still play in them at the beginning.

And later,

> What kind of people were the first Christians recruited from? Mainly from the "laboring and burdened," the members of the lower strata, as becomes a revolutionary element....There was absolutely no common road to emancipation for all these elements. For all of them paradise lay lost behind them....Where was the way out, salvation, for the enslaved, oppressed and impoverished, a way out (*Ausweg*) common to all these diverse groups of people whose interests were mutually alien or even opposed? And yet it had to be found if a great revolutionary movement was to embrace them all. This way out was found. But not in this world. As things were, it could only be a religious way out. Then a new world was embraced.[36]

These texts, the sheer extreme of Engels's speculations, are not without their relevance, even a historical one; but they are clearly circular, presupposing what they set out to demonstrate.

What they no doubt proclaim, and in no uncertain terms, is that "the masses think," that *the proletarian worldview is nothing other than the thought of the masses*, whose specific content (what we have called the "politics of labor") is not the result of a simple configuration of the class struggle but represents the conclusion to a long history (and a historical memory of its own). In this sense, this thought is not that of individuals; it is not the sum or resultant of individual psychologies (interests/motives/desires). Does this show the influence on Engels of a "social psychology" of the sort for which, at the time, certain reactionary theorists were drawing up a program?[37] I would say not, since we do not find in Engels any trace of the two constitutive elements of such a psychology: neither the idea that the process constitutive of the mass or crowd is its relation to a leader, an "agitator"; nor the idea that the thought of the masses is, in the last analysis, "religious" on account of a so-called elementary (archaic, primitive) religiosity that makes a periodic return in human social behavior. Rather, we find the inverse idea: that religious conviction, with its own ambivalence, is a given historical form of the thought of the masses. The line of demarcation between the two positions, however, could not be clearly drawn without constructing a concept of the *unconscious* as something other than the shadow cast by "consciousness," but that theoretically reflects both the imaginary of "salvation" and the interpellation of individuals (if necessary, by themselves) as bearers of the collective, institutional identity of the group, the social movement.

Engels's comparison never really breaks free from the positivist antithesis between illusion and reality, even when it willingly takes to task its most simplistic and dogmatic forms. Already, his insistence upon the heritage of classical German philosophy and utopian socialism in historical materialism is meant to be at odds with the scientism proper to the "organic intellectuals" of the workers' party (or rather inherent in the historical relation between "intellectuals" and "workers," constitutive of the mass party). But it still only refers to abstract intellectual productions. In making socialism not only an analogue of early Christianity but also the distant result of its transformation—through the revolutionary mass movements of the Middle Ages and the Renaissance, the peasant wars, the utopias of the English Levellers and Diggers, the struggle of the "Fourth Estate" in the French Revolution—Engels in fact inscribes the ideological relation to history within the very content of the proletarian worldview, or, if you will, within the mode of production of mass consciousness. But he only does this in order to confirm an evolutionist view of that history: in the end ("in the last instance"), sufficient cause for the transformation can always be found

in the "real conditions" of liberation, that is, in the development of the productive forces and in the simplification of class antagonisms by capitalism. If
real communism can grow out of imaginary communism—so he tells us—
it is because these conditions force the proletariat today to *leave illusion
behind*, to go through the looking glass of its dreams; it is because there
actually exists a pre-established harmony between the impoverishment
of the masses, the radical absence of *property* among wage workers
(*Eigentumlosigkeit*), and the radical absence of *illusions* in Marxist theory
(*Illusionslosigkeit*). It is because the proletarian is "the man without quali-
ties," contemplating his essence in the naked text of the theoretician, which
states reality "without alien addition," with neither regret nor hope. The
political content of mass thinking remains suspended within this pre-established harmony, which is basically always that of a radical negativity
(in which the persistent trace of the concept of alienation could easily
be found, for labor is to property what reality is to illusion), and which still
requires all the pedagogical and organizational work of a party to deliver it
and bring it to the fore.

The uncertainty of Engels's position is then clear. It can be seen, in a
rather academic way, as the expression of a double impossibility: the impossibility of maintaining a simply anti-Hegelian position, opposing the real as
practice to ideology as speculation; and the impossibility of returning to a
Hegelian position (or one perceived as such) in which practice and theory,
being and consciousness would come together in the "final" figure of a proletariat, the absolute truth of history—perhaps not *outside* any determinate
material condition, but nevertheless *beyond* all these conditions, at the end
of their development.

This dilemma would seem to be the source of the equivocal line taken by
Engels's epistemological reflections, which, without totally identifying with
either but drawing examples and concepts from each in turn, follow alongside both the "critical" path of neo-Kantianism and the "materialist" path
of evolutionism and naturalism. In this respect the very insistence of the
philosophical problem of the "unknowability of the thing-in-itself," or of
"relative truth" and "absolute truth," is not only an effect of the ambiance of
the times. It is an aporetical expression of the search for a "third path" that
never stops escaping from its own concept.

This third path, which should represent both a new philosophical position and a departure from the element of philosophy, is presumed to be
incarnated by the mass party as a unity of opposites: expression *and* transformation of proletarian consciousness; proletarian replica of the statist

forms of "ideological power" *and* practical anticipation of a communist civility in the course of the class struggle itself. We can of course consider this uncertainty simply to represent the intermediate historical link between a purely critical concept of ideology that would challenge all domination (Marx's concept at the beginning) and a completely inverse concept, which would prepare other dominations (under the name of proletarian and then Marxist-Leninist ideology). But such a conclusion would be a way to close again the question that Engels had opened, under the effect of the disturbance that the emergence of an organized class struggle produced in the traditional confrontation of politics and philosophy. It would do no more than lead us back to the traditional antithesis of a theoretical knowledge, free of ideological conditioning (*Wertfrei*), and a "party" position expressing a subjective "worldview." Is it not precisely the insufficiency and sterility of this opposition that Engels's project, in its very uncertainty, makes clear?

5

IN SEARCH OF THE PROLETARIAT
The Notion of Class Politics in Marx

At the beginning, we are confronted with a flagrant paradox. Starting with the "encounter" which took place in 1843-1844 in Paris (a theoretical as well as a personal and "lived" encounter), the concept of the proletariat summarizes all the implications of a "class point of view" in Marx. It is the main object of his investigation into the capitalist mode of production, into the specific form of exploitation born out of the transformation of labor-power into a commodity, and with the industrial revolution. It is the last term in the historical evolution of the forms of the "social division of labor." Finally, the concept of the proletariat is the tendential subject of the revolutionary practice which must "deliver" bourgeois society from its own internal contradictions. However, the argument that leads to this conclusion evolved considerably from the 1840s to the 1870s and 1880s. Above all, the very word "proletariat" almost *never* appears in *Capital* (vol. 1) which, whether one likes it or not, constitutes the basic text where the validity of Marxism is established. Moreover, this is true not only of the universal term "proletariat" as a singular substantive implying the representation of a personality responsible for a historical mission, but also of the more "empirical" plural term "proletarians." The latter is also almost absent from Marx's eight hundred pages, the result of twenty years of work and line-by-line corrections, and the text in which Marx wanted to concentrate his theory most systematically. In general, *Capital* does not deal with the "proletariat," but with the "working class" (*Arbeiterklasse*).

I need to be more specific in stating that the terms "proletariat" and "proletarians" are "almost" absent in *Capital*. In particular, I must carefully distinguish between the two successive editions of *Capital* published by Marx (first edition 1867; second edition 1872).[1]

In the first edition, the terms "proletariat" and "proletarians," with one possible exception (in the chapter on the work day, in relation to the factory inspectors' reports [*Capital*, vol. 1, 405]), only appear in the dedication to Wilhelm Wolff and in the two final sections on the "general law of capitalist accumulation" (concerning the "law of population" peculiar to the capitalist mode of production), especially the process of "so-called primitive accumulation" (about twenty occurrences in all). Only on *one* occasion do "the proletarian" and "the capitalist" confront each other (even though the latter is omnipresent in *Capital*).

The location is very consistent. These passages have in common their insistence on the *insecurity* characteristic of the proletarian condition. This insecurity is first seen as a result of the expropriation of "independent" workers from the land and then as a permanent consequence of large-scale capitalist industry. This fact partially explains the placement of the discussion of the "expropriation of the expropriators," which at first sight seemed so aberrant. These arguments point to the revolutionary reversal of the tendency begun violently at the beginnings of capitalism. However, this makes it all the more surprising to notice the absence of any reference to the proletariat in the body of the analysis dedicated to the labor process, to wages, and to the means of exploitation. All this happens as if the "proletariat" as such had *nothing to do* with the positive function which exploited labor-power accomplishes at the point of production as the "productive power," nothing to do with the formation of value, with the transformation of surplus labor into surplus value, or with the metamorphosis of "living" labor into "capital." All this happens as if the term "proletariat" only connoted the "transitional" nature of the working class, in a threefold way.

1. The condition of the working class is unstable. It is even a condition of "marginality," in comparison with "normal" social existence. A state of general insecurity typifies those societies which have become more

and more "proletarianized."

2. The condition of the working class perpetuates the violence which at first openly and "politically" characterized the transition from feudalism to capitalism. Capitalism legally normalized this violence by substituting a seemingly purely "economic" mechanism for it.

3. The condition of the working class is historically untenable. It implies another transition which will annul the preceding one and for which capitalist accumulation has already prepared the material conditions.

We should note, however, that these (rare) references to the proletariat in *Capital* belong to a very specific level of the text, one which allows the analysis of the mode of production to be embedded in the historical perspective originally elaborated by Marx in the revolutionary conjuncture of 1848. The dedication to Wolff is the symbolically affirmed continuity with the Communist League. Most important, the term "proletariat" is the "bridge" which makes it possible to quote significant passages of the *Manifesto* and *The Poverty of Philosophy* in the footnotes. Thus, such references constitute the beginnings of what, from 1870 on, will become "historical materialism." However, on account of this very fact, the references to the "proletariat" accentuate the difficulty in holding together, without aporia or contradiction, historical materialism and the critical theory of *Capital*, although these "two discoveries," as Engels calls them, constantly interfered with each other.

This problem takes on another dimension with the additions in the second edition (1872). There are two very significant references to the proletariat, still located at the same margins of the text, which reinforce the embedding effect of this historical perspective.

One is in the postface (*Capital*, vol. 1, 98), showing how the "maturity" of class struggles after 1848 caused the breakdown of the "scientific" problematic of classical economics by confronting it with the repressed political content of its own concepts. Thus, the "scientific" problematic is transformed, on the one hand, into "vulgar" economics (J. S. Mill), and, on the other hand, into socialism as the "science of the proletariat" (Marx himself). The question concerning a new relationship between science and politics (another name for "dialectics") is raised.

The second and most symptomatic reference appears in an added paragraph on the abolition of the laws against "workers' coalitions" (called Combination Acts, that is, antitrade-union laws) in England, brought about by the class struggle. It is the link between the preceding theme (the emergence of a "political economy of the working class") and the theme of the working class's autonomous political action and organization. It is the introduction into the text of *Capital* of a problem that had been strictly absent from it: that of the form of the working class's political existence within the limits of the capitalist "system," and of its effects on the very "functioning" of the system. At the same time, it suggests not merely a *historical* way (some kind of a "tendential law"), but also a *strategic* way to pose the problem of the conditions under which the political action of the working class can begin to go beyond the capitalist mode of production, or begin the transition toward communism.

To make this point still more explicit, one must refer to several relevant contextual statements. At the same time, however, its ambivalence will become clearer.

1) The detailed analyses which *Capital* dedicates to the length of the work day and to the "factory laws" (limitations on women's and children's work, etc.) undoubtedly form a major element in the definition of the class struggle. However, as I mentioned earlier, they do not refer at all to the "proletariat." Moreover, since they focus on the law and on power relations at the point of production and in the labor market, they introduce the bourgeois state in two ways: (a) as a relatively autonomous agency with regard to the immediate interests of the capitalists; and (b) as a regulating agency for social antagonisms (Marx speaks of "the first conscious and methodical reaction of *society* against the spontaneously developed form of its production process" [*Capital*, vol. 1, 610, emphasis added]).

In short, the working class is presented as the subject of an "economic" struggle, whereas "politics" is the concern of the bourgeoisie, inasmuch as the latter, through the state, is distinguished from the simple aggregate of capitalists, the owners of the means of production.

2) In 1865, *Wages, Price and Profit* defines capitalism as a "system" endowed with an *inside* and an *outside*, or which functions according to regulatory limits. Within these limits, the system is stable; beyond them, it must become another system functioning according to other laws. This is a way for Marx to articulate economic and political struggle: the former remains "internal" to the system, and the latter, by definition, contradicts it and goes beyond it.

However, this definition runs the risk of becoming nothing but a tautology. It could be read as a statement that the working-class struggle only puts the system in question from the moment when it itself goes beyond the trade union form (defined as the collective defense of the level of wages) to assume a political form and political objectives (reversal of bourgeois rule). It could also be read as an act of theoretical decision: by definition, class struggle is political insofar as it goes from the demands for "normal wages," for "the normal work day," etc., to the demands for the "abolition of the wages system." *Wages, Price and Profit* justifies this decision by describing the "double outcome" of the workers' economic struggle. On the one hand, it opposes the tendency of capital to decrease wages below the value of labor-power, a result which is simply defensive and historically conservative (like Sisyphus's rock which always needs to be pushed up again). In this sense, such a result serves the interests of the capitalist class much more than it serves the interests of the proletarians. At this point, however, the working-class struggle produces a second, potentially revolutionary result, far more decisive than the first. The workers' organization is reinforced, the workers' forces permanently come together; they are made conscious of revolutionary ideology, to the point where a break with the system occurs. This is indeed superb dialectics—although narrowly dependent on presuppositions which the history of capitalism was to nullify even while Marx and Engels were still alive: (a) the profits of capitalist production imply the maintenance of average wages at the absolute minimum; (b) the permanent organization of the proletariat is ultimately incompatible with the "system"; and (c) the class struggle, bourgeois as well as proletarian, irreversibly unifies the working class. None of this proved to be the case...

3) The addition made in 1872 to *Capital* fits into a very specific political context: the aftermath of the Paris Commune, the conflict within the International with the English trade-unionists and the anarchists, the resurgence of the concept of the "dictatorship of the proletariat" with a new significance, and the attempt to elaborate the theory and organizational principles of the revolutionary party.[2] Let us reread this addition:

> The barbarous laws against combinations of workers collapsed in 1825 in the face of the threatening attitude of the proletariat. Despite this, they disappeared only in part...until at length the "great Liberal party," by an alliance with the Tories, found the courage to turn decisively against the very proletariat that had carried it into power....It is evident that only against its will, and under the pressure of the masses, did the English parliament give up the laws against strikes and trade unions, *after it had itself,* with shameless egoism, *held the position of a permanent trade union of the capitalists against the workers.* (*Capital,* vol. 1, 903, emphasis added)

We recognize here the terminology of the criticisms of anarchism which more often than not bear an ironic tone:

> The working class must not occupy itself with *politics*. They
> must only organize themselves by trades-unions. One fine day,
> by means of the *Internationale*, they will supplant the place of
> all existing states. You see what a caricature he (Bakunin) did
> of my doctrines! As the transformation of existing states into
> associations is our last end, we must allow *governments, these
> great trade-unions of the ruling classes*, to do as they like,
> because to occupy ourselves with them is to acknowledge
> them.[3]

There has been a complete reversal with respect to the analysis of the factory laws which I mentioned above. Everything takes place as if the two antagonistic classes of society had traded places with respect to the "political" and
the "economic." Now it is the bourgeois class that restricts its horizon to
the economic struggle, or whose political organization merely represents a
corporatist or "syndicalist" (in the broad sense of the term) practice. On the
other hand, the mass action of the proletariat allows its own "political"
forms and objectives to emerge. If one prefers, it is the proletarian initiative
which, even when it only perceives itself as being simply trade-unionist,
forces the bourgeoisie to "engage in politics," to endow its state with a
political capacity to use, control, and repress the proletariat. This thesis is
consistent with the necessity for a working-class mass party, with the idea of
a "proletarian worldview," with the analysis of the Commune as the first
"working-class government" (*The Civil Wars in France*), with Engels's statement that "workers are political by nature" (*Critique of the Erfurt Program*),
and with the definition of communism as a resolution of the old historical
contradiction between *labor* and *politics* (a contradiction which was started
at the dawn of history by the democratic *and* slave-holding Greek city-state).
All these theses appear at the same moment in Marx's and Engels's "political" and "historical" texts.

The Antinomies of "Proletarian Politics"

The discursive configuration which I have just indicated can only seem highly paradoxical. All of Marx's writings suggest that the term "proletariat"
refers precisely to the political sense of his analyses, to the necessary tendency linking together the two theories of exploitation and revolution, and not
just to the conclusions of his economic or historical analysis. On the other
hand, we accept in *Capital* the most precise elaboration of this tendency.
However, such a configuration indeed means that the determinant concept

of the analysis can only appear under its own name in a position of relative exteriority, and even then it must be added afterwards. One can guess that this situation, if it clarifies some difficulties engendered by the analysis of the capitalist mode of production (that is, by the development of the *labor/capital* antithesis), can only, in turn, lead to more ambiguities. We must now show how this difficulty does nothing but reflect an omnipresent uncertainty in Marx. This is not so much a mark of weakness with regard to the dominant ideas as a mark of the break Marx undertakes with those ideas and its repercussions on him.

Marx's omnipresent uncertainty can be located at the theoretical level, but it is to be found principally at the level of the political action which he tried to conduct. Marx was never able to stabilize his discourse with respect to the concept of "politics."

By emphasizing the extreme positions, it is doubtless possible to retrace something like an evolution on this point. Thus, it could be said that the works of the "young Marx," including *The German Ideology* and *The Poverty of Philosophy*, are dominated by a negative thesis which is obviously not exclusively Marx's, but which puts him within the mainstream of the working-class thought of the early nineteenth century, opposing the "social revolution" of the producers to the bourgeois "political" revolution, free association to the political state, and so on.[4] This thesis makes politics and the state an alienated representation of the real conflicts and interests that constitute *society*. This implies that the "political state" be thought of both as an illusion or as the "locus" where all revolutionary practice becomes an illusion, and as the material instrument of an oppressive *domination* (according to all sorts of modalities: more or less archaic military-bureau-cratic rule; "the committee for managing the common affairs of the whole bourgeoisie" in the *Manifesto*; the final product of the "division of manual and intellectual labor" in *The German Ideology*, etc.). On the other hand, it can be said that the works of the "old Marx" after 1870, in what I once called the "period of rectification,"[5] are dominated by the opposite thesis, that is, a positive concept of politics. This is so, first, in the sense that the necessity of the proletariat's political organization is always stated in these works. The transition to communism is no longer the negation of politics, much less its "abolition," but rather its expansion, its transformation by the mass practice of the workers, who take it over (it is the sole object of the "second" dicta-torship of the proletariat to which, from this point of view, Lenin and Gramsci will always remain faithful). Second, this is so in the sense that the concept of the bourgeois state maintains the meaning of a domination, but loses the idea of an illusion, insofar as the power of the ruling class is now characterized by the existence and the structure of a *state apparatus.*

This evolution is real, but it is only tendential, and is primarily indicative of the existence of a permanent contradiction. Indeed, the initial period is not only the period in which the proletariat appears entrusted with a historical and revolutionary mission, since it has already been liberated from all political illusions. It is also the period in which Marx defines the revolution as "proletarian politics" by directly associating himself with the experience which seems to him the furthest from the "utopianism" of the prophets of the "end of the political": neo-Babouvism and Blanquism. The concept of "communism" then appears, at the end of a very rapid evolution, as the correction by one another of certain anticapitalist tendencies which claim to be political and others which claim to be "apolitical" or "antipolitical." The same applies to the conception of the political party that runs throughout the *Manifesto*, which contradictorily finds some of its origins in English Chartism, and others in French Blanquism.

Similarly, at the other extreme, a comparison of Marx's *Critique of the Gotha Program* and Engels's *Anti-Dühring* (with Marx's chapter)—despite their significant differences (the former obviously taking a stronger stand against state control than the latter)—is sufficient to establish that the period of affirmation of the necessity of the political is also, and contradictorily, the period during which the *denial* of the political finds its most striking formulations, those destined to have the greatest influence: Marx's vindication against Bakunin of the idea of "anarchism in the real sense of the term,"[6] as well as the borrowing of the Saint-Simonian catchphrase, "substitution of the administration of things for the government of men," introduced in a dialectical schema for the withering away of the state.[7] It is thus clear, as I said above, that Marx's discourse is, in this regard, literally contradictory.

The objection will probably be made that the contradiction can be resolved with a necessary distinction between the *realm of politics* (*le politique*) and the *realm of the state* (*l'étatique*), abusively conflated in the preceding summary. It will be added that Marx's texts (and those of the best Marxists) taken as a whole even provide a criterion for this distinction, which has the great advantage of dealing not only with the future or the ideal of a society without a state, but also with immediate actuality. The realm of the state would be defined as politics conducted *outside the masses* by an oppressive or manipulative minority. The political, in the strong sense of the term, would be the *politics of the masses*, conducted not only for them but also by them, and in this sense would be opposed to the realm of the state by definition. But even if we admit that this criterion is properly Marxist (which is doubtful, since it can be found in a large portion of classical political philosophy, where it appears as a shadow cast by the formation of the bourgeois state apparatus), far from solving the contradiction, it only reinforces it. As a matter of fact, it is sufficient to reread the texts mentioned above to establish the impossibility Marx always felt of defining once and for all, from the proletariat's point of view, the boundary line between the realm of politics and the realm of the state in this sense or, in other words, the boundary line between the "compromise" with the existing state forms and their revolutionary "use" against the ruling class.

The analyses of *Capital* with respect to the relation between the state and working-class struggles already displayed the same impossibility, and I will add that this is fortunate because Marx (Lenin perhaps even more so) thus shows us that the distinction between the realms of politics and the state can certainly have a regulatory function for revolutionary practice, but cannot, without lapsing into metaphysics, serve to categorize, once and for all, the strategies, the forms of organization, or the theories of the social movement. This distinction is useful only if it is submitted to the assessment of conjunctures and to the "practical criterion" of concrete actions. In this way, we begin to see that the contradictions, the vacillation of fundamental concepts in Marx, rather than simply masking a theoretical incapacity, conceal a dislocation between the historical reality which he brings to light and the necessarily "impure" discourse through which such clarification can be formulated. Why this dislocation is unavoidable remains to be understood.

The same conclusion would be reached from a study of the contradictions of Marx's political action (to my knowledge, such a study has never been done entirely). Contrary to the wish set out in the *Manifesto* ("the communists do not form a separate party opposed to other working-class parties"; and "in the various stages of development which the struggle of the working class against the bourgeoisie has to pass through, they always and everywhere represent the interests of the movement as a whole"),[8] the actual struggle could only develop against a series of rival political and ideological positions. Some of these positions were, at certain times, more truly a part of the working-class movement than Marx's positions were. I am even tempted to say that, taken together, these rival positions (those of Proudhon, Lassalle, Bakunin, the collectivists, etc.) have always been more massively accepted than his, even *after* the recognition here and there of a Marxist "orthodoxy." Practically, Marx had to take this situation into account, although he completely misunderstood its reasons.[9]

Let us mention only one example: the triangle formed by Marx, Lassalle, and Bakunin. In my opinion, one does not wonder enough about the fact that such indefatigable polemicists such as Marx and his faithful assistant Engels turned out to be incapable of writing an "Anti-Lassalle" or an "Anti-Bakunin," which would have been practically much more important than an *Anti-Dühring* or even than the reissue of an *Anti-Proudhon*. No personal and no tactical reason in the world will ever be able to explain such a lapse, a lapse which moreover was, as we know, heavy with political consequences. *They did not write it because they could not write it.*

A reading of those texts ("marginal notes" on the Gotha Program, "notes" on Bakunin's *Statism and Anarchy*), which in a certain sense constitute "rough drafts" of these aborted critiques, shows fairly well why such an impossibility existed. What is Marx's response when Bakunin systematically associates the totality of Marx's "scientific socialism" with Lassalle's "state socialism"? He has no other recourse than to reaffirm the meaning of the *Manifesto*'s democratic program, which, as a matter of fact, had allowed Lassalle to proclaim himself in its favor. Conversely, Marx also proclaimed himself, as against Bakunin, in favor of "real anarchism," which he supposedly discovered and defended "long before him." The high point of this "response" consists in the affirmation that Marxism and Bakunin's anarchism are the opposite of each other, which ends up admitting—an enormous concession—that they are constituted from the same terms. One would make capital the product of the state (and thus make the abolition of capital the result of the abolition of the state), the other would make the state the product of capital (and thus, etc.). Reciprocally, when Marx is confronted with the Lassallean theses ratified by the Gotha program—nationalism, statism, workerism (a combination which retrospectively appears to us as a striking anticipation of the so-called welfare state, which I prefer to call the national-social state, realized in most Western European countries in the twentieth century)[10]—he can certainly reaffirm the essential themes of class politics: internationalism, the autonomy of the working-class movement from the state, and the critical function of theory with respect to the institution of the party. But in the end Marx has no other solution than to resurrect the utopian ideological catchphrases ("from each according to his abilities," etc.) that constitute the common ground of antistatism (including anarchism), while trying to give them enough of a twist to reconcile them with his affirmation of the dictatorship of the proletariat. In doing so, Marx finds himself "trapped" in the mirror relation (statism/anarchy) from which he needs to escape.

In fact, what these still allusive analyses demonstrate is that Marx's "political" theory and action have no proper space in the ideological configuration of his time. For this configuration is itself a "full" space, devoid of any gap in which a specifically Marxist discourse could have established itself alongside, or opposite, other discourses. This is why Marx finds himself reduced to playing these discourses off against one another. In the same vein, practically, all of his political "art" consisted in building more and more massive organizations of the working-class movement, while playing different tendencies off against one another in an attempt to dilute their antagonism and add to their strengths, at least for a while.

Now, this space is entirely structured by a series of oppositions that can be translated into one another: first of all, state/society, but also capital/labor, state/capital, compulsion/freedom, hierarchy/equality, public interest/private interest, plan/market, and so on. The only possible "game" in such a space is to substitute one antithesis for another, or to identify alternatively with one of the terms against the other. Such is the game unconsciously played by all interested sides in the struggles in which the constitution of the labor movement is at stake. It is also the game Marx played, sometimes from a defensive posture, as we have just seen, and sometimes, when he thought he could choose his own ground, from an offensive posture, starting from a theory which he thought allowed him to dominate the way the cards were dealt, the conditions of the game (the genesis of the "ideas" that compose it, and the material basis of their constitution). Let us just suggest here that when Marx and Marxists think that they have mastered the political game which they inevitably must play, this game in fact escapes their control and comes back to haunt them.

However, this does not mean that one should be content merely to record and illustrate the inscription of Marxism in the space of the "dominant ideology" and the effects in return of this ideology upon Marxist discourse, which I discussed earlier in terms of vacillations, contradictions, uncertainty. This would be a little too easy. And under these conditions, it would be hard to understand why Marxism, or *something* obviously central to it, did not end up being digested, and blended into the banality of dominant ideas. On the contrary, Marxism has constituted for a century one of the permanent anchoring points for any critique of social domination (if necessary by passing through a prior "critique of Marxism" in its official form).

It seems to me that there are both theoretical and factual reasons for this critical function. The political "game" is not static. It is a process that must confront the unexpectedness of an excessive reality that contradicts its own representations. As a consequence, what is significant is the conceptual displacements, the effects of twisting of the dominant discourse that, in a given conjuncture, make its coherence vacillate. It is indeed the case that, if *no* discourse can be held outside of the existing ideological space, *every* discourse in a conjuncture or in a given relationship of forces is not, for all that, reducible to its logic and does not thereby function as a moment in its reproduction. The fact is that in the conjuncture in which we still find ourselves today, Marxism, or something of Marx's discourse, produces this twisting effect, and the decisive concepts, above all those in *Capital* which explain the logic of exploitation, figure as foreign bodies in the space of the dominant ideology. Marxism's decisive concepts, which are not reducible to the effect of "consensus" of the dominant ideology, thus impose a perpetual work of refutation, interpretation, and reformulation.

This is why we must examine what it is in Marx's reference to the "proletariat" that disrupts the binary representations mentioned above, and thus liberates another field of investigation.

Marx's Theoretical Short-Circuit

This irreducible element, it seems to me, is the *short circuit* established by Marx's analyses between two "realities" that the whole movement of bourgeois thought, ever since the beginnings of the "transitional phase" in the sixteenth and seventeenth centuries, tended on the contrary to *separate* from one another as much as possible—not only in theoretical discourses but above all by a multiplication of material institutions—*the labor process and the state.*

Bourgeois ideology elaborates a whole system of mediations between these two realities, each having its own history, its own "personnel," its own social finality. The law's resources play a critical role in these mediations, particularly the distinction between "public" and "private." The labor process is a private activity; its social function is only a result of this private activity, whether it is imagined as springing spontaneously from the division of labor and competition, or whether one establishes the necessity for regulatory intervention to limit the perverse effects of private initiative and to direct its ends. On the contrary, the existence of the state embodies a very different principle which expresses the necessity of a "totality," a central power and a common law, and which is organized according to various "political" modalities. The distance between these two extremes is insurmountable on account of an unavoidable institution called *property.*

Indeed, property is part of both realities, but according to two modalities that are irreducible to one another. On the one hand, property "commands" labor (as Adam Smith puts it) in order to provide for human needs. On the other hand, it receives a legal sanction, but its meaning is reversed: instead of "commanding" the existence of individuals, it appears as a faculty or capacity that *belongs to them*, as subjects of the state, citizens, or public individuals.

The importance of political economy as a tendentially dominant form of dominant ideology stems in particular from the fact that, through successive historical adaptations, it has made possible the practical organization of this disjunction and given it a "scientific" foundation. Political economy either encloses the equation of property and labor within the area of production (thus making "productive labor" the origin of property in general, which in turn allows for the justification of the organization of labor according to the owners' interests and logic), or it introduces more mediations to reach this justification—for example, utility, the relationship of equilibrium between production and consumption, etc.—thus widening its conception of the market. Under these circumstances, it is easy to see why the assumptions of classical liberalism (including its conception of the individual), which find their permanent verification in economic reasoning, have never presented any difficulty—in fact, quite the contrary—to the continuous extension of the state apparatus. On the other hand, it is easy to understand why Marx's endeavor, which started in 1843 as an attempt at a "critique of politics," was to become very quickly a "critique of political economy," the effect of which is not to confirm but to contest and *invalidate this separation* which political economy establishes (even though a whole part of the Marxist tradition has always misunderstood this).

It is in fact an essential part of the construction of the economists not to ignore such notions as "classes" and "class struggles," but to confine them to a single side of the separation: *labor and economics unite, politics divides* (or vice versa, depending on whether one believes in the omnipotence of "needs" or in the omnipotence of the "group"). It is therefore important to insist on Marx's constant assertion that "no credit was due to (him)" for having introduced the concepts of classes and class struggle.[11] What characterizes Marx's endeavor is that he reunited the two aspects against the evidence of bourgeois society, while drawing the utmost consequences from the first social struggles caused by the industrial revolution, and while anticipating to an amazing degree the future history of capitalism. Marx's endeavor is also characterized by his introduction of the political notion of antagonism *within* the analysis of the labor process itself (instead of keeping it on the margins, to the side of its consequences), and his making such notions the principal explanation for its historical tendencies. Marx paradoxically thought that the existence and the very identity of classes is the tendential effect of their struggle, thus opening up the historical question of their overdetermined transformation. Then, at the cost of subverting the meaning of the notions of "labor" and the "state," labor, with its own complexity, becomes the fundamental social relation, outside of which all political relations would remain unintelligible, whether conceived as contractual or as "pure" power relations.

I speak of a short circuit because Marx's critical endeavor, if it obviously opens up a whole field of analyses which was mysterious until then, also forces us to think against the self-evidence of social representation, to deny in a way the institutional distance that separates the "base" of the social organism from its "summit." However, this formulation is not simply an invention of mine; it seems to me to be the most rigorous way to read the provocative statement in which Marx himself explains how he conceived the object of "historical materialism":

> The specific economic form in which unpaid surplus labor is pumped out (*ausgepumpt*) of the *immediate* producers determines the relationship of domination and servitude, as this grows *immediately* out of production itself and reacts back on it in turn as a determinant. On this is based the entire configuration of the economic community arising from the actual relations of production, and *hence* also (*damit zugleich*) its specific political form. It is in each case *the immediate relation* of the owners of the conditions of production to the *immediate producers*…in which we find the innermost secret, the hidden basis of the entire social edifice, and hence also the political form of the relationship of sovereignty and dependence, in short, the specific form of the state in each case.[12]

The important word is "immediate": the labor relation (as a relation of exploitation) is *immediately* economic *and* political; the form of the "economic community" and that of the state "grow" simultaneously out of this "basis." There can therefore be no ambiguity: if there are "mediations," neither do they take place *between* pre-existing economic and political spheres, nor does one originate from a pre-existing other. Rather, the formation and the evolution of each of them occurs from their permanent common basis, which precisely explains the "correlation" that remains between the two. In other words, the relations of the exploitation of labor are both the "seed" of the market ("economic community") and the seed of the state (sovereignty/servitude). Such a thesis may seem blunt and debatable when looked at from a static perspective, if one reasons only in terms of given structures, and "correspondences" between these structures (or institutions). However, the thesis gains a singular explanatory power if the notion of "determination" is given a strong sense, that is, if it is considered as a leading thread to analyze the tendencies of transformation of the market and the bourgeois state in the last two centuries or, better yet, following the best "concrete analyses" of Marxism, to analyze the critical conjunctures which punctuate this tendential transformation and which precipitate its modifications.

In such conditions, what does "antagonism" mean? Without attempting to summarize the theory of exploitation, a task that would be both enormous and useless, a few of its notable characteristics can be pointed out to the reader.

What Marx calls exploitation is a process with two sides, neither of which has a privileged position over the other; they are designated by the two correlative terms *surplus labor* and *surplus value* (*Mehrarbeit/Mehrwert*). Surplus labor is the "concrete" organization of the expenditure of social labor-power, or the differential between necessary labor and unpaid labor, between the productivity of labor and the length of the working day/intensity of labor, which increases through the various stages of the industrial revolution. Surplus value is the "abstract" movement of the valorization of value, or the differential in the increase of capital. This is the "discovery" of the *Grundrisse*, given a "shape" in *Capital*. Marx calls this movement a "self-movement" of capital, but one should not be deceived by this word: "self-movement" is not a "supernatural power" (Marx) of capital, but a result. It is the effect of a social relation in which labor-power is treated as a "commodity," and occurs only to the extent that it can be so treated (for it does resist). In other words, self-movement presupposes a series of unstable *conditions*, some created in the sphere of production (labor discipline and habits, a hierarchy of skills and salaries, etc.), and others created "outside" of this sphere, in the "social" space supervised by the state. In the last analysis, all of these conditions exist only through class struggles, and all are eminently "political." It is then easy to see why, as capitalism developed and these conditions led to sharper conflicts and "regulatory" interventions by the state, they were progressively *recognized* as "political."

I have elsewhere called attention, following others, to the terminology Marx uses to describe the state "machinery" as well as the "machinery" established by the industrial revolution (or rather by the succession of industrial revolutions) to "pump out" labor-power. "The central machine (is) not only an *automaton*, but also an *autocrat*," writes Marx as he interprets Ure, "the Pindar of the automatic factory" (*Capital*, vol. 1, 544-45). This identity in terminology makes it possible, strictly speaking, to describe the compulsion to surplus labor as a "despotism of capital," but it undoubtedly poses a problem.[13] At the same time, however, this identity in terminology advances a double characteristic of capitalist relations of production which confirms their nature as indiscriminately "economic" and "political," or rather, as we can now write it, as *neither economic nor political* in the sense given to these categories by bourgeois ideology.

The first characteristic is that there is no "pure" process of exploitation: there is always some domination involved. In fact, the idea of "pure exploitation," the purely calculable difference between the value of labor-power and capitalizable surplus value, is nothing but an illusion resulting from the contractual form in which the "seller" and "buyer" of labor-power "exchange" their respective "properties." This point is very clearly explained in Marx's analysis of wages. But if this illusion expresses the *effectivity* of legal forms, which precisely prevents any consideration of the law itself as an illusion, it cannot, however, continue very long in the face of a reality inseparably composed of legal norms and power relations, and in which law and violence are constantly exchanging roles. It is in exactly the same way, at least in principle, that they exchange roles and pass into one another at the level of what is commonly referred to as "the state" or "political life."[14]

The other characteristic is essential to understand the novelty of Marx's concept of "social relation," the way in which this concept escapes the antitheses of nature and history, or nature and institution, like that of social "mechanism" and "organism" (or as is fashionable to say nowadays, "individualism" and "holism"). All these classical antitheses, in fact, presuppose that the social relation is conceived as a *communal bond*, even if this bond is capable of existing in two contradictory forms, one of which would be "correct," "true," or "essential," whereas the other would be "false," "perverted," or "alienated." In other words, these antitheses presuppose that the social relation is a bond between men that unites them or divides them as a function of the relation they have to a common idea (essence, origin, destination, species, descent, etc.).

In opposition to this conception, as Althusser has shown,[15] the analysis of exploitation implies that any social relation must be the organization of a material constraint upon social groups defined as a function of the nature of this constraint. Just as there is no "pure exploitation," there is no "pure antagonism" without materiality (that is, without unevenly distributed techniques and means of power). A discussion of the more or less necessary role Marx assigns to "violence" in his explanation of history and in his definition of revolutionary practice can begin from this point: this violence should no longer take on a metaphysical significance.

Marx's short circuit is the discovery of an immediate relationship, a correlation which develops historically through economic and political mediations between the form of the labor process and the state. Then the implications of the concepts of the *proletariat*, of "proletarian politics," and "proletarian revolution" can appear more clearly. The proletarian condition and proletarian demands are directly perceived, in the space of the dominant ideology, as "nonpolitical," even if in order to obtain such a result a whole arsenal of forms of state action must be deployed. The details of this are now, one hundred years after Marx, much better known, thanks to a series of works by both Marxist and non-Marxist historians. The class struggle and the working-class movement have considerably displaced this boundary, a boundary which is imaginary in its justifications but very real in its effects. Nevertheless, there is *always still*, on the side of labor, of the production and reproduction of labor-power, a sphere that is defined as "nonpolitical," which the state, in order to function as a ruling-class state, must keep "outside" of politics.

One can even wonder whether the counterpart of the gains of the working-class movement on this point has not been a permanent reconstitution of the "nonpolitical" sphere under new forms (precisely statist or "technocratic" forms). It is also possible to wonder whether this factual division (kept alive by a series of "cultural" as well as economic and institutional gulfs, a series which is inscribed in the organization of space and the organization of individuals' time) does not represent the bourgeois form of a much older division between the rulers and the ruled (which would justify Marx for having sought to include the capitalist mode of production within the schema of a hypothetical evolution of "class societies" since antiquity). In any case, the horizon of working-class struggles can only be formulated in these conditions in terms of a *politics of labor*, in three senses: (1) the political power of the workers (or better, of citizens inasmuch as they are workers); (2) the transformation of the forms of labor through political struggle; and (3) the transformation of the forms of "government" by the recognition of labor-power's capacities to expand (unlike productivism, which represses such capacities).

In creating this short circuit, Marxism thus produces not so much a "reversal," as the classical metaphor would have it, as a displacement of the representations of the "social." It deprives the notion of *property* of its central function (which it keeps, in a negative sense, in most of the socialist ideologies of the nineteenth century) and it replaces the "vertical" axis of the society/state relationship with the transverse network of effects and conditions of the *relation of production*. At the same time, Marxism creates a zone of unbearable tension in the space of intellectual confrontations. As I said above, since it is itself caught in that ideological space, Marxism is unavoidably subjected to a force of reintegration and reinscription in the representations it contradicts. The history of Marxism and its "crises" is comprised of a continuous dialectic of a deepening of the break and of a formulation of the theoretical means needed to conduct the reinscription. This history of Marxism starts with Marx himself, and it would be easy to show here how the famous "topography" of 1859, the schema of correspondence between the base and the superstructure, responds to this necessity. What it boldly identifies on one side, in terms of conflict and antagonism, it in fact dissociates on the other, reintroducing the classical idea of a series of institutional "mediations" between the "economic" and the "political," whose architecture would have to be "constructed." It is also obvious that this construction responds to the need Marx felt to deduce from the concept of class struggle a representation of society as a "whole," as an organism or a mechanism unified by *one* principle which would be, at the same time, *the* principle of its history. Quite independently of the ideological influences that might explain this "need" of Marxist theory (Hegelian philosophy of history, sociological evolutionism), one can say that it points out a true theoretical difficulty. Indeed, how can a social relation (the exploitation of labor) whose effects extend to *any* social practice be defined without identifying social practice *as such* with the development of this relation? On this point, we may not be any further along than Marx was. However, we may be more able to pose the problem, thanks to the very development of the contradictions of Marxism.

Classes and Masses: The Nonsubject of History

Perhaps we can now see with a new eye what at first seemed to be a paradox in the terminology of *Capital*—the eclipse of the word "proletariat" in the body of its analyses—and offer a new interpretation.

Capital is an *analytical* work which is presented in the form of a *narra-*

tive. Even if the narrative is not linear and has stylistic and logical breaks, a formal subject is necessary. This subject is "capital," or more precisely what I referred to earlier as the "self-movement of capital," capable of becoming an individual and collective character: "the capitalist." It is striking that the reference to the "capitalist class" appears especially when Marx wants to show how the antagonism between capital and wage labor prevails over the competition between "individual" capitals. As for the concept of the bourgeoisie, it appears mostly to give the capitalist class an individuality from the standpoint of universal history (role of the bourgeoisie in the disintegration of the "feudal" mode of production, in the generalization of commodity relations and in the socialization of the productive forces, historical limits of this role). However, this presentation always presents the bourgeoisie as a "bearer" (*Träger*) of the relations of production, even when it intervenes as an organized political force, that is, as a state. The bourgeoisie's historical individuality is thus presented only in accordance with the determinations conferred on it by the movement of "capital." Such is the very specific point of view which is designated by the allegorical reference to the "capitalist."

Under such conditions, the fact that the proletariat is not explicitly in question assumes diverse significations. The working class cannot be presented as facing capital symmetrically, as would be the case if the two terms were exterior to one another. Labor and, consequently, the totality of working-class practices linked to the expenditure and reconstitution of labor-power are *part of* the movement of "capital." In fact, they constitute its concrete reality. This theoretical asymmetry (the abstractness of capital and the concreteness of labor) precisely expresses the "class point of view in theory." The abstractions of "capital" and "the capitalist" appear as the theoretical condition which allows the concrete reality of wage labor to be discovered as the very object of investigation. The study of capitalism is not the portrait of the "bourgeois," it is not even the portrait of the "capitalist," it is the analysis of the process of exploitation, with all its conditions. This is why labor can stop functioning here, in contrast to political economy, as a central but undifferentiated concept and become a contradictory process. Second, the duality of the object of *Capital* (*neither* purely economic, *nor* purely political) would lead Marx to an insoluble dilemma if he were forced to personalize the proletariat at the same time as he developed its concrete analysis. Such a historical "character" would have had to define itself once again as either an "economic" or as a "political" entity. The proletariat would have had to define itself either as the *other* (or the adversary) *of capital*, or as the *other* (or adversary) *of the bourgeois state*, whose empirical manifestations and developed forms are different, even though they evolve in correlation. We know that, historically, Marx takes the term "proletariat" from a tradition that sees class antagonism as a *political* struggle. On the contrary, the term does not have a significant existence among economists.[16]

However, I would like to suggest here that if the proletariat is concretely present in *Capital* but without a unique signifier, it is because it always appears in the analysis in at least two modalities that cannot be simply and purely identified. To return to categories whose opposition we have already encountered, let us say that it appears both as a *class* and as the *masses*.

It would seem that this polarity is always linked to the approach of the problem of the revolution, or the revolutionary movement. In *The German Ideology*, at the limit, only the bourgeoisie is a "class"; the proletariat, on the contrary, is defined as a "mass," as the last product of the decomposition of society. This definition precisely makes it the agent for a *communist* revolution in which no "particular" interest (no "class interest") need be advanced. At the other end of the development, Engels's texts, which attempt to elaborate a definition of the "proletarian worldview" and answer the question of the "driving forces" of historical transformation, are based entirely on the pair formed by classes and masses. The proletariat becomes an effective revolutionary class when it organizes itself as a mass movement, which raises the problem of its own "consciousness" or "ideology."

Between these two extremes, some of Marx's concrete analyses, linked to the strategic evaluation of the conjuncture, are organized directly around this problem. Such is the case of the *Eighteenth Brumaire*, in which, as has long been noted, there is a true breakdown of the concept of "class" at the very moment that the problem of "class consciousness," or more precisely of the passage from "class in itself" to "class for itself," is posed. Not only do the "two-class" or "three-class" schemas explode in a series of subdivisions, but there also appears the astonishing idea that crisis (and revolutionary) conjunctures are those in which classes decompose as social groups defined by simple and distinct "interests" with a direct expression, or a direct political representation, especially in the form of well-defined parties. Marx declares at the same time that these conjunctures are also those during which the course of history "accelerates." These are periods during which the polarization of society into opposing camps in the class struggle really manifests itself. Then the conclusion must be drawn that the revolutionary polarization does not *directly* develop from the existence of classes, but rather from a more complex process (Althusser would call it overdetermined) whose raw material is composed of mass movements, practices, and ideologies. Marx does not exactly say that "classes make history," but that "the masses (or people *en masse*) make history."

If reference to the definition of the mode of production makes it possible to develop an apparently simple and specifically "Marxist" definition of the fundamental *classes*, the same is not true with respect to the *masses* (or the classes as they concretely exist in history and politics as masses). To stay only with the work of Marx and Engels (since it is a known fact that the problem has never ceased to haunt Marxism, from Lenin or Luxemburg to Mao), it is obvious that their usage of this term is not so different, most of the time, from the usage of their contemporaries, whether writers, historians or political ideologues.[17] This term notoriously keeps oscillating between the description of a social *condition*, in which the "communal bonds" of traditional societies are collapsing and a radical isolation of individuals is emerging, and the description of a *movement*, in which the diversity of conditions is covered over by a common "consciousness" or ideology which aims at the transformation of the existing order. In other words, on the one hand there is extreme disorganization; on the other, the utmost historical organization: the atomization of individuals versus the thrust of collective power.

I shall argue that in *Capital*, whether consciously or not, Marx attempted to overcome this dilemma, which obviously remains very abstract, but is also very typical of the opposite "fears" of the ruling classes and their intellectual elites. The description of the working class, in which he tried to integrate all possible information, aims both at characterizing a class structure "typical" of capitalism, *and* at explaining in reference to immediate actuality the process which tends to transform a more or less standardized "proletarian condition" into a mass movement.

The first aspect is organized around the notion of the *wage system*, or the capitalist relation defined as the "sale and purchase" of labor-power. This is incontestably the prevalent aspect in the general exposition of the mechanism of the valorization of value, and what makes it possible to affirm that "only variable capital (i.e. living labor) produces surplus value." It is thus closely linked to the representation of labor-power as a "commodity." But as it goes along, it takes on a series of assumptions or theoretical simplifications. An example is the justification of the reduction of "complex labor" to "simple labor" on the basis of a historical tendency toward uniformity and the interchangeability of workers, allegedly empirically verifiable—the Marxian variation of the idea of an "atomistic" or "individualistic" society. Another, more important example, despite the allusion to a "historical and moral element" in the determination of the value of labor-power (*Capital*, vol. 1, 275), would be the return to the economists' conception directly equating the value of this labor-power and the value of the "necessary" means of subsistence (that is, a quantitative theory of "real wages," rather than a historical investigation of the "making of the working class").

On the contrary, the second aspect implies the development of a whole series of historical analyses that take the concept of labor-power even further from the simple notion of a commodity. Here, the wage system is not a simple form any more; it is diversified and evolving. In the capitalist labor process, depending on the period at stake, depending on the branches of production which are unevenly affected by the technical division of labor and by mechanization, labor-power is not *only* a commodity (even as a "use value," or as a quality): labor-power also represents the division between manual and intellectual labor, the hierarchical combination of "skilled" and "unskilled" labor, the use of men, women, or children, and the attraction or repulsion of immigrant manual workers (the Irish in Britain providing the classic example). The *use* of this labor-power is not mere "consumption." It is unavoidably the *management* of these differences, and consequently management of the conflicts which these differences bring about both among the workers themselves and between the workers and capital, or, rather, its representatives. The analysis of labor-power undertaken here and the historical analysis of working-class struggles (on the length of the work day, the disappearance of skilled labor, "technological" unemployment, and the use of machines as a means to intensify labor) have a completely identical object.

It may be added that all these analyses are linked to Marx's use of the concept of "population." Marx had read very closely not only Malthus but also Quêtelet.[18] It is true that if the idea of a "law of population" of the capitalist mode of production were to be understood as a regulatory mechanism, it would again lead to a negation of the historical conjuncture. The fact that this idea cannot be dissociated from the study of the "industrial reserve army of the unemployed," which is not, as we know, limited to cyclical unemployment, is already enough to distinguish them. From this point of view, the concept of population in Marx is the mediation *par excellence* between the idea of "class" and the idea of "mass." And I could go so far as to say that "population movements" are the main basis of explanation for "mass movements." But then the eccentric location of the term *proletariat* in *Capital*, precisely where this problem of population movements is made completely explicit, becomes extraordinarily pertinent.

Let us try to specify not only the interest, but also the limitation of these analyses. Their interest lies in the fact that they allow us to dismiss the problematic of the "subject of history," without either rejecting the idea of practice as a moment of the transformation of social relations, or adopting the thesis of an indefinite reproduction of the mode of production as a constant system. As a matter of fact, the idea of the proletariat as a "subject" supposes an identity, whether spontaneous or acquired as the result of a process of formation and coming to consciousness, but always already guaranteed by class condition. The fact that the proletariat, which is both a "class" and the "masses," is not a subject, that it never coincides with itself, does not mean that the proletariat never presents itself or acts *as a subject in* history. However, this revolutionary action is always tied to a conjuncture, lasting or not, and only exists within its limits. This thesis opens up two practical questions: (1) what are the conditions and forms through which such an effect can occur? and (2) what enters a mass movement, from a determinate class condition, that makes it capable of being recognized practically as the expression of this class? Conversely, this thesis dismisses the speculations and puerile controversies concerning the irreducible difference between the "ideal proletariat" and the "empirical proletariat." It admits that the emergence of a revolutionary form of subjectivity (or identity) is always a partial effect and never a specific property of nature, and therefore brings with it no guarantees, but obliges us to search for the conditions in a conjuncture that can precipitate class struggles into mass movements, and for the forms of collective representation that can maintain, in these conditions, the instance of class struggles within mass movements. There is no proof (rather, quite the contrary) that these forms are always and eternally the same (for example, the party-form, or the trade union).

However, it is obvious that neither Marx himself, nor Lenin, Gramsci, or Mao escaped the representation of the proletariat as *the subject of* history. They are still read as if they were the perpetrators *par excellence* of this concept. There are several reasons for this, the most immediate of which is that they saw in the form of the party not only a *conjunctural* form of organization for the class struggle, but *the* essential form to guarantee the continuity of the class struggle and to overcome the vicissitudes of the history of capitalism and its crises, both heading toward the proletarian revolution or the seizure of power, and beyond this revolution. Under these conditions, it turned out to be extremely difficult, not to say impossible, to maintain the critical distance between the theoretical and strategic "centers" of the working-class movement.[19] This led, on the one hand, to the illusion of mastering the meaning of history or coinciding with it, and, on the other hand, to the illusion that the unity of the organization represented, *by itself,* the unity of the working class. In both cases this illusion was maintained only by a headlong plunge into the organization's construction of an imaginary representation of the "proletariat," and thus into an exercise of compulsion (first upon the organization itself) in order to conjure away the menacing irruption of the real.

The second reason is the impossibility Marx and Engels felt of thinking the dialectic of classes and masses *in terms of ideology* or ideological structures and not in terms of "consciousness" or "self-consciousness." Marx and Engels were never able to formulate the concept of *proletarian ideology* as the ideology *of proletarians:* neither as a problem of working-class ideology (national, religious, familial, legal), even when they were confronted with the question of the English "labor aristocracy" or with that of "state superstition" in the German working class, nor as a problem of the organizational ideology of the proletarian party (particularly the Social-Democratic Party). But this incapacity itself leads us to another aporia of Marxism. If it is useless to pose the problem of proletarian ideology in a critical way, is this not because, for Marx and Engels, the problem is tendentially without an object? "Classes" and "masses" are only provisionally distinct; the empirical complexity they show will soon be no more than a relic. In the end we are told that this divergence only characterizes precapitalist societies, or the "transition" to capitalism, but that it no longer exists once the capitalist mode of production functions on its own foundation and extends to the whole "world market." The thesis of the "simplification of class antagonisms" by capitalism can be recognized here, a thesis foreign to the profound logic of *Capital,* but essential to the philosophy of history presented in the *Manifesto.* This thesis implies both a reduction of all social antagonisms to a single fundamental conflict, and the continuous radicalization of that conflict.[20]

Now this thesis is, in turn, only an extreme formulation of what I will call the *ahistorical historicism* or "historicity without history" in Marx's thought, but which this time is concerned equally with whole sections of the theory of *Capital.* This means that the cost of the critical recognition (against political economy) of the *historicity* of capitalism (of the fact that capitalist relations are neither "natural" nor "eternal" but the product of a determinate genesis and subject to internal contradictions) is paradoxically an incapacity to think and to analyze capitalism's own *history.*

This incapacity plunged Marx and Engels into unresolvable contradictions concerning "revolutions from above." In the end, as Gramsci saw very well, the whole bourgeois nineteenth century can be characterized as a revolution from above, or a "passive revolution" carried out by "enlightened conservatives," like Louis-Napoleon (Napoleon III), Disraeli, Bismarck, or Cavour, who took the first step toward what would eventually become the national-social state, i.e., the true form of bourgeois hegemony. These "revolutions," under their very eyes, began to give the state a direct role in controlling capital accumulation and, through the embryonic form of a "social policy," the very conditions of proletarianization. At the same time, Marx and Engels got bogged down in the idea that the bourgeoisie was in the course of becoming a "superfluous class." They also got bogged down in the idea that "the bourgeoisie cannot exercise political power itself," instead of wondering how the functions and the exercise of political power contribute to the constitution or reconstitution of a bourgeoisie.

This incapacity meant that Marx could never really think that, in the history of capitalism, or in *historical* capitalism, the relation between capital and wage labor actually takes on new forms. The fact that they are still based on the monetary accumulation of capital, commodity exchange, and the purchase of labor-power, and that this form is extended (leading to a generalized wage system and consequently a modified "law of population"), does not prevent these new forms from being qualitatively different from those brought about by the first industrial revolution. Today, everyone knows that the working-class organizations (trade-unionist and even political) not only are not exclusive of the capitalist relations of production, but indeed constitute an organic aspect of their modern form (which has nothing to do with the myth of the "integrated" working-class, symmetrical to the myth that the party or the trade union is by nature a revolutionary organization). The aporias about ideology, politics and organization, and history thus finally prove to be directly connected. I would suggest that this is the price that had to be paid for opening the new continent of thought (as Althusser would say): the introduction of "classes" and "masses" (above all, proletarian classes and masses) not only as the object, but also as *agents* of history in their own right.

6

POLITICS AND TRUTH
The Vacillation of Ideology, II

The constitutive role of the concept of ideology in historical materialism corresponds to the emergence of the working-class movement as a real force in the political field during the nineteenth century, the effect of which was to reduce its initial complexity and to polarize it into two "camps." Conversely, the revival of the concept of ideology in the discourse of the social sciences and of politics itself also corresponds to this polarizing effect (which points out both its necessity and its limits).

In the beginning, the working-class movement is the "foreign body" of politics; as such, it has to be expelled. Later, when its inclusion in the public sphere becomes an irreversible fact, the whole of politics—discourse and practice—becomes organized around its inescapable presence. As for the theme of the "end of ideologies" (or "end of worldviews"), whether in a "decisionist" or a "skeptical" form (designating the critique of dominant ideologies as itself ideological), it too has corresponded, for more than half a century, to the attempt to relativize this effect of division of the political, and thus to the attempt to find a political structure (for example, "the nation" or "the market") that would be situated beyond or outside class struggles, and would therefore be more essential than class struggle, with all the ambiguity of such a project.

But the "party" is a profoundly ambivalent form. The history of the working-class movement, from the 1840s on, is a dialectic of the masses' integration within and opposition to the party form. The existence of the working *class* as a political force has never been able to do without this form (even under other names), but neither has it been able to confine itself to it. In fact, the party form bears within itself a fundamental contradiction, which is precisely the source of its historical necessity. It is not only the form in which the working-class movement resists assimilation into the dominant model of politics but also the form in which it enters into that model, with the goal of transforming it, like the Trojan horse. It is the only form in which the working class, and working people in general, can establish an organic relation with intellectuals in order to give body and structure to their own class (for no "working-class party" has ever existed except as the relative and conflictual fusion of a portion of the working class with a determinate group of intellectuals). Conversely, it is the only form in which intellectuals, the more or less disciplined and controlled "products" of the development of the bourgeois state, can establish a new social and institutional relation with "productive" workers.

That is why, when the crisis of the party form develops historically within the working-class movement, it is accompanied by a reconsideration of the Marxist (and anti-Marxist) discourse on ideology and a decomposition of the very concept of "dominant" ideology. In part, this reconsideration also constitutes a reactivation of the internal difficulties repressed at the moment of the constitution of the concept. The history of the problem of ideology, including when it simply repeats the oscillations of the initial formulation, expresses in a privileged way the historical contradictions of the party form. This is exactly what we are witnessing today.

The position of Marx and Engels, from this point of view, is very revealing. To what extent did they reflect upon the implications of this problem? It is here necessary to interrogate, for their own sakes, the concepts of proletarian *class identity* and *political autonomy* of the proletariat.

Party Form and Class Identity

On the one hand, Marx and Engels already show a tendency, as does the whole Marxist tradition thereafter, to formulate a concept that would grant the working class a practical recognition of its own historical "difference." As opposed to the philosophical concept of "class consciousness" (which, moreover, is not to be found in a literal form in Marx's and Engels's works), the idea of a "proletarian worldview" describes this perspective and can furnish it with a practical name. If it becomes inseparable from the goal of constructing a party, in such a way that the proletarian "worldview" becomes real in the twentieth century as a party view, it is because the proletarian worldview only exists within the framework of a struggle against the dominant worldview (or ideology), dissociating itself from the latter by way of a periodically reaffirmed symbolic scission, especially when its "frontiers" are poorly defined. It is so further because of the need to provide a historical continuity for the class identity that is a result of this break. The continuity must go beyond the revolutionary conjunctures in which it appeared in the full light of day, in such a way that the unity of the social body around a certain form of the state was shown to be a fiction, if it was not shattered altogether.

From the catastrophism of 1848-1850 to the evolutionism of the last period, the theoretical work of Marx and Engels is aimed at precisely that result: a steady distribution and accumulation, through a series of conjunctures, of the irruptive energy of revolutionary movements, which by its very nature seemed transitory. It is aimed at transcending the slackening effect of the counterrevolutionary phases in which capitalism expands, which Gramsci was later to call phases of "passive revolution." It is aimed at creating the conditions of a collective political experimentation and rectification of strategies. Finally, it is aimed at effectively anticipating the construction of new social relations. The base of this continuity, in their eyes, is the industrial revolution itself; its matter is formed in the meeting of exploitation with class instinct and the proletarian revolt, but its form can only come out of organization.[1] Party organization and worldview crystallize a relation of forces, mediate an effective conquest of power and appropriation of knowledge, without which it would be silly to believe that the masses could ever "make their own history." If this condition is achieved, class struggle in society can be carried to the limits of the "system" and beyond.

But is the position of Marx and Engels really as simple a plea for continuity as this presentation suggests? The impossibility of talking about a proletarian ideology (as will readily be done later within the Socialist and Communist parties) and the oscillation between the concepts of ideology and worldview can here be considered to be a decisive symptom. They do not mean that the concepts of class identity and proletarian autonomy are empty or objectless. But they redirect us toward the aporias also present, in the same period, within the definition of the party form. What remains unclear is the question of whether the conception of the party articulated by Marx and Engels, along with their definition of proletarian politics, ultimately represents something more than a *critique* of the different competing tendencies at the heart of the working-class movement (particularly the anarchist, "antistatist" tendency, and the "statist" tendency of post-Lassallean nationalist socialism). The strength of the Marxist position is that it exposes the "fetishism of the state," as present in its abstract negations as in its fantasies of reformist utility, and that it therefore clears an autonomous space for the problem of the politics of the working-class movement. Its weakness lies in only being able to manifest this theoretical autonomy by way of a permanent tactical compromise between those tendencies, or rather by way of a political "art" of struggle on several fronts, as a function of the conjuncture, at the very moment when the continuity of organization is being reasserted as a guarantee of the correctness of this theoretical autonomy. What is "scientific socialism" in practice? It is an anti-Proudhon, an anti-Blanqui, an anti-Bakunin, an anti-Lassalle, an anti-Dühring, *etc.*

The same aporia can be seen in the difficulty Marx and Engels experience in occupying a stable position within the organization as bearers of theoretical activity and scientific discovery concerning the class struggle. The same point would be valid for the most authentically revolutionary of their successors, who played the double role of "leaders" and "theoreticians" of the working class. Everything happens as if the asserted unity of theoretical "center" and political "center," or of theoretical direction and strategic direction (a unity already denounced by the anarchists as Marx's personal "dictatorship," thus furnishing in advance one of the elements of the future critique of "Marxist totalitarianism") had never been able to exist without immediately breaking up again.

In the period of the First International, Marx was the strategic arbitrator of a very embryonic movement, but only as a mediator and arbiter of conflicts between tendencies in the organization, not as a theoretician of the capitalist mode of production. In a way the division then occurred within Marx himself, in his own "subjectivity." In the period of social democracy, Marx and above all Engels were officially in charge of the party's theoretical direction but not, strictly speaking, of its political direction, which was in the hands of the "organic intellectuals" of the party apparatus, with whom they found themselves in a constantly ambivalent relation of conflict and mutual use, both trying to "unite" with the working masses. In the twentieth century, finally, the authentic "theoreticians"—placed by history and politics near or in the very center of "the decision," were to end up keeping silent, being excluded, or dying (in various ways), while the names of the "great" leaders were to become engraved "in the hearts" of militants, their giant portraits climbing to the starry heavens at their mass rallies. A series of well-known historical incidents illustrates this contradiction.

We can no longer believe nowadays that this only represents a historical lag, whether in the constitution of the working class as a collective intellectual or in the proletarianization of the political apparatus, since this contradiction is reproduced at every stage of the history of the working-class movement and Marxism. That is why, no doubt, the theory of the party form has never resolved the dilemmas of "spontaneity" and "centralism," except in some fragile intuitions of Rosa Luxemburg, Lenin, Gramsci, and Mao, at the time of the transformations, crises, and reworkings of this political form. In reality, the idea of the intellectual direction of class struggle can only be divided up, constantly, between the two discursive forms it must assume: the *program* (or even the slogan) and *theory*. Each is constituted as a way of "appropriating through thought" the historical process in course, but they do not do so from the same point of view, according to the "rules" of the same conceptual "game," the same division of labor, the same relation to the historical process and to the temporality proper to political experimentation.

The fact that Marx and Engels (just as, in their own way, Lenin or Gramsci) were uncomfortable with the reduction of either of these positions to the other, explains their resistance to the constitution of a political-theoretical "dogma." In this context, the very idea of scientific socialism still possesses for them a critical connotation—and a democratic one in the strongest sense of the term. It is not yet the way to claim the authority of science in order to legitimate their position of direction, still less the way to confer upon a caste of "Marxist" intellectuals, disciples of the author of *Capital*, the theoretical unction they need to monopolize the political direction (and to nourish the illusion that they are "directing" the course of events). It is rather an attempt, in the spirit of the Enlightenment, to make available to the masses, to the base itself, the instruments of its historical orientation and of the control of its class organization, against the rule of leaders, prophets, and other bosses. The regulative idea of the "thought of the masses" (and of the mass movement) was precisely what constituted the permanent index, the practical compass, of this mobility. In this way, the theoretical center would tend to be situated everywhere (as Pascal would have said), as a kind of noncenter. However, if the unity of theoretical thought (science, philosophy) and the thought of the masses is, indeed, the effect sought after by the proletarian worldview, it remains to this day the object of a postulate, that is, the more it remains empirically uncertain, the more it is affirmed as a unity of opposites. It ultimately proves impossible to maintain, from an objective as well as from a subjective standpoint.[2]

Historicity without History

In "The Vacillation of Ideology," I proposed that Marxism's conceptual oscillation between the two notions "ideology" and "worldview" be read as a symptom: the symptom of a practical contradiction, but also the symptom of a blockage in the theory itself, one with a progressively more immediate effect on analyses of the state and the so-called capitalist system. This blockage is quite evident (for us) in most of the texts by Marx and Engels that bear on the crisis, the wage form, trade unionism, and the difference between reform and revolution. Finally, what is at issue is the way *Capital* represents the historicity of the capitalist mode of production.

The striking fact about the theoretical forms I have described is that they never break free from either *the philosophical symmetry of truth and illusion* (or being and unreality), nor from *the political symmetry of society and the state*, even though new definitions are always presented as attempts to transcend that symmetry. It could be that these two schemata are intrinsically related and that the problems they pose may in fact be the same, since there is no "sublation" (*Aufhebung*) of society by the state (or vice versa) that does not announce itself as the truth of an illusion. Nor is there any map of the land of truth amidst the "ocean of illusion" (to borrow Kant's metaphor) without the institution of a tribunal, itself attached to the ideal of a political community.

A theoretical short circuit occurs when Marx posits that "it is in each case the direct relation of the owners of the conditions of production to the immediate producers...in which we find the innermost secret, the hidden basis of the entire social edifice, and hence also the political form of the relationship of sovereignty and dependence...."[3] In other words, the antagonistic social relation is in fact *neither* economic *nor* political, *neither* "public" *nor* "private" as the terms are classically understood. This theoretical short circuit also implies another distribution of the names of truth and illusion (another division of their respective "spaces" in history than that of mutual exteriority).

What we now need to examine—on the basis of a close reading of the texts—is the question of how it happens that the problematic of ideology, called forth by the critique of the state/society dualism (or if one prefers by the discovery that "all" economics is political, just as "all" politics—at least modern politics—is economic), should end up nullifying this critique and reinscribing the ontological dualism *in* the historical dialectic?

To the extent that the expressive relation between society and state finds itself under interrogation, we suspect that there is a fundamental incompatibility between historical materialism and this representation of a social system as the superimposition of two spheres, which derives from classical philosophy and political economy. In the last analysis, it is the *Marxist* concept of class struggle that contradicts this representation, in rendering invalid any conception of history as the expression of society in the state or, symmetrically, as the absorption of the state into society. The concept of ideology implies, in principle, the same critique, since it designates a relation of political domination inherent in the organization of labor itself as the matrix of the "universals" in which each historical period represents as a symmetry society and the state (individual and collectivity, people and nation, etc.). But in the end each new definition reproduces in its own way the same symmetry or dualism: it has only been displaced or formulated in a different way. The concept of class struggle is thereby buried again underneath the problematic of classical economics, political philosophy, and philosophy of history. Paradoxically, it is the concept of critique in Marx's work that nullifies the effect of a theoretical rupture or epistemological "break" of historical materialism. Hence, the vacillation proper to the concept of ideology maintains the theoretical vacillation of Marxism between the "before" and "after" of a break with the economic ideology and the "bourgeois" ideology of history that it denounces.

Engels's construction in *Ludwig Feuerbach* points this out in a rather significant way. Against an "economist" representation of history (which called itself "Marxist"; but could it be said that Marx and Engels had nothing to do with it?) in which the state is only the instrument of the ruling class in the class struggle, and the latter, in turn, the direct expression of a "law of correspondence" between relations of property and the development of productive forces, Engels, as we have seen, sketches the analysis of a dialectical interplay, designated by the difference between *classes* and *masses*. In posing as he does the question of the constitution of the masses as "motor forces" of history in the element of ideology, and defining the ideological process by way of its internal relation to the state, he introduces a concept that will carry us much further than the simple idea of a "retro-action" (*Rückwirkung*) of one sphere on the other. For the masses obviously exceed the sphere of the state, conceived as an apparatus of power, even as they determine its concrete forms. To specify this *internal* determination of the mode of ideological thought and of the state itself, it would be necessary either to carry out a "broadening of the concept of the state" that would make it structurally *encroach* on the sphere of society (this is Gramsci's method), or to try to think an "action at a distance," an "absent causality" of the state in the ideological process as a whole, that characterizes the irreducible complexity of what we call the "state," beyond and beneath the threshold of visible manifestations of "power" (this is Althusser's method). The import of the latter, of course, would be that it would give a stronger meaning to Engels's insistence on the "unconscious" character of the ideological process. The notion of the unconscious would precisely express this dual modality of the historical action of the ruling-class state, at once immediately manifest and visible in its coercive and administrative apparatus, and indirect and invisible in its effect on the ideology of the masses. This differential gap between consciousness and unconsciousness in social and political struggles would thus designate the very materiality of ideology, its mode of historical action.

It is not, however, difficult to see how the classical symmetry of society and state comes to be lodged at the heart of this sophisticated definition of ideology. It is represented there (very classically, for anyone who has read Hobbes and Hegel) by way of an account of the "genesis" of ideology from individual interests. That these interests are defined as *class* interests, that they are determined by the material conditions of labor and social existence of individuals, does not in the least change the fact that this genesis reproduces the classical model of the formation of the "general interest" (or the "general will") from the competition of individual interests. As we have seen, this is the idea of the *resultant of motives*. In other words, Engels's concept of ideology, by virtue of its theoretical form alone if not its political content, revives the liberal conception of the state arising from the contradictions of "civil society": what Hegel christened "the cunning of reason."[4]

Formally, the movement of the masses is to class antagonism in Engels what the state is to civil society in Hegel: its dialectical transcendence, or its actual totalization. In both cases there is a birth of historical individuality from "infra-historical" individuality, that of the economic classes and the empirical individuals they comprise. The very thesis (also a watchword) according to which "it is the masses who make history" therefore takes on a new light, as the equivalent of the role assigned by Hegel to the "great men" (and we must remember that on this point Engels thought it necessary to reduce the role of the "great men" to that of the masses). Engels's construction signifies that the masses are the real "great men" (or statesmen) of history; in this sense, it inverts the ideological, state-oriented theme that Hegelian philosophy had adopted. This inversion, however, preserves its Hegelian theoretical structure: the couple of the masses and ideology functions like that of the "great man" and the "spirit of the people" in Hegel, namely, as the "spirit of the age" effectively realizing itself. The trajectory in Engels (and Marx) that leads from class antagonism to communism through the action of the masses (or their historical individuation) exactly parallels, notwithstanding the difference in their contents, the trajectory in Hegel that leads from civil society to freedom in the state, through surpassing competition, and which is precisely what the individuality of the "great man" expresses. The myth of the great man is replaced by a symmetrical myth of the masses.[5]

I have previously noted the paradox that posits, on the one hand, the dynamics of mass movements in the sphere of ideology and, on the other, a revolutionary force without an ideology of its own. One might add that it is the concept of the *movement of history* or of *historicity* that is at stake here. For Engels's dialectic only ever had a temporary use. The theoretical distance between classes and masses, that is, between two modes of manifestation of the same social reality (one passive, the other active; or one as the *effect*, the other as the *cause* of the transformation of social relations) is in every case destined to be eliminated. In the historical movement of the proletariat, as Marx and Engels picture it, masses and classes ultimately coincide again.

Engels's comparison of early Christianity with socialism has exactly the same consequences. On the one hand, there is the complexity and irreducible heterogeneity of the "laboring and burdened," who join forces in the imaginary hope of Christian salvation; and on the other, there is the homogeneity and pre-existing unity of the modern proletariat, which alone constitutes the masses within bourgeois society. In the former case, the distance remains an irreducible one; in the latter, it collapses. Again, it is the thesis culled from the *Manifesto* (and projected onto the theory of *Capital* following Marx's own indications) of a historical "simplification" of class antagonisms that allows this reduction to occur. Proletarian mass ideology, as such, can be homogeneous with a directly political "class consciousness" and a scientific-materialist worldview because the modern form of exploitation is the tendency toward the constitution of a single "standard of living"

(*Lebenstandard*, a curious Anglo-German neologism of Engels's), "life-long wage-labor" for all, and the submission of the great mass of individuals to a process of proletarianization (and impoverishment) in which everyone becomes identical.

In this pseudo-historical argument the theory of capitalist exploitation reveals its own internal impasse. Marxism stumbles on a paradoxical limitation—and it is a very serious one—of its representation of history, which can be illustrated in a number of ways.

Historical materialism was based on the discovery of the historicity of the capitalist mode of production and its corresponding economic categories: the relation between capital and wage labor, Marx tells us, is not "eternal"; a product of history, it must some day disappear under the effect of its internal contradictions. However, what Marx was never really able to think (and Marxists after him only with great difficulty) is a *history of capitalism* in the strong sense, in which the relation between capital and wage labor (hence the class struggle between the bourgeoisie and the proletariat, and the very composition of the two classes) would take on new forms, still based on the accumulation of capital, but qualitatively different from those brought about by the first industrial revolution. This failure is quite clear in *Capital*: even if Marx does not provide any calculable time frame for the development of the contradictions of capitalism, these are nonetheless conceived of as "fatal" *in their immediate form*, that is, having no possible result other than a break with or destruction of the "system."

We are thus confronted with a theory that paradoxically combines the affirmation of the historicity of capitalism with its denial. Although the class struggle is presented as the necessary effect of capitalist relations of production, it nonetheless does not produce any determinate effect *on them* as long as a revolutionary transformation does not intervene. It only acts in the form of "all or nothing." It keeps capitalism identical to itself for as long as it does not destroy it. This denial is particularly evident in the analyses of trade unionism, aimed at showing that working-class "economic" struggles only regulate the "norms" of exploitation, and change nothing of the relations of production. This paradox of a *historicity without history* is resolved precisely by the proposition of "laws of evolution" that postulate the permanence of the system's structure even as they prefigure its negation.

There is a direct relation between this blockage and the difficulties we have encountered with the notion of dominant ideology. When Engels defines the "bourgeois worldview" by its *legal* basis, he invokes an argument borrowed from the history of the bourgeois struggles against feudalism, which were carried out in the name of the law and in the dominant form of legal discourse. He offers us no way of knowing whether this form stays the same indefinitely when the bourgeoisie becomes dominant and when the principal political problem becomes the struggle to maintain the exploitation of the working class. We can assume he thinks it does: for one, the general form of wage relations is still that of a "contractual" commodity exchange; and, second, the material instrument of the struggle is still direct-ly the state, which is instituted as the legal guarantor of private property in general. These implicit arguments, however, harbor the same paradox of a historicity without history (or, if you will, of an invariable essence of "cap-italism") as those regarding the relation of production itself. We certainly have two successive configurations for the conflict between worldviews: first, theological-feudal against bourgeois-legal, then bourgeois-legal against communist-proletarian. But the change has no effect on the contents of the bourgeois-legal worldview, which remains once and for all true to its origins (as if the law functioned against aristocratic privileges and working-class demands in the same way). In other words, the existence of the proletariat and its social struggle (that of the working-class movement) plays no role in the formation and transformation of the dominant ideology. Here, again, is the paradox of domination without the dominated that I discussed earlier.

The same theoretical obstacle can be seen with respect to the proletariat. If the relation of production is a constant, the working class has no history other than that of the successive extensions of the wage form. Henceforth, the question of proletarian ideology is also represented in terms of all or nothing: a submission of the proletariat to the dominant ideology *or* a liberation from illusions, consciousness *or* unconsciousness. Historically, there are *working-class* ideologies, bound up with different forms of exploitation, different locales and conditions of existence, origins and cultural (national, familial, religious) "traditions," but these remain here unthought and strictly unthinkable. They are no more than a mass of excep-tions and backwardness without real theoretical pertinence. Similarly, the fact that political organization, even when it is built with the aid of a scien-tific theory, produces mass ideological effects on the working class, to the very extent that it provides the working class with the means to acknowledge an "identity," remains beyond the grasp of historical and critical analysis. The working class becomes the blind spot of its own politics, leaving the field free for messianic ideologization.[6]

Let us take a bit of distance to contemplate this paradox. The Marx of *The German Ideology* (permeated with Rousseau, Kant, and Feuerbach) calls "ideology" the ahistorical (and antihistorical) universal into which a ruling class projects the imaginary eternity of its conditions of existence, which are also the conditions of its rule. The Marx of *Capital*, the late Engels of *Ludwig Feuerbach*, good readers of Hegel, critics of the "dominant" economic ideology from the point of view of the "ultimately" revolutionary class, see in capitalism's *historicity* the moving figure of its constancy, of its eternal self-identity. In *The Poverty of Philosophy* (1847), Marx wrote ironically of the essentialist naturalism of the economists, "thus there has been history, but there is no longer any."[7] And now it is our turn to be ironic: thus there is no more history, but there will be....A small detail—the fact that the concept of a "proletarian ideology" remains decidedly impossible to formulate—leads to a large result: "history" becomes the other name for eternity (and "materialism" the other name for idealism?).

The Mask of Politics

This reversal is directly translated by the inability to develop the dialectic of mass movements and class positions, which nonetheless emerges in Marx and Engels as the practico-theoretical kernel of historical materialism. On the contrary, due to the thesis of the "simplification of class struggles in the history of capitalism," they will constantly reduce this dialectic to nothingness by tailoring the historical individuality of the masses to the pattern of a purified class antagonism.

Thenceforth, even more profoundly, it is the concept of politics at work in Marxism that must be re-examined, beginning by applying to Marx and Engels their own distinction between "method" and "system," in which method is not simply what remains of a system once it has been deprived of its conclusions or goals, but rather what enters into contradiction with these conclusions and goals and as a result—sooner or later—brings on a crisis in the system.

In the different theoretical forms we have encountered, we have always found the idea of a *distance from the real*, of a thinking that takes off at a tangent from the real, toward a "lateral object" (*Nebenobjekt*), and therefore deflects practice toward a fictive end, a *Nebenzweck*. It has always been clear that this deflecting (or metaphorizing) operation has a political effect, in the sense of an effect on the class struggle, but we have seen both Marx and Engels hesitate to define it either as the distance of *all* politics from the real or as the distance from *a politics that would be the real itself*.

We must look, then, at the way ideological dominations or worldviews have been periodized. In the theological, medieval form there would be an implied division of the instances of power (and consciousness, and representation or discourse): on the one side, the feudal state, the organization of the ruling class of landed gentry; on the other, the Church, at once caught within the feudal system in which it is a link and rising "above" it, and therefore capable of bestowing a guarantee of sacred authority upon that system. If religious (Christian) ideology's distance from the real is explained by this division, one can draw out its consequences: although the feudal state (monarchy, empire) is explicitly represented as topmost in the hierarchy of rulers (feudal lords), the Church is legally and effectively, by the identical practices it imposes on them, a community of *all* the faithful, rulers and ruled; whereas, while the state constitutes a separate world of the rulers, the Church, which draws its unity from its reference to a mystical beyond, is at the same time the organizer of everyone's everyday life, of "society."

What happens when a secular bourgeois ideology (a profane wisdom, *Weltweisheit*, as Hegel, following Saint Paul, says) replaces this religious ideological apparatus? It seems that the division is reabsorbed. The Church, denounced as a "state within the state" at the same time as religion is denounced as a mystification, does not disappear but loses its role of guaranteeing authority when the state stops organizing itself around a caste. The state then stands on its own, at once "object" and "subject" of the representations of the dominant ideology; it functions *directly* as an ideological power. In other words, the state becomes the new Absolute. Legal ideology would thus be the direct expression of state rule; but it could also be said that it is pure mystification in the service of this rule: an absolute transparency corresponds to absolute manipulation.

In fact, Engels's description, confirmed by Marx's analyses of the bourgeois state, suggests another reading: there is a new splitting of what, compared to its feudal past, seems quite simple. But this time the splitting is generated by the machine of the state, as a differentiation between *state power* and the *legal order*. Once again this division, which structures class practices, covers over the distinction between the state, "organization of the ruling class," and civil "society," in which all those relations of exchange that allow for the circulation of commodities and men and that take the form of a contract are inscribed. It also allows an ideal term (the law) to function as a guarantee of state power: it allows the *political* to be formally distinguished from the *juridical*, which would be situated above the political, expressing at the same time the community of its subjects. Once again, finally, this division provides for the displacement or deflection of the goals of practice toward an ideal object (in this case the "rule of ends" of law, "justice," the rule of the "rights of man," Liberty-Equality-Fraternity, etc.), the more surely to attain its real goal, the reproduction of the established order.

This entire process would seem to illustrate a kind of "law" of the transformation of ideological dominations, a law of division-unity-division or (for unity is only a theoretical abstraction) a law of the displacement or substitution of divisions. What the intermediate unity actually designates is the moment of transition in which the form of the state is seen as what is actually at stake in a transformation, in "seizing power." It is the moment of transition in which two transformations coincide in practice: a transformation of the form of the state by the class struggle, and a transformation of the dominant representations of rule (for example, "secularization": the passage from sacred authority to legal authority, from the Christian state to the constitutional state, from the intellectual as cleric to the intellectual as judge or scholar, etc.).

We can call eminently political the moment in which this transformation reveals what is actually at stake (state power, the form of its apparatus) in a theory and mass historical practice. A theory of class struggle, or rather a concrete analysis of the forms class struggle takes in a determined historical transition, can show us, at any point in time, what its objective is. To describe the modality of the relation thus established between the class struggle and its representation as "political," we must resort to metaphors. Turning around the formulation we had previously advanced, let us say that *it is in the (historical) vacillation of ideology that politics appears*, but this time in the sense in which a form of ideological domination (the theological, for example) must be negated in its mass power, in its historical capacity to represent the real, so that another (the juridical, for example) can take its place. We can also use another metaphor, the *twisting* of the relation between state and ideology, which must be undone for the relation to be twisted again in the other direction, as a many-stranded rope twists one way and then the other under the effect of two forces.[8]

The bourgeoisie's accession to power (its transformation into a ruling class) thus already represented itself as political; it did not have to wait for historical materialism to forge the concept of the modern state. And this representation underlies its own "materialism," one whose critical force is directed against theology: it involves destroying the idea inherent in everyday human life, of a community of sin and salvation, in order to replace it with the idea of an immanent social bond, woven here on earth by men themselves into the exchange of commodities, the division of labor, contracts, government institutions, the constitution of the state, and its different "powers."

Under these conditions, what are the representations thrown up by the struggle of a new class, the proletariat, against the bourgeois state? They take the form of a "new materialism" whose critical force is directed, this time, against the idealism proper to legal ideology (against the ideological twisting of the real into the form of the law)—in effect, what can be called "historical" or "dialectical" materialism. These representations also introduce *another concept of politics*, which initially takes the form of the concept of *another politics*, irreducible to bourgeois politics: a politics of the masses, of labor, a communist politics. But can we not assume that this critique is accompanied by its own movement of ideological twisting? Or even that, if proletarian politics homogenizes what was present in the double form of the "political" and the "juridical" (in stripping "bare" the workings and political stakes of the law), it is also accompanied by its own division, its own displacement? This is whole question. Let us then explore this path.

To say that the unity of the political is divided afresh is to say that, in certain conditions, *politics itself can become the "mask" of politics*: it does not constitute a final term, a "solution found at last" to the enigma of class struggle (or history) but *one of its forms*, in which we still find symptoms of a distance from the real which has characterized the concept of ideology. We must give up entirely the idea of a "language of real life," this promised land of the critique envisaged in *The German Ideology*, whether one reads into the expression "language of real life" a reduction to what is before all language, to the "life" it expresses, or whether we find the converse, the ideal of an ordinary language, absolutely "true" and nonmetaphorical. Politics, including that of the exploited class, since it is always both practice and language, or practice within language, must be what is masked over indefinitely and what is unmasked in its own words, or rather in the use made of them.

It is not impossible to find in Marx and Engels moments in which this situation is "practically" recognized. This untheorized recognition of the internal contradictions of politics (one might suggest, in philosophical jargon, its intrinsic "finitude") is related, significantly, to their experiences of the dislocation between the language of theory and the operations of the political party—hence the example of the episode of the *Critique of the Gotha Program*, whose disappointing outcome (Marx's withdrawal of his critiques, later exhumed by Engels after their author's death began to turn him into a monument) is as interesting as is its point of departure (the debate on "statism" and "workerism"). If Marx's critiques went unpublished ("*dixi et salvavi animam meam*"),[9] it was probably under pressure from the party officials they might have embarrassed, but it was also, Engels tells us, because within this conjuncture the workers "read" into the program "what was not there" (the affirmation of a class position), and, because of this, these critiques would have lost their "usefulness."[10] But if the workers could read this class position it had to be there, at least in the form of words in which to invest a class practice; that is, it had to be present in a conjunctural *relation* with these words, or in the "line of demarcation" these words might trace out between different "class" discourses in a particular political conjuncture. Perhaps today we are less surprised by the possibility of such an equivocal reading, given that the history of revolutions in this century has shown how the words of religion or patriotism (even nationalism) can "bear" the class struggle, while at other times the words of the class struggle can bear only nationalism, if not religion. We do not believe any longer in the univocity of words, apart from their use.

Is this to say that, in the "sound and fury" of history, no practical, univocal difference ever appears, but only a succession of the ambivalent forms of a perpetual illusion? On the contrary, what appears are precisely differences, some of which are irreducible. The fact that, with the antagonism of the bourgeoisie and the proletariat, the juridical appears as a "mask" of politics, does not mean that the bourgeois critique of religious ideology is entirely negated. What fails is its pretense to be the ultimate truth of man or history. Similarly, the fact that proletarian politics is divided and covered over again from the moment it acquires its own autonomy does not negate the difference between law and politics revealed by the critique of bourgeois legal ideology. It simply signifies that this critique too is a moment in an incomplete process with no foreseeable end. From the point of view of this infinite process (which is retrospectively presented as a progression, even though it is neither continuous nor regulated by a pre-established goal), the succession of worldviews appears as a series of divisions and identifications of politics. And this figure—if it is not absolute—is still no more unreal than the present process itself.

Let us take this further. Bourgeois ideology, by confusing in the same category of Reason both legal and scientific discourse, has constructed a way of presenting "science" as a new form of the Absolute. Conversely, the fact that proletarian politics is based in the last analysis not on reason but on the irreducibility of class antagonism, as it is analyzed for the first time by a materialist theory, can allow a recognition of the objectivity of scientific knowledge within its limits, extracted from the oscillation of "all or nothing" (subjectivism/objectivism, skepticism/speculation). Under these conditions, the fact that the concept of ideology in Marx and Engels is ultimately constituted by a denial of the essentially metaphoric nature of language explains how a metaphysics of truth (or of the meaning of history) is built up around it. This does not, however, require—as the "postmodernists" would have it—substituting a generalized skepticism (through which other metaphysics, even other religions might reappear) for the critique of ideologies. It is not a question of *substituting*, by means of a hyperbolic transcendence of "grand narratives" and "worldviews" (or, if you will, in a highly problematic "withdrawal from the political")[11] the metaphoricity of language for the identification of ideological differences, but of *inscribing* ideological effects as differential effects within the historical element of language.

If there is once more a division and a covering over of proletarian politics, what are its operative terms? First, it seems to me there is a continuous play of distinctions and confusions between economics and politics. This distinction/confusion is symptomatically present in the Saint-Simonian formula taken up by Engels in the *Anti-Dühring*: "the government of persons is replaced by the administration of things, and by the conduct of processes of production"[12] (which has been interpreted both as the catchword of a "self-regulatory" society without a state and as the substitution of the industrial imperative for the conflict of capital and labor). It can be equally read into the watchword *abolition of labor* in the works of the young Marx and in the later call for a (communist) *politics of labor*. Doubtless this distinction/confusion is nothing but the prolonged effect, *within* "proletarian politics" itself, of the ideological and institutional dualism that structures "bourgeois politics," which I evoked above with respect to Engels's analyses.

Above all, however, this same distinction structures the way the working-class movement has practiced politics against the "legalism" of bourgeois politics: not simply by disavowing the juridical form but by *distinguishing* the law from legal ideology so as to avoid becoming a prisoner of existing law through legal ideology, so as not to "believe in the law" but to *use* it, in a "Machiavellian" way, by "turning" it against the ruling class (either in forms of mass unionism or by way of universal suffrage). So, while the practice of the working-class movement has tended toward reformism, revolution has become its point of honor and its myth—*what is believed in order not to believe in legal ideology.* And it is in this period—that of the first crisis of Marxism, from 1895 to 1905—that the ideologies of organization are instituted (still active today: "Sorel" against "Lenin") to represent at times the union and at other times the party as *the truly revolutionary form*, the only one incompatible with the system (while the other is supposed to remain inside it) and hence the sole bearer of the proletarian worldview. Both these representations, moreover, can seem Marxist, whether in the name of the critique of economism or by virtue of the struggle against "constitutional illusions," "parliamentary cretinism," or "Jacobinism."

But what matters most here is the fact that the distinction/confusion of the economic and the political, even if we cannot locate it very precisely, structures the functioning of the bourgeois state itself, its relation to "society." Far from changing anything, the extension of modern "social policy" and "economic policy" (in what has been called the "interventionist" state or the "welfare state," and which it would be better to call the national-social state), have only confirmed the insistence of these categories. The new institutions (social security, planning, etc.) had to be inscribed, not without a certain amount of acrobatics, in the field of these pre-existing representations. Economics has become the principal area of state intervention in social practice. It is also, contradictorily, what poses an unceasing obstacle to the efficacy of state intervention, to its "decisions." This is what we call the "crisis": all political discourse, as we know, turns on how its "cause" will be assigned, even on how responsibility for it will be imputed, either *inside* or *outside* the sphere of the state and its regulatory or interfering interventions. This transformation, however, cannot be separated from the effects on the bourgeois state of the development of a mass working-class movement. Nor can it be separated from the way in which, forcing the bourgeois state to reorganize itself as a function of its existence, the working-class movement has seen its own aims being displaced and finds itself displaced within the field of politics. The same words ("reform," "revolution") that, in given historical conditions, designated a real political objective, have now come to mean a lateral or metaphorical object, a "*Nebenzweck*." This is either because the struggle has *already achieved* this objective, albeit in an unrecognizable form (that of the "national-social state"), or because *it can no longer be achieved*, the conditions that made it "thinkable" and historically practicable having been destroyed by the class struggle.[13]

Behind the indefinite displacement of ideological forms we will thus discover the displacement of the conditions of the class struggle. Both processes can be thought within the notion of a permanent *divergence* of real history with respect to the "direction" drawn for each period by the resultant of social conflicts in the sphere of discourse. It is remarkable that, in their critique of utopianism, as well as in the aporia of their proletarian worldview with no specific content, or their proletarian ideology thought of as *nonideology*, Marx and Engels left open a double possibility: either the myth of a definitive escape from ideology (or of a "science" without ideological conditions or effects), corresponding to the myth of the end of history, or the concept of a "materialist critique of politics," yet to be determined as a function of the ways in which politics itself forever masks its reality and its illusions.[14]

Of the "Truth" and the "Whole"

If the real process (what we understand as history) *never sticks to the straight path* toward which, on account of its own internal ideological tension, it seems to tend, then every simple representation of an outcome (that is, of a salvation, even a worldly one) is necessarily a lure, a *Nebenzweck*, even if it is the necessary form of collective practice. What is real, however, is exactly *that a transformation takes place* in this form. It is a series that diverges without limit, not one that converges on an ideal limit. A bifurcation in an unforeseen form, it results from the instability of social relations and the retroaction of social struggles on their conditions of possibility.

The representation of historical *convergence* of time (the convergence of the "series" that gives historical time its scansion) is one of the great commonplaces of the philosophy of history, which, in the modern age, goes from Leibniz to Teilhard de Chardin ("everything that rises must converge").[15] In Marx and Engels it is present in the secular figure of the Hegelian "negation of the negation." It underlies the extrapolations of the tendencies of capitalism toward its "general crisis" (whereas we now know that history tells the story of the change of form or even of the change of the function of crises), toward the growth of the "conditions of the revolution" (whereas history tells the story of revolutions that happen *elsewhere*, in places where these conditions are not met, and do not happen where "the conditions are met"). Witness, in its echo forty years later of Marx's post-1848 expectations, Engels's "forecast" (in which there is an astonishing combination of theology and technocratic positivism):

> For the first time in history, a soundly knit workers' party (*eine solid geschlossene Arbeiterpartei*—which can also be understood as a "tightly closed party") has appeared as a real political force (*als wirkliche politische Macht*)...a force whose

existence and rise are as incomprehensible and mysterious to governments and the old ruling classes as the flow of the Christian tide was to the powers of decadent Rome. This force develops and expands as surely and inexorably as did Christianity before it, so much so that the equation of its rate of growth (*die Gleichung ihrer wachsenden Geschwindigkeit*)— and hence the moment of its ultimate triumph—can now be computed mathematically. Instead of suppressing it, the anti-socialist legislation has given it a boost.[16]

This evolutionist representation also underlies the epistemological notion of an absolute truth as a "process of integration" of relative truths (or relative errors) as it was put forward by the *Anti-Dühring*.

The metaphysics of "truth" and "totality" thus continues, beyond the rupture, to haunt historical materialism. Nevertheless, this sort of contradictory configuration merits being studied in the singularity of its conditions and its time, rather than being referred to the "origins of Western metaphysics" by a mechanistic application of the philosophy of Heidegger. This does not mean that this configuration is proper to Marx alone: what is more likely at issue is a contradiction that—from the time of the almost simultaneous constitution at the beginning of the nineteenth century of a "secular" philosophy of history and an evolutionist biology, of a state "economic science" and a formal logic (or a mathematics of language)—has been at "work" upon the relations between the sciences and politics.[17] But the position occupied by Marxism in the play of this contradiction is nonetheless original.

This metaphysics, if it cannot be "suppressed," can at least be counteracted if we keep in mind both the irreducibility of the antagonism and its nonteleological character (thus its incompatibility with any expectation of a "final solution"). It is only in the "current moment" that historical reality can be appropriated in practice. Lenin clearly designated this point by defining Marxism as the "concrete analysis of a concrete situation" and by substituting for a conception of absolute truth—as the "progressive integration" of relative truths, following a predetermined curve—a conception of the moment of absolute truth present in each "relative truth."[18] Taking this further, we can say that any "truth" is both a *conjunctural fact* and an *effect* of the conjuncture, in several senses.

Truth—or, rather, *the true*, whenever and wherever it arises—is an effect of conjuncture, in that it contradicts the "dominant" forms or criteria of universality, that is, it embodies a practical criticism of ideology. Thus it is produced in the very element of ideology. One can read in the same way Hegel's thesis that makes all truth the *aftereffect* of a negation through defining it by its essential recurrence (*Nachträglichkeit*), which is precisely not the glorification of a "*fait accompli*," since the *fait accompli* presents itself as "accomplishment" in the very forms of the dominant ideology. All that is "certain"—but it is at least something—is that there is something in ideology incompatible with a certain practice of ongoing transformation (and with a certain form of social communication). Inasmuch as it signals this practical effect—not definitive, but irreducible—the concept of ideology is materialist and breaks free of the circle of dogmatism (originary or final truth) and skepticism (no truth, or truth as pure mystification, moral fiction, elaboration of desire, etc.). If the primary *ideological effect* is to change all knowledge into obviousness or an illusion of universality, the primary effect of the *concept of ideology* is to *divide the concept of truth*: between a concept of truth that postulates its autonomy and one that acknowledges its practical dependence on the conjuncture; or to put it differently, between a concept that designates as truth (if need be in order to deny its possibility) the fantasy of a self-consciousness absolutely contemporaneous with itself and a concept of the true as a process of knowledge, implying a noncoincidence, an irreducible noncontemporaneity of discourse and its conditions.

In the case of historical struggles, the "true" is also an effect of conjuncture in that it is produced as an encounter, an exceptional condensation of the class struggle and the mass movement, two realities that remain relatively *heterogeneous*. No effect of knowledge (or "truth" in the materialist sense) arises from what remain only mass movements, unified by an ideological faith and essentially defined—even when they weather well, or inspire a revolution, or smash the established order—as fluctuating forces, always ambivalently attracted to and repulsed by the state. Nor can truth arise from the stable or stabilized configurations of the class struggle, which nurture the dogmatism of the established order, or the symmetrical dogmatism ("subaltern," as Gramsci put it with a ferocious lucidity) of the resistance of the oppressed organized in their trenches, each one characteristic, in short, of what the same Gramsci called the processes of "passive revolution." Indeed, one can ask whether these processes are not really the ordinary state of history in its self-misunderstanding, whether there really are *exceptions*. Admittedly, we will never prove in advance that there are: we shall always have to content ourselves with the "contingent" fact that they have taken place.

What makes true knowledge (or at least some of its conditions) arise is the unpredictability of their coming together: these are the "days in which the masses learn more than in years," of which Lenin, following Marx, spoke (days, however, can themselves be years if it is the case that the problem is not chronological but structural: the metaphor of "crisis" that underlies this formulation would have to be re-examined). Either, as Marx brilliantly analyzed for the revolutions of the nineteenth century, class antagonism ends up polarizing, displacing, and radicalizing the mass movements, or, above all, as Lenin, Gramsci, and Mao saw much more clearly, the mass movements determine a class struggle that had remained hypothetical until that point and provide it with its concrete content. I say "above all" because it is probably for lack of having envisaged this reciprocity, in spite of their dialectic, that Marx and Engels generally applied a reductionist conception of the class struggle. This prevented them from concretely developing the critical idea of a historical process whose causality would not express the destiny of a predestined subject (proletariat or other), but rather would express the contradictory articulation of the masses and the classes—which are never quite the same even "in the last instance." To parody Kant, it could be said that without the mass movements the class struggle is empty (which is to say, it remains full of dominant ideology). However, without the class struggle, the mass movements are blind (which is to say, they give rise to counterrevolution, even fascism, as much as to revolution). But there is no pre-established correspondence between these two forms, no universal "schematism." The true is then produced as the critical effect of the unpredictable that obliges the class struggle to *go back over* and correct its own representations (and its own myths).[19]

I would like to draw two further conclusions from these hypotheses. The first is that the great theoretical lure in the history of Marxism has been constituted by the ever-developing and ever-aborted project of a "theory of ideology." This project cannot be circumvented since, without a concept of ideology, there exists neither "historical materialism" nor a "class point of view" in theory. It can be said that after Marx and Engels this project is rooted both in the dissatisfaction that the constant vacillation of their concept of ideology provokes, and in the temptation to "develop" the descriptions of the effect of ideological "inversion" of the real that they propose into a coherent theory, articulated with that of capitalist exploitation and of the state. Neither Marx nor Engels, however, seems to have thought about such a theory (unless, perhaps, it goes by the name "dialectic"). The constitutive instability of a founding concept, even if it produces a series of theoretical obstacles and aporias, is not exactly a conceptual *lack* that could be filled.

Rather, this project is the symptom of the relation to Marx—the father—maintained by Marxists and of the contradictions of that relation; it is, at the same time, the closed field of their confrontations or antithetical "deviations." We should remember how this project is constituted (Bernstein is the first within the revisionist camp to formulate it in these terms, but, just as quickly, Plekhanov takes it up in the orthodox camp, opposing social psychology to the development of consciousness, the lesson of Taine to that of Kant, etc.) and what forms it later takes, right up to Sartre and Althusser, during what can be called the classical period of Marxism (the formation and dissolution of the parties of the Second and Third International, whose theoretical base was essentially the same). Sometimes this project is "economist" and sometimes it is "anti-economist." Paradoxically, it can be both at the same time (as it is in Lukács and, in general, in all theorizing that tries to use the commodity form dialectically against the mechanicalness, the evolutionism, or the reductionism of class, as was already the case in Engels).

What I would like to emphasize here is that the idea of a theory of ideology was only ever a *way ideally to complete historical materialism*, to "fill a hole" in its representation of the social totality, and thus a way ideally to constitute historical materialism as a system of explanation complete in its kind, at least "in principle." This ever-reviving project must be read as a kind of symptom. The necessity to complete the social whole is indeed the ambition, avowed or not, of all sociology, of all "social science," and not of Marxism alone (it is at this point that its *ad hoc* concepts arise: "mana," "the symbolic order," "systemic constraint," etc.). This is necessary in order to be able to locate the cause entirely in a given representation, in a structural schema of the social totality, whether in one of its parts—identified as the *site* of "determination in the last instance"—or in the reciprocal interplay of all the parts, of their overall complexity or *Wechselwirkung*. And if the missing link must be designated "ideology," then it is because this term, turned against its initial use, comes to connote the imaginary correspondence between the practice of organization and theoretical knowledge in a "program" that could be formulated once and for all. In this sense, the return of teleology in Marxism and the project of a "theory of ideology" (or of a "Marxist science of ideologies") seem to me always to be strictly correlative. One could even suggest that they have always served to compensate for the horizontal division that the class struggle introduces into society by means of another fictive unity (a more abstract one, it is true), a principle of vertical totalization in the schema of theoretical explanation. The "Marxist theory of ideology" would then be symptomatic of the permanent discomfort Marxism maintains with its own critical recognition of the class struggle.

I think that we can and should uphold the contrary: that programs and plans are never fulfilled, although they are sometimes adequate to their conjuncture (what Althusser suggested calling practical "correctness"); that the "theory", or rather, *the concept of ideology* denotes no other object than that of the nontotalizable (or nonrepresentable within a unique given order) complexity of the historical process;[20] finally, that historical materialism is incomplete and incompletable in principle, not only in the temporal dimension (since it postulates the relative unpredictability of the effects of determinate causes), but also in its theoretical "topography," since it requires the articulation of the class struggle to concepts that have a different materiality (such as the unconscious).

Such a position seems to me to be consistent with the idea, argued above, of an effect of "truth" *in the conjuncture.* In political terms, this implies not an absolute separation or natural antagonism of knowledge and decision, or organization, but the impossibility of a total "fusion," acquired once and for all, of theoretical and strategic functions. If it is the encounter, or the conflict, between theory, or rather between theories and practices, that gives rise to both knowledge and "politics," then it is certainly necessary, from time to time at least, that theory be produced *outside* the organization. It may even be that there are more opportunities—and not fewer—within this parallelism for the social division of labor to evolve, and that theory (as a social activity) will increasingly cease to be a monopoly of individuals or of castes, a business for intellectuals, in short, for those Marx, in the beginning, called "ideologists." For if proletarians or, more generally, the people from below are no longer portrayed either as completely lacking ideology (*Illusionslos*) or as the potential bearers, by nature, of a "communist worldview"—providing revolutionary theories with an ideal guarantee—they will themselves have more, not fewer, opportunities to introduce and test their ideas (the "thought of the masses") in the battlefield of politics, from which they had been excluded in their own name.

PART THREE

FRONTIERS OF CONTEMPORARY POLITICS

Questioning the Universal

7

FASCISM, PSYCHOANALYSIS, FREUDO-MARXISM

My intervention—which obviously does not come from a psychoanalyst—is intended to point out that a reflection on psychoanalysis's relation to Nazism (what it suffered from it, what it thought of it, how it was transformed by it) cannot omit mention of what has been called "Freudo-Marxism." This term is equivocal by definition, not only because of the variety of individuals and positions that it encompasses, but because of the theoretical emptiness of the object that it seems to designate. Everyone seems to have already judged the case, those who would reject both Marxism and psychoanalysis as uncertain speculations (for this critique is valid *a fortiori* against their combination) as well as those who have rallied to either one or the other (the two points of view being considered obviously antithetical). Still, I will argue that this judged and rejudged trial in fact leaves a question open.[1] And if there can be no question of beginning the adventure of Freudo-Marxism over again in different circumstances, perhaps the appropriate thing to do would be to reformulate the question from which it stems, to recall its necessity, and to identify exactly what leads it into a dead end, that is, what renders the enterprise impossible. Perhaps it is precisely this status as a necessary impossibility that gives Freudo-Marxism its interest today, at a moment when the abundance and cacophony of discourses on contemporary racism and its "filiation" with Nazism are more striking than their efficacy and precision.

Actually I will not apply the category of necessary impossibility to "Freudo-Marxism" as a whole, but to a single author, Wilhelm Reich, and to the one book which, situated in the exact conjuncture of its composition (1933) and reread in the France of the 1980s, appears truly symptomatic: *The Mass Psychology of Fascism*. This work, as is well known, along with the militant activity whose basis it claimed to establish, was immediately rewarded with Reich's exclusion from the two organizations of which he had been a member, the International Psychoanalytic Association and the German Communist party (a section of the Communist International), two organizations that were confronted, each on its own terrain, with the problem of explaining Nazism and intervening against the threat it posed to their *raison d'être* and their physical existence. It would be absurd to turn this double rejection into a theoretical argument, according to which Reich would have been rejected and eliminated because he told the truth. But it is also too easy to sanction it indefinitely *a posteriori* (as if the lucidity of the orthodoxies had been proved) and *a fortiori* to justify it by the "delirious" evolution of Reich's later theorizations. What should be much more striking to us today, rereading his analyses, is the strange status of a discourse that doubtless is *false*, but that *hits the mark*.

This discourse hits the mark with respect to psychoanalysis because it poses the question of its "politics" at the very moment that it becomes an object of political debate. More precisely it poses the question of a politics which would be *neither* a tactic of investiture of existing medical institutions, *nor* a project of transformation into a "worldview" with the ambition of guiding the transformation of society, but a politics that would find a point of articulation with the social forces (classes, masses, "parties") already constituted in history, in the battles of democracy and in the confrontation with the state. This question is incontrovertible in the conjuncture of Nazism's rise to power, precisely because Nazism establishes a social order radically incompatible with the knowledge of the unconscious and with the practice of the analytic cure: a social order, Reich was to say, that in a sense stages and instrumentalizes the unconscious. The moment to oppose it with a "pedagogy," the teachings of a science to come, following Freud's enlightened program, had already passed. Reich is not the only one, as is well known, to have sought in Marxism the recognition of this politics and its "real" forces. The failure of his attempt left, once again, only two possibilities: political indifference (or, if you prefer, the possibility for analysts and their patients, constituted as a small "society" within the larger one, to "choose," according to their preferences, temperaments, or social position, either conservative, reformist, or anti-establishment political roles), and interpretive politics, that is, a commentary in psychoanalytic language upon events and social formations.

This discourse also hits the mark with respect to Marxism, because it designates *in its heart* and in its evolution the cause of the possibility of the victory of Nazism. This thesis—"excessive" by definition—takes several forms. It locates the origin of fascist movements (including Nazism) in the failure of proletarian revolutions within a conjuncture of world crisis. It also shows the "socialist state" and the party that corresponds to it (of the Soviet type) to be authoritarian structures of the same nature as fascism and therefore powerless to oppose radically different forces to it and disintegrate it from within, from the society over which it establishes its mastery. These are two variants, in short, of the model of "counterrevolution." But above all, this thesis goes back to a point prior to these events and phenomena in order to formulate Marxism's blind spot: its own myth of "class consciousness," and its correlative incomprehension and denial of what it itself calls "ideology." Wilhelm Reich goes far beyond merely pointing out a theoretical *deficiency* in Marxism (because it lacked an adequate conception of ideology it was unable to understand the power of an "ideological movement" like Nazism). What he dares affirm is that historical materialism (the only "real" one at a given moment) *denies out of principle* the reality, the "material force" of ideology as an "emotional" or affective structure of the masses, distinct from the "consciousness" they have of their conditions of existence, and as a consequence denies the irreducible *split* between class condition and mass movements. But mass movements are the very matter of politics (politics does have a matter) and this is why fascism was able to construct itself directly upon the exploitation of the contradiction internal to Marxism and the political practices inspired by it, simply turning against Marxism the collective "subjectivity" whose revolutionary role it exalted. For things to have happened otherwise would have required the intervention of a *third* element capable of displacing and upsetting this mimetic relation: an element drawn from Freud which, in particular, would have allowed an analysis of the role of sexual repression in the structure of "authoritarian" institutions, as a function of which (within which, but also against which, in a movement of "revolt") emotional solidarities develop.

Let us pause here for a moment. Without debating Reich's conception of a "sexual sociology" inspired by Freud (but opposed to Freud's own humanist "philosophy of culture"), it is possible to confirm retrospectively how much (and how tragically) he hit the mark with respect to Marxism. Reich said that Marxism had been unable to explain why the impoverished masses went over to nationalism (rather than to revolutionary class consciousness), which opened wide the possibility for Nazism to crush the class struggle under nationalism. Today we know that Marxism never recovered from this defeat. What has been called the "crisis of Marxism" is a process with many episodes, in a sense coextensive with its whole history (just as a "crisis of Freudianism" is in some sense coextensive with the entire history of psychoanalysis), since it begins with the very constitution of a Marxist "science." But the turning point of this crisis was precisely the confrontation with Nazism and European fascism in general: because Marxism did not fight fascism *politically, on its own base* (as a revolutionary class force), and never gained any theoretical grasp on its functioning, and above all because, after the fact, it interpreted and presented this defeat as a victory (for example interpreting the military victory of the U.S.S.R. as a victory of "socialism" when it was in fact a victory of nationalism or state patriotism). One of the results of this was the fact that the scission of Marxism (between communism and social-democracy), which fascism and Nazism had systematically exploited (and in which all the anterior forms of the crisis were crystallized), was not overcome but consummated at the end of the experience of "antifascism," since it was now inscribed in the very institutions of the system of states and the "camps" of world politics. Reich is one of the rare *theoreticians* of Marxist formation (with the Gramsci of the *Prison Notebooks*) to have seen this turning point and attempted to anticipate—if not prevent—its consequences by means of a critique of the conspiratorial vision of history to which the orthodox problematic of class struggle had led: above all the idea of racism and nationalism as *ideological instruments* manipulated by the ruling classes against the proletariat, supposed to be "naturally" revolutionary. What we can also read retrospectively in this critique and in Reich's insistence on the "emotional armature" of the family and the state is a critique of a Marxist individualism and sociologism ("whiggism," the British would say) that has never ceased to conceive of the state as an artificial, parasitical structure (an inessential "superstructure"): whence its proleptic conviction that the symbolic and material collapse of the state in a period of war and revolution would be experienced by the proletariat (and by "society" in general) as a liberation of its essential forces. But the German and European crisis of the 1920s and 1930s showed exactly the opposite to be true: the collapse of the state, as legal authority and coercive apparatus, engenders not a power to act, the "free association" of individuals, but rather emotional panic and the need of individuals to recognize themselves *en masse* in the "charismatic" figure of a simultaneously ferocious and maternal leader. Reich's analyses contain in this respect a revealing oscillation between two tendencies: a renewal of the libertarian myth (in particular of the idea that the proletariat as such is foreign to the archaism of authoritarian family bonds, just as it is foreign to nationalist "honor"), but also a critique of the anarchist illusion still alive within Marxism (manifested by its fluctuations between proclaiming the "nothingness of the state" and attempting to do "everything by the state").

Thus Reich doubly hits the mark in the designation of the insufficiency and impotence of his own theoretical references, of his own strategic "positions" (perhaps because, wanting to be a member of two organizations at once, without reducing either of them to being a mere instrument of the other, he cannot entirely idealize either of them). It must be asked whether this effect of being on target was possible *despite* the dangerous proximity of his own biologism (a biologism of "work," of "sexual economy," and of "genital happiness") to the biologism of the enemy he was fighting (a biologism of "race"), or if, paradoxically, in a given conjuncture, it is not a *consequence* of this proximity. Let us hazard the hypothesis that, in the presence of the efficacy of Nazi racism on a mass (and thus historic) scale, which is not just any "omnipotence of ideas" but precisely an ideology of nature, it was necessary to move onto the enemy's ground in order to be able to get any sort of hold on it, in order to manage to think the banality and normality of Nazi institutions (the state of a charismatic leader in which the permanent tendencies of the modern state, both "nationalist" and "social," are quite simply recomposed) in the very heart of the crisis, of the dramatic circumstances of the state of exception. This was necessary in some sense, then, in order to think the norm in the excess, and in its apparently abnormal, inconceivable form. In the same way, Gramsci was able to go beyond the impotent banalities of orthodox Marxism about the reactionary function of Italian fascism by taking seriously the theme of the "national-popular will." At least at that moment, only the theoreticians who took the risk of approaching the adversary's language, who sought a trace of truth in it, were effectively able to escape impotence, at least intellectually.

Reich's biologism only secondarily constitutes a speculation on life, on the "natural energy" that penetrates individuals. Even this theme, moreover, would deserve a careful analysis, for in the register of metaphor, or even fantasy—a fantasy that paradoxically opposes the representation of orgasm, or sexual happiness, to the "irrationalist" and "mystical" thesis of a bond of *jouissance* between the leader and the masses—it also constitutes, in its own way, a naturalist approach to the *transindividual* dimension of the social relationship in which the unconscious is implicated. In *The Mass Psychology of Fascism* biologism is only the theoretical and ontological horizon of an articulation between the history of the family and the history of labor. But the *family* (and particularly the working-class family, which makes a real worker distinct from an ideal proletarian insofar as his "labor power" must be reproduced individually, and not merely sold, bought, and consumed like a "commodity") is precisely what, right from the beginning, Marxist analysis has reduced and finally excluded from the determining factors of the historical process, in order to be able to figure the "social relation" in the illusory fullness of a pure class structure. And symmetrically, *labor* (the *division* of labor) is precisely what Freud excluded from the definition of the "social bond" (except to idealize it by subsuming it as such, thus at the cost of a certain moralism, under the category of the "reality principle") in order to be able to think the social bond in the illusory fullness of identification, that is, of the imaginary.

Reich fills these two "lacks" (or, he makes each lack fill the other). Confronted with the Nazi state in formation which "mobilizes" the people as a community of heroic workers ("soldiers of labor" who are also worker-soldiers) and, simultaneously, assigns to it the destiny of conserving the German family (for the family is identified with the very substance of millenarian "Germanness"), Reich seeks a synthesis of two "authoritarian" institutions. In the end his reasoning comes down to thinking that if the repressive state involves both a discipline of production that seeks to break the resistance to surplus labor, and a transposition of infantile affects onto the person of the party leader as head of state, which implies the official institution of the family as the guardian of the race and of sexual discipline (or "morality"), a common element must be postulated. In the end it is this element that Reich calls biology or sexual economy, an archaic or originary unity of history and the unconscious, or of the class struggle and sexuality (and thus kinship). Apart from the content, the unifying procedure is the same for all Freudo-Marxist enterprises. In Marcuse's work the same function is held by the notion of *culture*, as it is in Althusser's 1964 text "Freud and Lacan." Deleuze and Guattari call it a desiring machine.

It is interesting to note that this fictional (but not unproductive) synthesis corresponds exactly to what Foucault, in the first volume of *The History of Sexuality*, called the repressive hypothesis. Foucault, caught in a game of mirrors with Reich, which is in fact implicitly based upon the urgency of the same questions (racism, "bio-politics"), was to conclude that the repressive hypothesis is indissociable from Marxism and psychoanalysis in themselves, but it is more a result of their addition. But at a deeper level this synthesis can be understood as a reconstitution of the unity of man, a metonymy of "human nature." Our suspicion is that the Freudo-Marxist articulation of work and the family is the specific form taken by the question of human nature when the state reconstructs itself by means of a racial politics. A naturalist formulation comes to the fore, but a structural reading is equally possible, which holds open the question of institutions as systems of collective subjectivization. The state (or more precisely the nationalist state, the state as an apparatus for the nationalization of society) is neither an enlarged "family" nor a generalized "factory," no more than it is, as certain of Foucault's formulations might lead one to believe, the envelope or armature of a "disciplinary society." In order to characterize the specific behavior of "men within the state," however, the overdetermination of the subjective process taking place in the family by the capitalist domination of labor power must be analyzed at the level of the structures themselves. As neither one nor the other goes without saying, politics effectively does have a history.

Doubtless, in the Marxist tradition, the theme of the *masses* is not proper to Reich. It is omnipresent as a political slogan: "the masses make history." This means that the masses make revolutions, which at the limit is a tautology: not so much because history and revolution would be synonymous, but above all because the masses are the opposite of the state, and revolution is the dissolution of the state. But in that case "mass" is only another name for class, or rather for the purely active class, the class in the course of becoming a "subject." In the same way, the idea that what historical materialism is lacking is a "theory of ideologies" and of their specific efficacy returns ceaselessly from Engels to Gramsci and beyond. Most frequently, however, it returns in the perspective of "consciousness," that is, as the requirement for a knowledge of the *individual* submitted to the ascendancy of the *social* structure, a knowledge of how much "freedom" the individual retains with respect to the collective determinations (division of labor, commodity relations, class antagonism). Reich reverses this problematic in two ways. He posits that the lacking ideological factor is not the expression of economic rationality but its other (which he calls "irrationality"), and identifies it with a form of primary socialization that precedes individuality. "Ideological force" is then no longer the derived effect or phenomenon of the class struggle, reducible to a class—that is, a group—psychology (itself a reflection "in consciousness" of the class situation), but in fact the prior material with which the class struggle works and which it more or less completely rationalizes. Social being is not what is obtained by abstracting from ideology, but what is woven out of it together with economics. The gap between the theoretical configuration of classes and their own being (in) masses becomes structural, and it can acquire the function of a historical causality.

The denial of this gap (tied to a utilitarian, and not a materialist, anthropology) is at the origin of Marxism's recurrent inability to account for the autonomy of the state, or rather for its tendency to autonomization, particularly in the form of the nationalization of the "petty-bourgeois" family, from which comes the representation of the people as a generalized "national kinship," what can be called a fictive ethnicity.[2] This is why the questions raised by Reich—if not the answers he gives—should appear particularly pertinent to us at the moment when, speaking of Marxism, we ask ourselves about the relative functioning of nationalism and racism. It is indeed these questions, or questions of this type, that must be posed when it becomes clear that the "racist community" is both the antithesis of the "class community" and the model that returns within it (as in the representation of "class origin," and more generally the whole metaphorization of social differences in terms of hereditary differences, implicitly or explicitly sexualized). This same process can be seen in the extreme forms of nationalism (such as the Nazi ideology of the chosen people as a "master race"), which combine the idealization of imperialist goals, without which no collective violence (and in particular "total war," interior and exterior) could be sustained, with the practices of eugenics and population control that tend to raise the "worker" above the "slave" (or the *national* as "worker" above the *foreigner* as "slave").

Can we detect at least the beginnings of an analogous dialectization with respect to Freudian theory? Let us look at *Massenpsychologie und Ich-Analyse*. In a sense what is absent from historical materialism is here presupposed from the beginning: what, with Lacan, we can call the transindividual (and thus transferential) character of the unconscious (in opposition to the idea of an "individual unconscious," but also of a "collective" or "popular unconscious"). This can be clearly shown merely by considering the diagram at the end of chapter 8[3] as representing not a parallelism of individual "psychic personalities" with analogous structures, but precisely the outline of a "social" structure upon which the organization of the psyche into distinct instances (and thus the formation of a personality) depends. In fact the schema shows the simultaneity of three phenomena: the identification of different "egos" (thus the formation of their imaginary community); the substitution, for each ego, of a loved (or desired) "object" for the ego ideal; and the unification of different ideals on account of the fact that, in the substitution, it is one and the same "exterior object" (or real object, be it a leader, an institution, or a historical dogma) which fills this imaginary place. The progression Freud follows in its construction is not causal but pedagogical (the exterior object is identically loved by each ego *as* a narcissistic object would be). But if we ask what could make a single "exterior object" (what is more, an object whose reality has as heterogeneous modalities as those proposed by Freud) able to be substituted *simultaneously* for a multiplicity of ideal egos, we are led to make the model function in an inverted, *retroactive* way: this effect is only produced *on the basis of* the identification of the different "egos," that is, on the basis of their ideals having been placed in common. One more step will lead us to the hypothesis that the very constitution of the "ego" (described by Freud as tied to the ambivalence of repression, to the double pressure of a desire and a censorship, or of an id and a superego with whom you have to "negotiate") is the effect rather than the cause of the process of collective idealization. It could even be suggested that this whole process is commanded by the fact that the so-called exterior object is really a complex structure, represented *at once* by persons, by institutions, and by beliefs or ideas: in short, a structure of "social relation." This would provide a better explanation than an individual psycho-genesis would of the ambivalence of an ideal instance, inscribed after the fact by Freud in its various denominations (superego, ideal ego). The circular character of the analysis, as Freud himself sometimes indicates in the text, would become clearer: rather than an explanation of the structure of the masses *on the basis* of the individual psyche, it would be a question of an explanation of the individual constitution that *always already includes* a "mass" structure. This is implicitly the path on which Freudo-Marxism, and Reich, engages us.

But this path in turn obliges us to put into question the immediate, "genetic" reading of the Freudian distinction between "primitive groups" (*Masse*) and "organized," "artificial" (or secondary) groups. Only the latter are institutional, and consequently only they offer the "ego," as a possible "object," a combination of persons inscribed in a social role (such as that of the leader) and of constraining norms and general ideas (thus of ideals: patriotism, the love of one's neighbor in Christ, being one of the elect, etc.) tied together in a discourse. Structurally they are *prior* to the "primitive group." In fact there is no "primitive group" except as an effect of ambivalent identification, constantly induced by the existence of "artificial groups." The "primitive group" *as primitive* (originary) is a mere naturalist myth. This in turn can only have distorting effects on the analysis of "artificial," that is, historical, groups and institutions. This fact directs our attention toward the singular restrictions that Freud places on their designation.

As long as "artificial groups" can be considered simply as examples, as *particular cases* on the basis of which the analysis will move back to the fundamental problem of identification, the completeness of their description is relatively unimportant. But once what is aimed at under this name is the institutional structure that ties together, in a single temporality, the constitution of the individual psyche and the relation of collective identification, Freud's ellipses can no longer remain unquestioned. To put it schematically, "army" and "church" are here *state* apparatuses that dare not say their name. Or rather: their association evokes, in a partial manner, an ideal state apparatus (combining the function of organizing violence and the function of sacralizing the law), but it leaves out, and thus in fact excludes, the question of what *unites* them, the question of the "sovereign" institution from which army and Church draw their permanence.

Several reasons can be imagined for Freud's singular elision of the problem of the state hovering behind his own analysis of the masses. We will suggest only two possibilities. On the one hand it would probably not be possible to identify *in general* "artificial groups" with the social institution without asking again how the family (or certain historical forms of the family) functions as an institution, that is, without putting in question a concept of the family that, at least implicitly, reduces it to being no more than the crystallization (not to say the projection) of the roles prescribed by the Oedipal complex (and their possible individual variations).[4] On the other hand it would not be possible to call the horizon common to all "artificial groups" the *state* without directly applying to this horizon the concept of ambivalence that Freud links with the process of identification. The state would then appear *in the present* as the true "primitive group," that is, as the site of unsurpassable conflicts and latent violence. It is striking that Freud, in the end, explicitly recognized conflict within culture (civilization's "discontents"), but carefully avoided recognizing it in the state, *a fortiori* designating the state as an institution for control of the masses that engenders both security and insecurity or violence. What we discover here in Freud is less a "psychologism" (as a superficial critique would have it) than a "sociologism," understood as a hypostasis of society organized into a state *beyond* social conflicts (as if society could not be conflictual *in itself*).

It is doubtful that Reich's theorization allows us to escape these difficulties. For it is characterized precisely by the conflation, or naturalist reduction, of the dimensions of the institution that give the "object" its historical complexity. Taking Nazism at its word out of fear of once again missing the reasons for its efficacy ("We must get into the habit of paying strict attention to precisely what the fascists say"),[5] he believes that repressive authority is immediately "real" and "imaginary," that is, that it coincides with the *person* who wields it and figures it. He therefore moves from the idea of a historically necessary articulation between the patriarchal family and the nationalist state to that of a homology or even a structural identity between the two. He thus renders incomprehensible both the difference between a fascist *movement* and a totalitarian *state* and the contradictory coexistence, within this state, of a double policy of conservation of traditional family structures or reactionary "familialism" and destruction of these same structures by eugenics, the inquisitorial control of marriages and births.[6] In the same way, having tendentially identified the structure of the unconscious with the social organization of sexuality, he finally returns to the utopia of a psyche without an unconscious by making the objective of politics the removal of repression itself. This utopianism is coherent with the idea that what must be opposed to fascism's mobilization of the masses is a "proletarian mass" freed from "mysticism," from the "emotional plague," by work democracy and the sexual revolution. The demand for politics turns into its opposite: a new version of the end of politics or of the nostalgia for the golden age. Still, the "delirious" effort can incite us to keep alive just a bit longer the critique of the conception of the social bond sketched out by classical psychoanalysis.

The identificatory relation formalized by Freud in terms of transference of the object of the "ego" to the "ego ideal" indeed institutes in the imaginary a *superhuman* figure, both all-powerful (thus menacing or punishing as well as benevolent or gratifying) and beloved, an archeo-paternal figure superimposed on the individual father. It is precisely when he includes the social dimension in his topography that Freud makes explicit this reference to the "superhuman." The analysis of the historical configurations of racism (or better, of racism-sexism, if it is true that they are always closely linked) obliges us to ask whether such a figure can in fact exist independently of figures of the *subhuman*. To put it another way, is it indeed true, as Freud suggests, that the "omnipotence of the father" is the corollary of "the equality of the sons"? It is strange that Freud referred to "Nietzsche's superman,"[7] making it the other name of the archaic figure of the father, without even evoking that of the subhumans. It is even stranger that, describing the sexual ownership of women as the fantasmatic stake of the rivalry between the "father" and the "sons" which generates the ambivalence of their relation, he did not at any point evoke the position of women themselves in the transindividual structure bound together by identification (in which all the "egos" are implicitly masculine). But in fact there are only supermen where there are also subhumans, who are themselves split up into several categories: on the one hand foreigners, slaves, colonials, and workers, constituted into a special "race" in the imaginary of industrial societies, and on the other hand, precisely, women, equally liable, from antiquity to the present day, of being perceived as a "race" opposed to that of men, and who have always been particularly forbidden from acting as a "mass." This configuration is not reducible to the opposition between father and sons, nor to the dialectic of the similar and the different.

If it is true that the experience of the fascist movements suggests a sort of collective "acting out" tied to the anxiety produced by situations of crisis or social transformation, the actual content of their ideology and their policies suggests that the topography within which this psychic dynamics would become intelligible must be completed by a dimension that Freud ignored. Can the subject's "irrational" oscillation between the fear or revolt that a discretionary (state) power inspires in him, and the recourse to an even more authoritarian and personalized state be understood if we do not suppose that individuals (in fact, men) have a constant unconscious fear that the power that collectively maintains them *above* the various "subhumans" is not also capable of precipitating them into the ranks of the latter by its arbitrary decisions? Or yet, in another possible configuration, is it not necessary to suppose that they unconsciously fear discovering or facing up to the *emptiness* of this "superhuman" place of authority (instituted by the state, occupied by the "head of state"), upon which nonetheless depends, by a tie of love and institutional recognition, their condition as men, that is, their collective elevation above subhumans and particularly above women? We must recognize that, following a long tradition, Freud constructs his representation of the social by *isolating* the sphere of the family, where the relation between the sexes is constitutive, from the sphere of public institutions, where it is repressed (to the benefit of a purely masculine "identification").

But the figure of the subhuman—here too racism, including its Nazi form, is revealing—is indissociable from the representation of the body, individually and collectively experienced in a relation to violence and aesthetics as well as to sexual desire and death. Insisting on work poses the question of the points of intersection between two series of fantasies of the "fragmentation" and "re-unification" of the body: one series tied to sexuality, to the presence or absence of the symbolic member, the other tied to manual labor, and even more to the mechanized labor of the modern age. Contemporary fascism is bound to racism by an aggressive projection of the "virile" type, by the spectacular organization of a sort of *jouissance* in common of bodies, not only in the behavior and staging of mass movements, but also in the enterprise of the regeneration of bodies. Here too there is a double reference: to the male and to the worker, all the more rickety a construction in that men are uncertain of their sexual role and workers are physically and intellectually exploited. Thus, if the Freudo-Marxist addition of a "primary" sexual interpretation of the fantasy and a historical reduction of social relations to the conditions of exploitation does not produce a genuine synthetic theory (except, once again, by invoking nature and life), the factual overdetermination is indeed the field in which Marxism and psychoanalysis are confronted by Nazism with a reality test. This field, it seems to me, is purely and simply that of political alienation in its materiality.

8

RACISM AS UNIVERSALISM

As soon as I had proposed this title, as an attempt to appeal both to the political scientists (because of racism) and to the philosophers (because of universalism), I became aware that I had put myself in a difficult position. Now I will have to sustain this paradox. My anxiety was increased a few days ago when an American colleague told me quite simply that she had always considered French philosophers to be professional *provocateurs*. But it is too late now to retreat. And it would not be very courageous to mitigate the formula, for example, by introducing a question mark at the end.

And after all, I mean it. Or more precisely, this is a formulation to which, to my own surprise, I was led in the course of recent reflections on today's new varieties of racism, and of rethinking antiracist politics by trying to understand why in some cases it is so desperately ineffective.[1] And I thought that I should at least make an attempt to carefully examine this formula: what reasons could have suggested it; exactly what do the only-too-obvious objections which it raises presuppose; what arguments could we propose to support it; and in case this examination leaves a door open, in what direction would such a formula engage further research, and under what conditions could it be considered a good working hypothesis.

But allow me to start again, in a different way. All this is a matter of language (I do not say a matter of linguistic conventions). It has to do with the use of certain formulas as context-bound or context-free sentences. And it very much depends on the initial choices you make of certain terms as entries. Let me be more concrete. When you speak of racism as universalism, or as *one form* of universalism, or as implying certain universalistic assumptions, you provoke astonished reactions, because everybody—including the speaker himself—has in mind that racism and universalism are *opposites*, that racism is indeed an *extreme* form of particularism. I will have to deal again with this idea of *extreme* form, or extremity. But right now let me say only the following: there are other opposites of universalism, for example, sexism or nationalism. I choose these terms on purpose because we will see that they are *not* in fact independent from the issue of racism. What racism, nationalism, and sexism seem to have in common is that they are all categories which, from an intensional or an extensional viewpoint, divide the universality of the human species into exclusive transhistorical groups which are supposed to be separated by *essential* differences, or to become self-conscious and act *as if* they were separated by essential differences. We must add: such essential differences are always at least tacitly understood and institutionalized as hierarchical differences.[2]

Now what would have been the reactions if I had proposed to talk about *sexism as universalism* or *nationalism as universalism*? Most likely you would have said: O.K., we agree, we know that already, since the case has already been argued and we made up our minds concerning the limits or conditions within which such formulas can be used. As far as sexism is concerned, several interpretations are possible. There is a weak interpretation, which sounds more or less like the following: sexism has been a component of every culture till now in the history of mankind, and as such it has framed the *representations* of the unity of mankind, by imposing a generally male-chauvinist bias, for which the very name *man*kind testifies. But there is also a strong interpretation, whereby sexism is not only responsible for an alienated picture of the unity, but for the very notion of *universality*, as it has been elaborated by what we call reason or rationality in the Western tradition.[3] The difficulty, as is well-known, is that it is very difficult to oppose that form of sexism without developing some sort of countersexism, in which, not by chance, sexual difference very often becomes expressed in terms which picture the genders as quasi-races, drawing on very ancient myths.

The reason for this double-bind situation might very well lie in a fact that is particularly important for Freudian theory, namely that all individuals are deeply, or primordially *bisexual*: but this situation is impossible to live with, therefore an "identity" or a "self" has to be built by *choosing* a gender; which in turn, despite biological evidence, proves not quite possible, unless something like a supplement or an excess of either maleness or femaleness becomes incorporated into the self, either by personal elaboration or by social education and role, or by both.[4]

How about nationalism, now? The case is perhaps even clearer. Leaving aside such issues as ethnocentrism in ancient societies, and concentrating on the modern sense of "nation" and therefore nationalism as a modern phenomenon, we may agree on the following: nationalism admittedly is *particularistic*, inasmuch as it claims that national entities have different roots, that they must keep control over their *own* members who "belong" to them in some strong sense, and that they must remain isolated from one another in order to preserve their identity, which leads to a struggle for life and a hierarchy of nations according to an alleged scale of values. But nationalism as an ideology is *also universalistic*, and this in at least two senses, which will prove to be intrinsically connected.

First, nationalism is usually associated with the idea that there should not exist natural or inherited differences between the men who belong to the same nation (I am not speaking of women…), for example, with the idea of justice or equal opportunity for all the nation's sons. Indeed, in the modern era, nationalism has probably been the strongest ideological current which supported the idea of formal equality, even in some case substantial equality, thus removing notions of castes and status groups and local privileges (I am not saying that it did actually bring about equality).

Second, nationalism has almost always taken the form of an ideology of *the elect nation*, be it in terms borrowed directly form the biblical, Judeo-Christian tradition, or in other terms which are nonetheless easily recognizable.[5] The elect nation is obviously a Janus-faced notion, in which particularism and universalism are inextricably linked. But it is more than that: in order to lead humankind to its own salvation, or to bring it peace, or civilization, or liberty, this nation has to think of itself (through its "organic" intellectuals, the working of its "ideological state apparatuses," etc.) as immediately universal in its singularity: in fact it has to *empty* this singularity of any particularistic feature or mode of being and *fill* it with universalistic elements, usually a secularized version of the great universalistic religions, with their messianic notion of human brotherhood. Again this leads in fact to building a concept of the universal which only the notion of election has made possible.

As you know a beautiful presentation and, at the same time, a critique or relativization of this ideology can be found in Hegel's vision of the *Volksgeister* as "moments" of the *Weltgeist*. But, to remain in the same crucial period, the most typical and, up to our day, the most influential of all elaborations of the theory of the elect nation is the one which was proposed by Fichte in his *Addresses to the German Nation* (1808).[6] What is striking in Fichte's universalistic nationalism is not only that it incorporates in a central manner the egalitarian motto, thus truly reconstructing a messianic framework; it is not only that Fichte's nationalism is explicitly antiracist, antibiological; deeper than that it is totally opposed to any genetic or genealogical notion of the national entity: it is the most radical argument against the "natural" concept of nationhood (or the concept of nationhood as a natural descent), in favor of a "spiritual" concept of nationhood, more precisely a spiritual-linguistic concept of the nation in which it is language, communication, and the ethics of communication which incarnate the collective spirit.

This radicality certainly does not protect Fichte against the more than ambiguous political implications of his doctrine, as we may see in a moment, but it leads us to a remark of particular importance to our subject. Inasmuch as nationalism and racism are related notions, and have a long history of practical interaction, what seems to be the case is that *racism* deprives *nationalism* of its universalistic character or, if you like, that racism reveals the nonuniversalistic component of nationalism, which was hidden within it, thereby obstructing the primacy or even the manifestation of the universalistic component. It does this in at least two ways. *One*, by introducing divisions and discriminations inside the so-called national community, which more often than not are also institutional inequalities and persecutions—just think of the Black and Hispanic people in the United States, of the Jews in Europe (especially Germany, Poland, Russia, etc.)—it reconstitutes the "status groups." *Two*, by precisely identifying the alleged national character, or singularity, with some hereditary element, pseudo- or quasi-biological, or even cultural, it in fact segregates the nation itself, or, to put it better, the *ideal nation* inside the nation, from the community of mankind. If it were the case that, in some definite sense, or in some definite conditions, nationalism necessarily leads to racism in that way,[7] the argument implicit in my title, racism *as* universalism, would be seriously undermined. That is, unless we were to add a new twist, and discover that things are in fact more complicated, more ambivalent than that, and that racism is not simply one possible expression of the particularistic element of nationalism, but rather that it is—among other things—a symptom of the contradiction between particularism and universalism which primordially affects nationalism, a symptom of the double-bind to which any claim of *identity* as *national* identity, both individual and collective, is unavoidably subject. Therefore it acquires relevance *on both sides* of the contradiction.

Before I develop this point, allow me again a detour. I am not apologizing for this because, as you know, I consider my own formulas as working hypotheses which have to be twisted and examined from various angles. Allow me to invert the proposed formula: not racism as universalism, but *universalism as racism*. Well, that is even more provocative, but in a sense it sounds more familiar to us. We may agree or not, but, just as for sexism, we have become accustomed to discussing the issue. Again there are weak versions and there are strong versions (I mean in the logical sense).

By weak versions, and I go quickly, I understand the idea that universalism was *used* in a Machiavellian way to cover and implement racist policies, to justify in a fake scientific manner racist ideologies, to rationalize institutional racism, to impose the domination of some cultures on others in a racist way: the list of phenomena would range from social darwinism in its successive forms to the educational policies of assimilation or Westernization of the so-called native populations in the colonial empires and after decolonization; to this we can add that such political and ideological processes work effectively *only* if those who carry them out actually *believe* in their legitimacy and, indeed, in their truth, or in their being grounded in true doctrines. Therefore, universalism itself has had to be elaborated in such a way that it provides "logical" foundations for racist or discriminatory or at least imperialist practices: this is the case with the ideology of the "white man's burden," certainly with Eurocentrism, possibly with individualism (and it is not quite clear whether communism does not work in the same way).

But this leads us to the strong version. The strong version of the argument is once again the one which *questions* the notions of universalism, universality, or universal with respect to their internal constitution and their implications, preferably in a historical manner. These notions indeed have a history (which does not mean that we will be able to reduce them to any pre-established pattern of historical genesis), and that history is not quite as clean, as harmless as we might hope. The case has been repeatedly argued, and in its best presentations it has nothing to do with cultural relativism, it goes far beyond that. Various historians and philosophers have shown how deeply rooted in the notion of mankind, the human species, the progress of human culture—as they were elaborated in that great blossoming of universalism, the Enlightenment—were anthropological prejudices concerning races, or the natural bases of slavery, and indeed the very notion of race, which at that period first acquired its modern meaning.[8]

The more rigorous and demanding a philosopher is—both morally and intellectually—the more decisive his achievements are for this issue. Therefore if we want to test the solidity of the argument, we had best look at somebody like Kant, the philosopher of the "cosmopolitan point of view," and certainly the most rigorous defender of universalism in the period. We might discover that there is a striking parallel between his basic distinction of "reason" and "sensibility" (or "transcendental" and "empirical" concepts of the subject), and his so-called pragmatic anthropology, in which the characters of sex, people, and race are thought of as natural categories, intermediaries between the individual and the species (thus *mediating* the concrete "belonging" of the individual to the species). In Kantian philosophy, to establish universality (*Allgemeinheit*, which in many places also means equality) as an *ideal* (hence a final goal for the "progress" of mankind) above all the empirical differences, requires that the ideal be rooted in *nature*.[9]

But the example which I would prefer to analyze in detail (if I had time for that) is the case of Aristotle. This really is the origin of what we understand as universal rationality: in a sense we cannot but think of thought and action in Aristotelian categories. Now there is an absolutely intrinsic connection between these categories, notably the category of individual substance (as the synthesis of matter and form) and the category of essence or definition (as a univocal linguistic expression of the substance), and the *political* definition of *man*: man in essence is "a living being who uses language" (*zôon logon ekhôn*), therefore "a being by nature living in and for the city" (*zôon te phusei politikon*). But this expresses a perfection or superiority of the individual, whose core is constituted by a double, or even triple relationship which is presented as a hierarchy *in nature* itself, in the very concept of "nature": the relation of man to woman (or masculine to feminine), the relation of master to slave (or intelligence to instrumentality), and the relation of father to son (or maturity to immaturity), each of which displays some aspect of the fundamental relation between "activity" and "passivity." Now, to focus on the second relation, the relation between the intellectual master and the instrumental slave is perhaps not exactly racism in the modern sense, but it already illustrates and prepares many of its most typical features, including the ethnicization of social inequalities, the somatic projection of moral judgments, and the identification of differences among men with differences between man and animal. What such a discussion would show, in my opinion, is not that Aristotle "was a racist"[10] (although he certainly was pro-slavery under some conditions) and that these prejudices distorted his philosophical rationality; not even that he represented a combination of true or ideal universalism with contingent particularistic views; but rather that as soon as universalism *ceases* to be a mere word, a would-be philosophy, and becomes an effective system of concepts, it necessarily incorporates in its very center *its opposite*, I would even say its *extreme* opposite. The *logos* itself is not to be defined without being conditioned by an anthropological and ontological hierarchy.

This example would show us even more than that: that no *definition* of the human species, or simply the human—something which is so crucial for universalism, or universalism as humanism—has ever been proposed which would not imply a latent hierarchy. This has to do with the impossibility of fixing the *boundaries* of what we call "human," or fixing the boundaries within which all human beings could possibly be gathered. You may remember that Aristotle had enormous difficulties in deciding whether slaves were animals or humans, because of their alleged unilateral relation toward language (as slaves following the instructions of their masters or supervisors, they should be able to listen, but not to speak themselves: be designated as "living tools"). At the same time, symmetrically, he felt the necessity to introduce in his politics and his conception of wisdom another uncertain limit between humans and godly individuals. We have the same difficulty today with humans and their new tools, with human brains and machines, or *robots* ("artificial intelligence"). In fact no "definition" of the human as such, or "the position of man in the universe," could ever be attempted which did not include the infinite process of demarcation between the human, the more-than-human, and the less-than-human (or *Supermen* and *Untermenschen*), and the reflection of these two limits *within* the imaginary boundaries of the human "species." The question can never be avoided, neither in practice nor in theory, of whether some men or women (especially women, who are more likely idealized and despised) look more like superhuman or like subhuman beings, be it because of natural characteristics, or because of personal and social functions, behaviors, and habits. We are back to the question of identity, at a deeper level. We do not need to be Nietzscheans in order to recognize that the *imagoes* of the *Übermensch* and the *Untermensch* (or the last man) will never cease to return in our attempts at defining *man in general,* or the essence of the human, or, to put it in Spinozist terms, the *general idea of man.*

But if the distinction of the superhuman and the subhuman is not racism as such, it certainly is one basic component of racism, one which precisely remains as a structural constant throughout the history of racist ideologies, passing from a genealogical to a biological to a cultural and "differentialist" problematics.[11] And if the attempt at defining a "general idea" of man is not universalism as such, it certainly is one basic component of universalism, at least moral or ethical universalism throughout history (and the possibility of universalism apart from morality or ethics remains to be proved).

Now this does not prove that universalism *is* racism, nor even that it is *racist per se,* a formula which philosophically is untenable, because it would imply that universalism is a substance that can be qualified. But it proves, at least in my opinion, that you cannot find a clear-cut *line of demarcation* between universalism and racism or, if you prefer, you cannot designate *two sets of ideas* with no intersection, one in which you would put all the (potentially) universalistic ideas, and the other in which you would put all the (potentially) racist ideas. If you like you can express this in a Hegelian terminology: universalism and racism are indeed (determinate) contraries, and this is why each of them has the other one inside itself—or is bound to affect the other *from the inside.*

This, in my opinion, is more accurate, if less simple, than the idea of a *complementarity* between universalism and racism, or more generally, between universalism and particularism (including racism, sexism, and nationalism) as was proposed by Immanuel Wallerstein, among others.[12] To speak of complementarity means that in the *same* world, or system, or world-system, you will have at the same time universalistic ideas or ideologies *and* racist/sexist/nationalist ideas, and that you will be able to refer them to complementary aspects of the system: for example, on the one hand the universality of the commodity form, exchange relations, the accumulation of capital, and on the other hand the national form of the state monopoly of power, or the necessary divisions of the labor force along gender, age, and ethnic lines. You will get to the idea that there is a functionality in this complementarity, which prevents you from hoping that one side will suppress the other: more precisely a political functionality, whereby universalism compensates for the "excesses" of racism (or its "extremities") and racism compensates for the "excesses" of universalism (both of them, of course, from the point of view of the existing order). And you will get to the idea that if one side (for example, racism) is to be overcome, in fact it is the whole system, consisting of both sides, which has to be overcome and replaced by a *third* term.

This, indeed, is true historical relativism. But if you do not think in terms of complementarity, but of contraries affecting one another from the inside, you will be led to the idea of an even tighter unity of both sides. But on the other hand you will not have to admit functionality (which, to me, seems unlikely precisely in the "extreme" cases, which badly deserve more of an explanation, or which clearly *escape* their own functional aspects (for example, Nazism). On the contrary, you will be led to the idea that although this contradictory unity is resistant and has very ancient origins (I mentioned Aristotle), although stable, its evolution is not predictable, and above all it might be *transformed* also from the inside, which is politically more cogent than the idea of overcoming the whole system. What I would like to say is that there is no *essence* of universalism: we do not know exactly how universalism could exist without being affected from the inside by racism or sexism, but this is not to say that it is unthinkable. Perhaps such a transformation would have to start with a different way of handling such categories as, precisely, the "universal," "difference," the "singular."

Of course the reason why Wallerstein and others would introduce the notion of complementarity is the urgent necessity to understand why, in today's world—an officially decolonized world, which is supposed to have eliminated Nazism, which may even have entered a process of relativization of the nation as *the only* legitimate political entity, but which at the same time is more deeply than ever divided along lines of exploitation, or poverty and affluence, or new poverty and new affluence, etc.—the flames of nationalism and racism (or so-called religious fundamentalism) are bursting out everywhere in basically the same way. Racism has become universalized. It is a concrete *Weltbild*. I might have started simply by saying, racism *is now universal*. But it is not a mere playing on words to say that if racism can be universal empirically, it has also to be universal theoretically, meaning that there has to be an element of paradoxical universality in it.

Which leads me to the last two points I wanted to introduce today. One concerns racism and knowledge, or rather racism, sexism, and knowledge; the other concerns racism and nationalism again. So we will return to the questions which were raised at the beginning.

For almost two centuries now, racism has been criticized from a "rationalist" point of view, that is, as a prejudice or a form of false consciousness. With very few exceptions, even the psychoanalytical and sociological approaches (of which the famous *Authoritarian Personality*, by Adorno and his collaborators, remains one of the best examples)[13] have not really altered this pattern: they have simply looked for the roots, or the causes, or the conditions of prejudice and false consciousness either in pathological personality or in social alienation and conflicts. So we have been left with the dilemma of a critique of racism as a prejudice or an error (be it massive and powerful) and a justification of racism as a natural (or social-natural, or historical-natural) necessity, such as is provided by racial ideologies themselves (sociobiology is a remarkable example of this). I want to bypass this dilemma, at the risk of making the practical situation appear more difficult.

I think that racism is a genuine *mode of thought*, that is to say, a mode of connecting not only words with objects, but more profoundly words with images, in order to create concepts. Therefore to overcome racism in one's personal experience or in collective experience is not simply a matter of abandoning prejudices or opening one's eyes to reality with the possible help of science; it has to do with changing one's mode of thinking, something much more difficult.

The more we become involved in discussions and militancy on the racist issue, the more we are struck by the fact that racism embodies a very insistent *desire for knowledge.* It is not only a way of legitimating privileges or disqualifying competitors or continuing old traditions or reacting to situations of violence, it is a way of asking questions about *who* you are in a certain social world, *why* there are some compulsory places in this world to which you must adapt yourself, imposing upon yourself a certain univocal *identity* (something much more compelling than a *role*); and it is a way of asking and answering questions about *why* we are violent, why we find ourselves unable to resist the compulsion of violence going beyond the "rational" necessities of competition and social conflict. The answer provided by racism to all these questions, which are vital indeed, is this: it is because we are *different*, and, tautologically, because difference is the universal essence of what we are—not singular, individual difference, but collective differences, made of analogies and, ultimately, of *similarities.* The core of this mode of thought might very well be this common logic: differences among men are differences among sets of *similar individuals* (which, for this reason, can be "identified").

In this broad sense, racism has an unlimited range of applications and a day-to-day function to perform. Even class situation (or maybe, in today's world, above all class situation) will be understood that way, which is very clear in the idea of *class origin.* But it is not only a question of understanding, or a desire for knowledge which becomes fulfilled by a system of differential categories (what we might call, after Lévi-Strauss, the "savage mind" of modern societies). It is also a process of building a community. The whole process of racist thinking is about creating lived ties and affects and common evidences among people in a society where, for example, kinship has ceased to be a central social structure. This might account for the fact that racism in all its historic forms is obsessed with the imagery of kinship, the rules of exogamy and endogamy as applied to entities which are not "families" or tribes, but nations or sections of nations (nationalities).[14]

I would summarize by saying that the racist mode of thinking basically *produces its own community*, the racist community, together with an interpretation of the social world in which this community is situated (in which the individual is situated *through* his community). Now again this makes the situation more difficult. The racist community has more than analogies with the male-chauvinist community, or the community of males. As feminism has progressively started to demonstrate, the issue with sexism is not, or not merely, to resist male chauvinism or to struggle against male domination: it is to have the male community destroyed from the inside. Similarly, the issue with racism, in the long run and in everyday situations, is to destroy the racist community from within, a community which is both institutional *and* spontaneous, based upon collective privileges (many of them—but not all— imaginary) and the individual desire for knowledge.[15]

But as soon as you have reached this point, you are unavoidably led to the question: are they in fact *different* "communities"? Should not we say that the male community and the racist community are one and the same "community"? I cannot discuss this question at length, but I would give a positive answer in principle. They are or they have become inseparable. This seems to me unavoidable if we want to understand why, in fact, all the categories of racist imagery or the racist perception of the world are sexually overdetermined, why all the *anthropological universals*, as I would call them,[16] which work in the production of "racial differences"—from the notion of heredity to that of aggressivity, or sensuality, or bestiality—are overdetermined with sexual metaphors. And this would lead me back to the question of universalism, inasmuch as it has to do with the process of idealization of individual "differences," or the self. This is a strange paradox indeed. Racism and sexism taken separately may very well appear as particularisms, because they divide the human species and claim that the divisions and hierarchies are "natural"; but racism and sexism taken together, working together, knit together in history, produce *ideals* of humanity, *types of ideal humanity* if you like, which one cannot but call universal: be they moral ideals (for example "mastering" one's own passions in a manly and civilized manner) or aesthetic ideals (living physically and morally according to the demands of beauty, making oneself a "work of art," etc.).

But ideals and idealization are at least a good part of the clue to the combination of racism and nationalism, and this is my last point. The whole question should be discussed by considering whether there are any nations, whether there ever has been any nation *without a nationalist ideology* enjoying successive forms before, during, and after the process called "nation building," a process that necessarily combines the creation of a nation-state *and* production of a social entity in which national solidarities, or rather dependencies, regularly prevail over other social groupings, above all those which have to do with class conflicts. My answer is *no*, if only because I have never found any means to draw the line of demarcation between "patriotism" and "nationalism," or if you prefer between clean, moderate, defensive nationalism which only aims at preserving an identity, and dirty, excessive and aggressive nationalism which leads to imperialist policies or to internal oppression of ethnic minorities.[17] It was never anything other than a question of *degrees*, or, to put it better, of *conjunctures*. Of course these degrees and conjunctures matter enormously, just as it matters enormously to consider whether we are dealing with a nationalism helping people to resist some foreign (or even "domestic") oppression or a nationalism trying to impose and perpetuate oppression.

But I do not think it is enough to say that there are no nations without nationalism and that therefore nationalism is everywhere—both inside states and among them—since all states in our world are now nation-states.[18] Nationalism, as we know, is about the creation of national *unity*. National unity is endangered by class struggles, and by the fact that nation-states encompass historical groups that have different traditions and a relative autonomy. There are different and powerful institutions that help create that kind of unity, above all, the army—wars are the traditional ordeal for national unity, an all-or-nothing trial—and the school system, which universalizes language, or substitutes sociolinguistic particularities for ethnic particularities, a hierarchy of "cultural" uses of the national language(s) for a coexistence of "local" idioms.[19] These institutions do not work in the same way everywhere: in a sense they must work in a different way everywhere, as part of national "identity."[20] These institutions work powerfully: they almost succeed in creating what is required, what I call the fictitious ethnicity which is supposed to "belong" to the people, the national community, in order for it precisely to be a "community," for individuals and above all families to "belong" to it *as a community*.[21]

No modern nation has an ethnic basis, meaning a permanent and homogeneous descent from prehistorical kinship groups or alliances. As modern nations arose, ethnicity in this sense—if it ever existed in a *pure* way—was progressively destroyed. The process is still going on with respect to local differences, but it is everywhere well advanced. But all modern nations have to some significant extent succeeded in creating a fictitious ethnicity. Nevertheless, I said that the national institutions and the nationalist ideology *almost succeed, but not quite.* This is neither the place nor the time to explain completely why. I would maintain that class antagonisms and struggles are a major reason. Not simply an external reason, an obstacle which nationalism would be too weak to overcome, but also, as I said before, because there is an intrinsic relationship between nationalism as an ideology and the notion of social equality, which makes nationalism very contradictory in this respect. You might say that the building of the nation-state, even when it becomes a welfare-state, is closely associated with class domination, but nationalism as an ideology must include some denial of the class differences, which leads to an internal contradiction. Call it "populism" if you like. In any case my idea is that this situation unleashes a permanent process of displacement and escape. You need more nationalism. You need a nationalism which is, so to speak, more nationalistic than nationalism itself: what I would call in the language of Bataille an *excess* of nationalism, or in the language of Derrida a *supplement* of nationalism *within* nationalism itself.

It seems to me that racism, in spite of all its historical differences, is unified by the fact that it simply *is* this supplement, or works as this supplement and excess. Now if you only think of the most obvious cases, not excluding the case of Nazism, you will discover a strange thing: in order to work as a supplement of nationalism within nationalism, racism has to take at the same time very contradictory forms or directions. It has to work and build itself as a *supernationalism*, that is, to define along lines of racial or cultural "purity" what the imaginary core of the nation is (the true English, the true German, the true French race, *la Hispanidad*) in order to impose its domination and preserve it from contacts and miscegenation with alien elements. This obviously reinforces the side of particularism. But it *also* has to symbolically inscribe the national character, the alleged destiny of the nation within the broader framework, potentially universal or universalistic, of some *ideal entity* which comes long before the nation and goes far beyond it in space and time: the Aryan or Indo-Germanic race, the white man,

Western civilization, the Arab-Islamic nation, etc., are similar entities. We meet again with the fact that there is no intrinsic end to this process: the excess does not suppress the contradiction, it merely displaces it. Sometimes it carries it to explosive antagonism.

This is, basically, how I see the issue of racism as universalism: neither simple nor conclusive. We need a practical conclusion, however. It can be at least negative. I do not think that we can effectively face racism with the abstract motto of universality. Racism has already (always already) occupied this place. So the struggle is *inside this place*, to transform universalism, not to abandon it—I never said that—for this would amount to surrendering without combat.

9

WHAT IS A POLITICS OF THE RIGHTS OF MAN?

For a long time now in politics we have been hearing about the rights of man, which is to say that politics and its diverse "subjects" have been *recalled* to the rights of man, to their universal value and unconditional necessity. The rights of man have become, again, the absolute of political discourse.

But little or practically nothing is heard about the *politics of the rights of man*, no questioning of its conditions, its forms or its objectives.[1] Why this discretion? Either such a notion is considered to be self-evident, to pose no particular problems—the politics of the rights of man being, tautologically, nothing but a politics that draws its inspiration from them and that tries with more or less success to put them into effect everywhere. Or it is considered to be contradictory, for (since they are either its absolute or its principle) the rights of man are always either beyond or above politics, in the technical or pragmatic sense of the word (in the sense in which, to speak like certain contemporary philosophers, politics (*la politique*) as it is conducted, or as we are subject to it, is not to be confused with the political (*le politique*) as it is instituted or theorized). Whether to deplore it or to congratulate oneself upon it, it will then be said, "there is no politics of the rights of man," "the rights of man are not a matter of politics."[2]

Nevertheless I suspect that things are a little less innocent and that, if so little is heard about the politics of the rights of man, it is because, in a very precise conjuncture, such a notion would be embarrassing. It would quite simply bring out the contradiction and principal deficiency affecting the notion and the very being of the rights of man today. Is a discourse of recognition really what they in fact lack most, what maintains skepticism about their necessity and even causes them to be dismissed as illusory? Is it not rather *a politics of their own*, not simply politics with a view toward their proclamation, but the very politics of their realization and implementation?

Perhaps there are conjunctural reasons for this state of affairs. The situation in which the problem is posed and the obstacles it raises before us would have to be examined from this point of view, and the history of the question itself rewritten. Has a politics of the rights of man *ever* existed anywhere? Is it not, as is said, merely utopian, or rather can we see it at work, in a more or less pure, more or less effective, more or less repressed or fettered fashion, in certain times and certain places?

But it is also possible (and I will say from the outset that this is my own position) that beyond these conjunctural reasons there are intrinsic or, if one prefers, logical reasons. It is possible that the very *concept* of a politics of the rights of man is so burdened with internal difficulties that its formulation, and accordingly its consistent, thoughtful application, is permanently running up against redoubtable aporias. Then one of our first tasks—a properly philosophical one, not to lose sight of the difficulties of the conjuncture but the better to face up to them—would be to seek to elucidate and to lay out all of the uncertainties, enigmas, and *aporias* of the politics of the rights of man.

This would probably be the only rigorous way to respond, without artificially closing it, and in a way that is itself authentically political, to the question, "What is a politics of the rights of man?"

On the Conjuncture

A few words should still be said about the conjuncture. I will characterize it by a triple *after*: after the end of "totalitarianism," after the beginning of the crisis of the "welfare-state," after the "return" of war. But in reality each of these suggestive formulations calls out for detailed corrections.

After the end of totalitarianism. Not only, as was said during many years, is the *crisis* of the regimes that called themselves "actually existing socialism" irreversible, but their collapse is universal.

The point of no return had perhaps been reached by the beginning of the 1980s, probably even by the beginning of the 1970s, with the failure of what, in a superb formula, Regis Debray called "the revolution in the revolution," otherwise known as the great, mutually opposed movements of internal *political transformation* of communism or of "actually existing socialism" (notably the "Prague Spring" and the Chinese "Cultural Revolution"). Thenceforth criticism could come only from the outside, or from reference to an exterior model. The combination of the dictatorial state, ideological imposture, and corruption and inefficiency in vital domains of the economy could no longer but lead to the collapse of the "system." Still, this event is ambivalent for two reasons. First of all because, in putting an end to the negation of elementary rights and of the freedom without which there is no politics, it also ruins (for how long?) the idea or the imagination of an alternative to the order of "liberal" capitalist states. Second, because we may know, or think that we know, what it is destroying, but we do not know—and doubtless will not for some time—what it is constructing in the way of a "society" or a "state."

After the beginning of the crisis of the welfare-state. This diagnosis has become banal, it circulates in the public forum and has even become a major topic in debates among politicians. Yet here too there are reasons to raise questions about dates and particularly about what effects can be foreseen.

Does dating the point of no return of the "crisis of the welfare-state" from the 1970s mean that this was the point when we entered the beginning of the end of a certain system of social and economic equilibriums that went hand-in-hand with a certain distribution of powers? Or does it mark the "end of the beginning," the fact that capitalist societies have now acquired the means to prevent economic fluctuations from turning into collapses, without, however, acquiring thereby the capacity to *cancel* their social effects (instead they are displaced in time and space)?

As for these effects, there is every reason to think that they will be profoundly different in the "center" and on the "periphery" of the world-economy. The welfare-state, an elaborate and very unequal result of prosperity, social struggles and their institutional mediation, only ever existed in the "center." But while it is true that this crisis is accompanied by massive phenomena of disindustrialization and unemployment, accentuation of inequalities and "exclusion," "new poverty" and regression of trade unionism, which can always put what is called "social calm" back into question, it is doubtful that this will end up in the competition of each against all and limitless individualism. More likely, confronted with the "Third World" or the "South" (which will contain all or part of the former "socialist camp") ravaged by "deregulation," the rival but interdependent states of the "North" will doubtless seek a way to conserve or reconstruct a certain degree of economic planning, both public and private. Not only will they seek to improve the financial instruments that allow them to control conjunctures, but also to preserve the sufficient correlation between economic, social, scientific, and technical research policies that is an essential condition of power. It is by no means certain that they will all succeed. If it is nevertheless true that the welfare-state was intrinsically a national and social state (national *because* social, social *because* national), one might wonder whether the evolution of its crisis will not lead to an accentuation of this imbrication of the *national* and the *social*, which would end up in the (minimally viable) paradox of societies that are economically "open" to the world, but that are "closed" from the point of view of social rights and the organization of citizenship.

After the return of war. Finally, but this is in an entirely different form than the one that haunted us more or less intensely during the period of "cold war" and "balance of terror."

Whether we then adhered to scenarios of catastrophe founded on the extrapolation of the arms race and the hypothesis of the autonomization of its logic, or, without adopting this deterministic point of view, we were content to take note of and to fear the growing instability of the balance of power, we thought that war would "return" in a worldwide, nuclear form.[3] This eventuality has by no means purely and simply disappeared; the weapons are still there. But we have seen war return in other forms.

First, there was the "Gulf War." Projected at the beginning as a confrontation between two imperialisms—one "small" but no less to be feared (Iraq), and the other very big, in the course of becoming the sole "superpower" (the United States)—technology and the diplomatic impotence of other countries turned it into a gigantic "regrettable accident" by the "international police." Tens of thousands of men died, crushed in a few days under a concentration of weapons of extermination unrivaled since World War II and Vietnam, while public opinion was packaged by the control of televised images. Afterward the massacre continued for several weeks in Iraq itself as the victor and his allies looked on, on account of the arms left to Saddam Hussein and the incitations to revolt that President Bush had heaped upon his opponents.

And now there is the resistible "ethnic" (or rather ethnico-religious) war currently turning Yugoslavia into a bloodbath, turning the "democratic transition" (or "transition to capitalism," according to the interpretation) into an unleashing of inexpiable community hatreds and a regression into a past that was believed to be definitively overcome, that had at least been repressed for fifty years. Europe looks on "powerless" (at least this is what we are told), except for fanning the flames with economic intervention, "private" or "clandestine" arms shipments, and the speeches of some of its spiritual leaders. Atrocious in itself, this war cannot fail to have repercussions elsewhere: but what will they be? Will it constitute a terrible warning for neighboring countries, where the same conflicts are growing? Or will it signal the start of a whole series of "local" or "civil" wars?

These two events cannot be amalgamated: they do not stem exactly from the same process, even if they are both inscribed in the underside of the "new world order." Still, taken together, they force us to reflect. Much is heard of growing individual and collective insecurity in our "postindustrial" societies: a facile theme, perhaps already worn out. But is not the most important form of insecurity this violence, militarization, and finally, banalization of extermination that seems to be happening, making it even more difficult to tell the "zones" and "periods" of war and peace apart? This calls for yet another reflection: should we in fact be talking about the "return" of war? Did it ever go away? Are we not above all frightened by the fact that it has moved up another notch in its murderous efficiency, and by the fact that it has drawn nearer to us? I say *us*, this time, as an inhabitant and citizen of Europe: for you citizens of Latin America have been living for much longer with internal and external war, or near it. Is it not finally time to face up to the fact that, for decades, and notably in the "Third World," under the global constant of great strategic balance, extermination large and small never stopped? It is in any case no longer a question here of a *possible* cataclysm but of *real* war, and the question is to know how to go about living with it, and whether we will accept living with it. This is a major question for politics, a major question for the "rights of man."

Let us then leave aside, at least for the moment, the conjuncture, and return to what I call the aporias or intrinsic difficulties of the very *concept* of a politics of the rights of man. Many questions should be raised, all of which would require their own analyses, even if they have many points of contact. Today I only want to raise two of them, which seem particularly revelatory to me: the question of the *limits of democracy*, and, under the heading of a concrete illustration, the question of the *forms of property*, as an intrinsically political question.

The Limits of Democracy

Everyone can tell that such a formulation can cover several aspects of the political problem. There are, on one hand, *de facto limitations*, which weigh heavily. What are called democratic rights, that is, a set of civil liberties and individual and collective powers whose definition has been progressively developed since the origins of the political institution (in Greece and elsewhere), and which the universalist "revolutions" of the end of the eighteenth century "founded" precisely upon an absolute, "natural" notion of the rights of man—these democratic rights are more or less recognized and guaranteed in the framework of modern states. Let us say that they *fluctuate* considerably (and dangerously) in space and time, that is, they are conquered, lost, and reconquered to a greater or lesser extent. Naturally there is nothing aleatory or spontaneous about this fluctuation; it is not a meteorological phenomenon. Here in Chile you are quite aware of this, having paid dearly for the knowledge.

There can be no doubt that one of the most important parts of the notion of a politics of the rights of man is the set of actions, forces, and forms— which it is difficult to describe other than as forms of struggle, even when this struggle is essentially peaceful—which work here to establish, there to re-establish, in their integrality, the respect of human persons and democratic rights, in opposition to their limitation or their suppression. Wherever dissidents are excluded from their work, imprisoned, and tortured, wherever political police (whether called the KGB or the DINA)[4] spy on, kidnap, and intimidate citizens, wherever poor children are shot on sight on street corners, wherever sexual, racial, and religious discrimination rule, the rights of man do not exist. And since resistance to these violations of the rights of man—which begins from individuals themselves but can only be collective—by definition forms a part of a politics of the rights of man, since this resistance never ends, we already have the first element of an answer to our question: the politics of the rights of man has always already begun, there is *always already* a politics of the rights of man. And in this sense it is probable that there will always *still* be one, be it only preventive: for we have learned to rid ourselves of the idea of an irresistible, irreversible progress of the rights of man through history.

But I am also thinking of other limits, which are not the *de facto* limitations imposed upon a democracy whose requirements are perfectly well known if not always recognized, but which are the *boundaries* of democracy, the borders of its unknown, that is, the limits that correspond to the question of just how far it can and ought to extend, and in what direction, to the question of just what happens when, in order to realize it or simply to confirm it or conserve it, it becomes necessary to go *to the limits* of democracy, intellectually and practically.

My argument is that the concept of a politics of the rights of man, in its specificity and with its own difficulties, begins to arise when, without leaving politics—on the contrary in the medium of politics and with its instruments (which are neither those of religion, ethics, science, nor economics)—we go to the very limits of democracy.

In truth this already originally characterizes the moment of the *Declaration of the Rights of Man*: as a publicity campaign, an act of making public without any real historical precedent, by which assembled individuals, taken as a representative "body," *publicly granted themselves their own rights*, it is an eminently political act. We should remember that, even if it has not always been valorized by political philosophy (for political philosophy since Plato has a strong tendency toward "aristocracy," if not oligarchy), the notion of democracy is considerably *older* than that of the "rights of man." Democracy did not need such a foundation, such a notion, to begin to think and to organize itself, even if, retrospectively, we can read in Greek or classical definitions of democracy a concept of right and of justice that cannot be entirely reduced to a privilege, a status, the counterpart of collective obligations and civic duties, or the necessity of protection.[5] Nevertheless, when the "rights of man" are declared as such, one goes to the limits of democracy (thus one both goes beyond its simple organization and shows its conditions of possibility) precisely in that an essential *limitlessness* characteristic of democracy (which forms the whole difficulty of its institution) is expressed.[6]

And, what is perhaps even more significant, is that the rights of man cannot be declared without being stated and defined from the outset as the "rights of man *and of the citizen*." Now, the notion of the citizen, of the activity of the citizen—for the concept of a "passive citizen," however much currency it might have, is a contradiction in terms—indisputably connotes politics. It even gives it its name.

In other words a declaration of the rights of man and the citizen, *the* declaration of the rights of man and the citizen (for in the strong sense there is only one, progressively elaborated in the course of history), is a radical discursive operation that deconstructs and reconstructs politics. It begins by taking democracy to its limits, in some sense *leaving* the field of instituted politics (this is the primary significance of the references to "human nature" or natural law), but in order to mark, immediately, that the rights of man have no reality and no value except as political rights, rights of the citizen, and even as the unlimited right of all men to citizenship. The right to autonomy and to the protection of "private life" is itself a political right: this is the renewed lesson of the history of all modern dictatorships. Earlier I tried to characterize the "proposition" that underlies this operation as the "proposition of equaliberty," that is, as the proposition that affirms a universal right to political activity and recognition for every individual, in all the domains in which the problem of collectively organizing possession, power, and knowledge is posed. I will here restrict myself to emphasizing again the three following points:

1. Equaliberty means that politics is founded on the recognition that neither freedom nor equality can exist without the other, that is, that the suppression or even the limitation of one necessarily leads to the suppression or limitation of the other. This might appear to be self-evident, but we know that in given historical conditions the construction of social forms that are both egalitarian and libertarian does not go without saying; it is on the contrary a task that is always being begun again, it is *the* political problem *par excellence*, and most often bristling with obstacles. Philosophically at least (thanks to Spinoza and to a few others) we know that what this implies is the necessity of moving from the point of view of limitative, mutually exclusive rights to expansive, mutually multiplying *powers*.[7]

2. Equaliberty implies universality: in this sense the democratic limitlessness of which we spoke above signifies that democracy is not only a constitutional state embodying equal—that is, uniform—rights, making no distinction of persons, conditions, or ranks among its own members, but also a historical process of the extension of rights to all humanity. We know, however, that historical states are instituted communities of interests and passions, that they therefore imply a principle of closure, if not exclusion (not to speak of the interior barriers or categorizations they bring with them). Here still, consequently, there is an intrinsic difficulty. A politics of the rights of man, in the wake of this already political act that is the *Declaration of the Rights of Man and the Citizen*, is a politics of the universalization of rights (and not merely a morality, an ethics, or even a religion of their universality).

3. Equaliberty implies, as we said, a universal right *to politics*: a right of

everyone *on his or her own behalf* (which signifies, among other things, that no one can be liberated or emancipated by others, from "above," even were this "above" to be right itself, or the democratic state). This then is the right of every man and every woman to become the "subject" or agent of politics, setting out from the specific forms of his or her activity and life, from the old or new forms of constraint and subjection to which he or she is submitted. It is in this sense that, against a well-established tradition, I proposed that the famous rallying cry of the preamble of the rules of the International Association of Working Men (1864), "That the emancipation of the working classes must be conquered by the working classes themselves,"[8] should be read as a faithful translation of the proposition of equaliberty, and consequently of the *Declaration of the Rights of Man and the Citizen*.[9]

This signifies, quite concretely—and history for the last two hundred years has constantly taken it upon itself to show to just what extent the question touched a nerve—that rights-claims cannot be circumscribed to any pre-established domain. As a consequence no social category or "social question," that is, no conflict of powers or project of liberation inscribed in any social relation whatever, can be indefinitely excluded from politics. This has been clearly seen with slavery, with colonization, with the inequality of the sexes and the domination of women, with education and the access of all to culture, and with the exploitation of salaried labor, even if, in all these domains, the "revolutionaries" of the eighteenth century thought that they had erected prudent safeguards, and even if none of these questions can be considered to be definitively dealt with today, nor even completely accepted as political questions.

This is *a fortiori* true of rights-claims that must eventually appear as claims of "rights of man" or that are in the course of doing so. For if the "rights of man" must, at a certain moment, be thought of as "natural," that is as unconditional or inalienable, this evidently does not mean that they have no historicity, nor even that their list has been set out once and for all, for this list depends on the history of the "natural conditions" within which social relations develop. For this is the very history of the practical discovery and enunciation of an *unconditional* (or, if one prefers, of a truth) in the *given*, determinate conditions of politics.

Let us try to put these questions to the test of a more concrete question: that of property. I choose it intentionally, among other possibilities, on account of the paradoxical combination of relevance and irrelevance that it presents: profound irrelevance because, since the collapse of socialist states and parties, the "ideological" debates on the mode of property to be incorporated into the structure of the state itself seem to have been decided "by history"; yet still profound relevance if it is true that, on all sides, practice is coming into contradiction with the traditionally taught definitions, to the point that it is becoming more and more difficult for politics to abstain from *thinking* property as such.

What Is Property?

Coming after Rousseau, who saw in it the origin of inequality among men, Proudhon said that property was "theft." No one will be astonished in these conditions that he denounced as an absurdity that the *Declaration* of 1789 placed it on the same plane as freedom, equality before the law, and security.[10] And we should recognize that there is indeed a problem here: in what sense is property a "right of man"? In what sense is it a "right of the citizen"? How is it to be explained that it has never ceased to have justice or equality claimed *against it* (under the name of the right to existence, of the right to employment, more recently of the right to environment, etc.)?

Unless, beneath the homonym of the term property, there are really *two* distinct notions at issue, corresponding to two different problems: on the one hand (art. 2), the "natural and imprescriptible right of man," on the other (art. 17), the "inviolable and sacred right" of which "no one can...be deprived, except when public necessity...obviously requires it." In the same way, for example, freedom is posed in articles 1 and 2 as a universal characteristic of persons (which has no need of being acquired), whereas its application to "the communication of thoughts and opinions" requires the principle of repression of "abuses" to be stated (art. 11). What remains unclear is why, foreseeing practical limitations on the right of property (or discovering *exceptions* to it, if not abuses), the *Declaration* did not specify *which property* was at issue, what it concerned (certain goods or usufructs for example).[11] Is it a question of uncertainty, lack of foresight, even dissimulation or latent contradiction? Or is it a question, on the contrary, of a margin wisely left for adaptation to historical conditions, so that the identification of the citizen as "proprietor" does not thereby signify that citizenship should be measured by property? But is that not essentially what was to happen?

Nothing is more obvious than the fact that the debate on the forms, limits, and attribution of property, or, as Saint-Simon would say, on the difference between the "right of property" and the "law of property," is a political debate *par excellence*. For the last two centuries people have taken sides, "classed" themselves by attacking it or defending it. Property then appears as both the object of contention that gives politics its maximum reality—its weight of social conflicts and interests—and as what permanently leads it back to its boundary and tends to make it go outside itself: both in the sense that it refers to "extra-political" (economic) constraints, and in the sense that it refers to naked power relations. For the stakes here to be those of the rights of man, however, it is sufficient that property appear as the very example of a *right* that has been turned back into, or that always tends to turn back into a *privilege*, and that this "regression" coincides with the installation of politics in a social constitution for which the role played by the rights of man is only that of a symbolic, founding reference.

Already in 1789, property as inscribed under the heading of the rights of man has a counterpoint that is heavy with social conflicts: the question of the means of subsistence, and more fundamentally still, that of the *right to existence*.[12] To the extent that it is interpreted as an exclusive right, as a "private" property that in practice takes the form of a monopoly and whose instrument is money, it confers upon its holders an absolute power over the life of others, which at the limit can become a right of life and death. Between those whose living is provided by property and those whom it kills, a mediation becomes necessary. The debate is joined among those who affirm that the solution resides in an extra measure of power to be conferred to property, which would become the only title under which society could be governed, and the prior *condition* of all other rights (and whoever has no money should get a job if he wants to eat!),[13] those who demand that a humanitarian or social counterpart (without which a right becomes precisely an abuse) be fixed, and finally, those who affirm not that the right of property must be abolished—for, let us note, none of the parties to the debate formulate such a demand[14]—but that it must be *subordinated* to the right of the community, to the principle of egalitarian distribution of the means of existence that founds and guarantees the community.

But a decisive redirection is produced when, half a century later, the question of the right to existence is taken over and advanced by the right to employment. It is in fact at this moment that a veritable dilemma is introduced, prohibiting the two theses in the debate from *simultaneously* claiming to be inspired by the "rights of man," or obliging them to declare themselves *for or against* the very idea of a politics of the rights of man.

It is well known that the claim for the right to employment, if not the notion itself, is Fourierist in origin.[15] Fourier and his successors begin from the fact that the human existence of individuals (not only their subsistence but the exercise of their passions and the establishment of their mutual relations) henceforth depends upon their being "workers": they propose in sum to interpret the right to property as *the right to receive work*. It is thus crucial that, at the very least, the proprietors of capital cannot hire and fire at their pleasure, and ideally, that property be organized so as to guarantee permanently to all citizens the quantity and type of work that they need. At the limit the proprietors *of capital* fulfill a "public service," in the service of the property *of all*. It is equally well known that, when the question, brought before the public forum by the Revolution of 1848, was debated in France as a political question, it was decided negatively.[16] Two paths were open from this point: either, from the liberal perspective, to make the rights of man in general the metaphysical guarantee of unconditional private property, which is practically equivalent to the absolute "command" of labor by capital; or to denounce in the very notion of the rights of man a bourgeois notion, a class discourse—at best a mystification and at worst an instrument of exploitation. Whence the socialist project of "going beyond" the simple rights of individual man by abolishing "bourgeois" property, and instituting the collective property of the workers, the condition of their "free association."

In a sense this dialectic, historically determinant, is still only a negative, exterior dialectic, in which the rights of man are posed against politics and politics in turn is posed against the rights of man. This is doubtless due to the fact that the notions and forces involved were from the beginning torn between a purely juridical conception and a purely economic conception of "property." Nevertheless, the real history of the relations between "private property" and the "collective worker" (Marx) did not remain in this standoff. Once the question of the right *to employment* (*au travail*) (while waiting to be reopened by the socialist revolutions and their repercussions in the capitalist world)[17] was decided by the victory of the "bourgeois" thesis, there began a much more obscure, day-to-day history, made of advances and retreats, which is that of the rights *of labor* (*du travail*). That is, by these arrangements, wrestled away in a hard-fought struggle, the worker—whose labor power has been bought and sold like a "commodity"—unable to be recognized as a "citizen in the enterprise," obtains the right not to be a slave, but to become a "man" again in the labor process itself (and in his life insofar as its conditions depend upon work). To the extent that this made the modern national state into a *social* state, incorporating individual and collective "social rights" into its constitution, opening a space of collective negotiation and politico-economic debate, there was a practical recognition of the *citizenship of the worker*, or if one prefers, of the fact that the citizen as such is *also* a worker. In any case the decisive point is that it was the national state that thus declared that modern *citizenship is impossible without a regulation of the conditions in which the right of property is exercised*. At bottom, if one reflects with a bit of distance, it can be seen that this conflictual regulation or "new social contract," despite flagrant irregularities, characterizes *both* the "liberal" and "collectivist" regimes. The former did not succeed in completely avoiding collective property (which they had to recreate as public property wherever they had tried to eliminate it) any more than the latter were able to eliminate private property (they had to legalize its persistence, at the risk of their own political crisis). Everywhere there tolled the hour of what could be called, deforming a Fourierist phrase, "composite property."

I will not linger any longer on this history, which is undergoing new episodes before our eyes, for what I want to get at is the following point: in reality liberal individualism and socialist collectivism have a common presupposition identifying property with the *unlimited disposal of goods*. (This is a simple relationship between men and things, or man and nature, which exactly illustrates what Marx calls "fetishism.") Whereas liberalism attributes this disposal to the "individual," socialism attributes it to "society," a collective subject that can be incarnated by the state or other institutions. But this interpretation is by no means implied by the actual text of the *Declaration* of 1789 (whose astonishing theoretical power we must once again recognize). The *Declaration* begins in a Lockean manner by posing a *generic* right of property, which is certainly not of "collectivist" inspiration but is also not reducible to "private" property. The latter, by definition, only concerns the disposal of objects by an already given "subject," one constituted elsewhere. But the sense of the preliminary formulas of the *Declaration* is precisely to define in its essential characteristics and thus to *constitute* this "subject," this citizen-man.[18] "Imprescriptible" property is one of these essential characteristics: which means that the idea of a citizen-man who is a "nonproprietor," "devoid of property," or dispossessed would be a contradiction in terms. It is obviously necessary that this property not be empty, that it have, as Hegel would say, an "actuality," that is, that it concern goods or services, means of labor, objects of consumption and enjoyment. But even before the appropriation of things has been determined in this way, before it has been decided whether it is to be exercised in a private or collective fashion, it thus appears as the condition of a *property of oneself*, of a free disposal of one's forces and of their employment. Only such a notion of property, *yet to be determined*—just as freedom, equality, resistance to oppression and security are to be determined in their means and juridical modalities—would truly be part of the system of the rights of man. We can then (and this is doubtless what current circumstances themselves oblige us to do) *reopen the dialectic of property*, this time as an *internal* dialectic: not in order to suppress its contradictions, but to generalize them and set them in motion—and this in several ways.

First of all we can put back into question the general identification of private property and individual property—and as a consequence dissolve their undifferentiated opposition to "collective" property, whether it be state property or not. This identification is properly speaking a *fiction*, that is an efficacious juridical construction, which allows all exclusive disposal to be referred to an ideal "individual." But the real functioning of this category is exactly the inverse of what is suggested by legal ideology: it is not proprietors who by nature are individuals or groups of individuals, it is individuals who, among others, fall under the exclusive, limitative category of "private proprietor," and who on this condition can exclusively appropriate such and such an object, such and such a right or power. From this point of view collective property and particularly state property—except precisely when it is associated to obligations, to the goals and constraints of "public service"—is in itself nothing but *private* property (what I would hazard to call *collective private* property). And the conflict that can oppose it to the properties of "private persons" is only a conflict between competing exclusivities. In both cases one can witness the *expropriation* of individuals in the very forms of the triumph of "property" (which is, as Marx had seen, the inevitable tendency of societies founded upon the exploitation of labor).

The constitutive link between the property *of things* and the property *of oneself* is a double-sided activity by which a subject "forms" or constitutes itself by engaging in relations of use, transformation, or enjoyment with natural as well as cultural objects. Combining the lessons of Adam Smith and Hegel, Marx saw that this activity, as such, is a "social relation," that is, that it is a possibility for each individual to the very extent that, in diverse degrees, it is shared with others—*common* to several individuals or to several groups of individuals (which does not mean that it is without conflict, competition or antagonism). He further showed that this activity turns around into its opposite, from a movement of appropriation into a movement of expropriation, when private property abolishes this transindividual aspect or places it beyond the reach of individuals (when, for instance, the "collective powers" of labor, including its powers of decision and organization, are entirely attributed to capital, and the necessities of their own organization are "thrown back" on the workers as pure exterior compulsion).[19] But there too the "solution" cannot consist in formal collectivization, which only displaces and at the limit reinforces this separation.

Marx, the virulent critic of the *ideology* of "the rights of man," is exactly in the line of a *politics* of the rights of man when, carefully guarding against positing the thesis of a simple reversal of private property into collective property, he defines the "expropriation of the expropriators" as the *re-establishment of individual property* in general "on the basis" of the "socialization" historically realized by the capitalist mode of production.[20] But for Marx— faithful in this regard to the theoretical tradition of socialist ideology and its critique of alienated labor—the only activity that realizes the double appropriation of oneself and of things is precisely productive labor. We have since learned to recognize alienation in consumption and even alienation in enjoyment.... And from the experience of an *expropriation* of individuals in the object of their consumption or their enjoyment we can deduce the concept of a corresponding *appropriation*. It would then be necessary, in this perspective, to think a generalized appropriation that includes all the forms of the relation of the "self" to "things" (and of the relation to "others" by the intermediary of things) insofar as it is expressed in a property. Doubtless such an appropriation goes beyond the juridical framework and can only be realized as the institution of a *way of life*, posing the limits of the respective shares of the public and the private, of work and nonwork, of individual and collective consumption. As such, this is precisely what can be called a frontier (to be explored) of politics.

But the dialectic of property must be reopened in yet another fashion. Even when a compromise has been sought to regulate it, the conflict between the cause of private property and the cause of public property, or between the "right of property" and the "right to employment" has always been conceived of in *dualist* terms, as if this were the only possible alternative. It has thus been forgotten that the very terms of the opposition presuppose an arbitrary decision: that every object, every raw or refined material, every natural or artificial (or even immaterial) "thing" is effectively appropriable (whether by an individual or an institution) in the form of an exclusive disposal. And despite some difficult cases—paradoxical "exceptions"—what can be called the *principle of total possession* of objects[21] has reigned unchallenged, and has appeared as the corollary of the constitution of individuals as free proprietors, of their realization in and by property.

Ever since old theological or theologico-political notions such as the "eminent domain" of God or of the sovereign over the entire earth have lost all significance, what has posed problems (and is today undergoing new developments) has above all been the possibility of extending the application of this principle of total possession to the human person itself, particularly when the human body, the use of its services and its capacities enters into commodity circulation. But the question was never again posed whether the principle of total possession brings with it intrinsic limits, that is, whether there are not "objects" that, by nature, cannot be appropriated, or more precisely that can be appropriated but *not totally possessed*.

But this is in fact the question that arises today in the center of the aporias of property, and whose repercussions point up its intrinsically political character, in such a way that also makes clear, retrospectively, that it had always existed but had been repressed or marginalized.[22]

This question first arises *negatively*, by way of "ecology" in the broad sense, that is by the recognition of the harms that turn the "productive" balance sheet of human labor into a "destructive" one, and that suddenly make manifest that the use of nature is submitted to practically no law. By "nature" should be understood here precisely all the nonpossessable materials that are nonetheless an indispensable component of all "production," all "consumption," and all "enjoyment." Their existence is only noticed when they are lacking (by the potential or ongoing exhaustion of certain fundamental "resources"), or when they are transformed into waste that cannot be eliminated, or when they produce effects capable of endangering the life of individuals and of humanity, which can be neither controlled nor repaired by the owners of their "causes," even when these owners are superpowers or multinational conglomerates with a worldwide reach.... There then arises the necessity to institute, and, first of all, to conceive of, a control on the use of certain resources or certain "universal" goods, and to give it a juridical foundation in a notion like the "common heritage of mankind."[23]

But what is this notion if not *the return of eminent domain*, the only difference being that it no longer has a theological foundation, that it is no longer attributed to a person transcending the laws and the life of the polity but is constituted in a secular or immanent mode by the presumed agreement of men themselves. The common heritage of mankind is thus exactly *the other of money*, what could be called, to parody Marx, the "general nonequivalent": neither private property nor public or collective property, but *universal property*, "without a subject," or without any subject but the *fiction* of a unified humanity,[24] a fiction that is perfectly *real* from the moment that it becomes the condition of any appropriation and is translated by restrictive limitations placed upon private or public property as exclusive right of disposal. Universal property in this sense is thus by no means a suppression of the "right of property" in the name of external ethical, economic, or political principles. Nevertheless, far from representing an enlarged application of the principle of total possession, it on the contrary marks its limit, the impossibility of subsuming everything under the right of exclusive property. It has nothing in common with a public appropriation, a national or supernational state property in whose terms a "social" power would *exclusively* dispose of certain goods. It would rather represent the form in which property would become once again virtually "imprescriptible" for "man," taken both individually and collectively.

This is the negative aspect. But we should note that it is a *self-limitation* of property that is at issue, and this can only result from social power relations and their institutional mediation: it thus immediately has a positive aspect. Moreover, it is indeed property, a moment of the appropriation of things, that is at issue; but this property consists in a regulation of men's activity upon "nature"—better yet, it consists in the reciprocal control of the collective activity of men (or of human groups) on nature. The real content of the universal property of nature is nothing but a *universal politics* of mediation of the interests and ends of public and private property. And more and more it appears that it cannot be enacted by unilateral or authoritarian means. It at least potentially includes a new political practice, democracy's crossing of a frontier (and of many borders), since it cannot exist without the participation or contribution of *all* "proprietors," even the poorest and most oppressed.

I have discussed at some length this point, which touches on current debates, but, without developing it fully for itself, I want at least to point to the other approach by which the virtual recognition of universal property is occurring today: namely, the effects of the "mechanization of intelligence," indissociable from the universalization of means of communication. In reality intellectual activity, or better the *intellectual aspect* of human activities, which accompanies all technology and all culture, has always been in a contradictory relation to private property. All appropriation presupposes an intellectual activity, in that it occurs through learning rules, knowing techniques, exchanging information, etc. But the "material" of this activity (whether it be called "ideas," "consciousness," "knowledge," or "discourse") is as such transindividual: it escapes exclusive property, or at least it always bears with it a non-exclusive remainder. At the limit the concept of an "exclusive knowledge," of a public or private *monopoly* of knowledge, is a contradiction in terms.[25] This obstacle to possession can nonetheless be turned in different ways, which are as much tied to relations of domination as they are to technical inventions: what then become objects of property are the instruments of this activity or of its communication (radio and television networks, newspapers, publishing houses, but also schools, libraries, research centers, even typewriters...) and its products (submitted to the system of copyright or public distribution). But techniques of assistance to thought and of global communication in "real time" are on the way to making most of these instruments inoperative. They too create an increasing quantity of *that which cannot be possessed or mastered*, which does not put an end to appropriation but becomes its condition. Data and methods are irresistibly "disseminated"; the "paternity" of the results of scientific and technological research can no longer be defined in an exclusive fashion— neither can, as a consequence, the property of objects that incorporate an ever greater amount of crystallized knowledge.

Different individuals can experience this situation, which puts back into question what Paul Henry called the "postulate of the individuality of the thought process,"[26] as either a dispossession or a liberation. The great collective proprietors (firms, states) regard it as a threat, which is why they are trying to control its effects by reintroducing monopolistic and secretive practices, combined with practices of exclusive training and development of employee "loyalty" for individuals who are the bearers of knowledge or the agents of its utilization and transmission, etc.

As can be seen again here, the problem is purely political: in order to *possess* it is necessary to *know*, but in order to know it is necessary to be integrated in cosmopolitan institutions that are less and less "separable" (as Aristotle would have said) from the networks of the communicative machine, and that are riven by tensions between compartmentalization and openness, authoritarianism and democratization. It then becomes impossible in practice, and more and more difficult even to conceive of in theory, to pose on one side a right of property that would deal only with things, or with the individual concerned with the "administration of things" (with the *societas rerum* of the jurists of antiquity), and on the other side a sphere of the *vita activa* (Hannah Arendt) that would be the sphere of "man's power over man" and man's obligations toward man, of the formation of "public opinion," and of the conflict of ideologies. Property (*dominium*) re-enters domination (*imperium*). The administration of things re-enters the government of men (if it had ever left it). And the *form* in which the "intellectual property of mankind" is instituted, controlled, distributed, and developed becomes the condition of each social group's temporary, local disposition of its objects and products.

Let there be no misunderstanding: the appearance of universal property, in its different forms, does not in any way put an end to the existing forms of property among which, since the beginning of the modern era, possessable objects have been divided. Nor does it put an end to the political antagonisms surrounding property that polarize social life when private property's successive *opposites* are affirmed against it: the right to existence and the right to employment, as a condition of their effectiveness, call for all or part of the right of property to be transferred to the state. What these antagonisms show is that *all* "property law," which divides property into public and private domains and thus regulates the hierarchical relation between property, labor, social security, and environment in a determinate fashion, is based on a determinate distribution of power. What the current debates on the common heritage of mankind or on monopolies of data (and technology) show, on the contrary, are the intrinsic limits of the principle of total possession. And what they bring forth as a repercussion is a "generic" notion of property, which fundamentally, in the totality of its conditions, remains a transindividual process. Whatever the mechanism of appropriation may be, individual or collective, there is thus *always already politics* in the division into or mediation between the different forms of property, none of which can eliminate the others. And in a certain sense politics itself is nothing but the permanent mediation between these different forms, private and public, exclusive and non-exclusive.

This *becoming-political* of property, without which it could not truly be considered to be a "right of man" (because it would never imply a "right of the citizen"), has already begun when its distribution appears as the key to the distribution of the means of existence and of labor itself (since the latter is not only a means of existence, but also a means of conquering personal dignity, or "independence," and thus getting out of a state of social "tutelage"). It is affirmed when a concept of "universal property," by imposing limits on the principle of total possession, opens up on active citizenship as the condition of the effective appropriation of nature.

Still, as long as such a concept is only perceived negatively, as a symptom of impotence (unless by inversion it is projected into a new mysticism of nature—which seems to be the danger of some current ecological doctrines), it is not only of blockage, conflict, or antagonism but of a veritable aporia of politics that we must speak. And we cannot say today that we have found our way out of this aporia: we can only say that it imposes itself upon us, so that if it is ignored—that is, if it is repressed—there is no more politics.

Perhaps it can now be seen more clearly in what sense I thought I could say that the very definition of the rights of man, which determines their politics, cannot be abstracted from a history, which in a sense is the very history of "human nature," or, if another vocabulary is preferred, "social relations." In reality the only vocabulary that is truly proper here is that of politics. This is why I will summarize by saying that a politics of the rights of man goes to the limits of democracy and takes democracy to its limits to the extent that it can never be content to conquer or to provide a juridical guarantee for civil and civic rights, however important these objectives may be, but must necessarily, in order to attain them at a given historical moment, *extend* the rights of man and eventually *invent* them as rights of the citizen (which implies conceptualizing them, declaring them, and imposing them).

This operation of inventing rights, or of continually setting their history back into motion, without which the concept of a politics of the rights of man in the strong sense is meaningless, is by definition a *risky* operation. It brings with it an intellectual risk, but also a practical, even existential one. It always supposes, whether one likes it or not, that an existing social order is put into question, even if it be the democratic and juridical order of a constitutional state that, within certain limits and within a certain field, institutes freedom and equality. We must not fear to employ the term once again: it supposes an insurrectional act, in the sense in which insurrection (which is more than revolt and anything but rebellion) is opposed to the stability of a constitution, and yet prepares and founds it. In insurrection, be it controlled, be it nonviolent, what is at stake is the necessity and the risk not only of popular *sovereignty* but above all, once again, of popular *power*. This is in the end the aporia, or in any case the difficulty, of the politics of the rights of man: the risky putting into the balance of the power that makes and unmakes constitutional orders through the invention of new rights, or the extension of rights, at the limits of democracy. It is the risk that arises once it has become clear that a simple *adaptation of rights* to the "evolutions of society" (evolutions of the market, of technology and productive forces, of morals, beliefs, etc.) is impossible. It is the risk of collective error, with infinitely greater consequences than those of any individual error whatsoever. It is the risk of having to confront the multiform violence of an established order "defending" itself and, what is doubtless even more difficult, of having to confront the consequences and the effects upon oneself of a "counterviolence," in which so many revolutionary endeavors have been lost (which means that they have tragically been both infinitely close and infinitely far from a politics of the rights of man). But it is the risk without which every right, even the right of peoples to existence, security, and prosperity, can be irremediably lost.[27]

NOTES

Preface

1. This means: what is the principle of its internal unity? I have examined this formulation more extensively in another essay which, to keep reasonable length, could not be included in this book: "Ce qui fait qu'un peuple est un peuple: Rousseau et Kant," *Revue de Synthèse* 110 (1989): 391–417.

2. He was himself perfectly well aware of that, as witness his (and Engels's) many references to the theory of private property as a source of alienation exposed in the *Discourse on the Origin of Inequality*.

3. If we follow Althusser's reading of Rousseau (see "Rousseau: The Social Contract [The Discrepancies]," in *Montesquieu, Rousseau, Marx: Politics and History*, trans. Ben Brewster [London: Verso, 1982], 111–60), the *Social Contract* can be seen as an *aporetic* (perhaps desperate) attempt to *re-create* the conditions of political autonomy, which are also the conditions for autonomy of politics.

4. I would dare to suggest that, without the theoretical challenge and the practical importance of Marxism, a *liberal* "economic" conception of politics (from Hayek to Rawls) would not have existed in the twentieth century.

5. I should ask the reader to take into account the different dates the essays were written to explain a number of discrepancies in their contents and positions. Since they testify to ongoing, unfinished research, I see no point in correcting or wiping out these discrepancies, which are part of the process; to which I should add that I have always considered an essay as an experiment in thought rather than a way of laying down or constructing argu-

ments for a preestablished thesis.

6. See Etienne Balibar and Immanuel Wallerstein, *Race, Nation, Class: Ambiguous Identities*, trans. Chris Turner (London:Verso, 1992).

7. The seminal importance of the *Addresses* for the whole history of nationalist discourse up to today can hardly be overestimated: every day you find evidence of its direct influence, from France to Japan, and from Arab to Latin American nationalism.

8. As distinct from ancient, platonic idealism, which is not a theory of the realization of moral (or human) ends, but a theory of the beautiful order of the world.

9. To combine the discussion of teleology with the discussion of the ambivalent recognition of the role of the masses in history is therefore the main "original" idea of this book. It involves studying "ideas" (in the sense of ideologies) as the "element" in which masses evolve, *and* the "element" in which teleologies are constructed (be they religious, juridical, socialist, etc.). Teleology could be called the great "complexity reducing" pattern in the life of the "masses," provided one understands that the masses *themselves are this "complexity"* which has to be reduced (in a sense this is exactly Spinoza's analysis of "imagination," a representative process which is both individual and collective, and projects "order" where in reality there is complexity). It strikes me that, although the concept of "mass" (admittedly not a very *univocal* one!) has been persistent in contemporary thought (to the point that a whole "discipline" was founded only to study "mass phenomena" and their impact on politics: namely "social psychology"), a precise and comprehensive *history* of the concept "mass"—starting with the Greek *to plethos* or *hoi polloi* and Latin *multitudo*, and extending to the modern conflicting notions of "the masses" (which is rather positive in revolutionary discourse) and "crowd" (which is rather negative, in the conservative discourse)—does not exist.

10. To the same sequence also belong the various entries I wrote for the *Dictionnaire critique du marxisme*, ed. Georges Labica and Georges Bensussan, 2nd ed. (Paris: Presses Universitaires de France, 1985): *appareil, classes, contre-révolution, critique de l'économie politique, dictature du prolétariat, lutte des classes, pouvoir, droit de tendances.*

11. Of course it is even less challenged by "analytical Marxism," in spite of its professional skill, since it is not primarily interested in the real *text*, but only in the *arguments* which can be "found" in it (i.e., abstracted from it), therefore it is constantly guided by the ideal of the system.

12. This, of course, is likely to produce a new insistence, both "from above" and "from below," on the necessity of "smashing violence."

13. "From Class Struggle to Struggle without Classes?" in Balibar and Wallerstein, *Race, Nation, Class,* 153–84.

14. It is perhaps a paradox, but also a major historical achievement, of socialism, and particularly Marxism, with all its insistence on the "class character" of politics and the unique mission of the "proletariat," that it was more effective than any other modern ideology in *bringing together* individuals and groups *from different classes* (including the bourgeoisie, particularly intellectuals), and allowing them to "make politics" collectively, beyond the ossified structures of the division of labor and education, of professional and cultural hierarchies.

Chapter 1 • Spinoza, The Anti-Orwell: The Fear of the Masses

1. Antonio Negri, *The Savage Anomaly: The Power of Spinoza's Metaphysics and Politics,* trans. Michael Hardt (Minneapolis: University of Minnesota Press, 1991). See also the commentaries published in *Cahiers Spinoza* 4 (Winter 1982–83). I regret not having been able to take account of the book by André Tosel, *Spinoza ou le crépuscule de la servitude:*

Essai sur le Traité théologico-politique (Paris: Aubier, 1984), which appeared after the composition of this essay, and whose different perspective is equally stimulating. Several questions raised below could have been clarified.

2. This study takes up again and develops some ideas which I had presented at a colloquium at Urbino, *Spinoza nel 350' Anniversario della Nascita*, October 1982. The proceedings of that colloquium have been published as *Proceedings of the First Italian International Congress on Spinoza*, ed. Emilia Giancotti (Naples: Bibliopolis, 1985). I want to thank, in turn, Olivier Bloch, Jean-Luc Nancy, and Philippe Lacoue-Labarthe for having provided me with the opportunity to return to this work in their respective seminars.

3. Pierre Macherey, *Hegel ou Spinoza* (Paris: Maspero, 1979).

4. In the *Political Treatise* Charles Appuhn (*Oeuvres* [Paris: Garnier-Flammarion, 1966]) translates *multitudo* as *masse, multitude, population, peuple, masse du peuple*, etc., which is hardly rigorous, but illustrates the polymorphism of the notion. Sylvain Zac (*Traité politique* [Paris: Vrin, 1968]) generally translates *multitudo* as *multitude* but also as *population*. Madeleine Frances (*Oeuvres complètes*, ed. Roland Caillois [Paris: Gallimard, Bibliothèque de la Pléiade]) translates *multitudo* as *la masse* (and on rare occasions as *population*). Pierre-François Moreau (*Traité politique* [Paris: Editions Réplique, 1979]) systematically translates *multitudo* as *multitude*, except in Chapter IX, 13, in which he remarks that "the term has a more statistical than political meaning." I shall return in a moment to the possibility of reducing this last distinction.

5. Baruch Spinoza, *Ethics*, in *The Collected Works of Spinoza*, trans. Edwin Curley (Princeton: Princeton University Press, 1985), 1:567. I have returned to this crucial proposition—the very core of Spinoza's political anthropology, in my opinion—and dealt at length with the remarkable structure of its twofold demonstration, in my book *Spinoza et la politique* (Paris: P.U.F., 1985), 91–105.

6. See *Theologico-Political Treatise*, XVII: "However, in order to correctly understand the extent of the sovereign's right and power, it should be observed that its power is not limited to the use of coercion based on fear, but includes every means by which it can induce men to obey its commands. It is obedience, not the motive for obedience, that makes one a subject....Obedience does not concern external action as much as it does the soul's internal action."

7. Gilles Deleuze, *Expressionism in Philosophy: Spinoza*, trans. Martin Joughin (New York: Zone Books, 1992), 273–301.

8. For an inventory of *multitudo* in Spinoza and the evolution of the contexts in which it appears, see Emilia Giancotti-Boscherini, *Lexicon Spinozanum* (The Hague: Martinus Nijhoff, 1970), 2 vols., 2:728–29.

9. The central concept of *conatus* has no simple and satisfactory French (or English) equivalent. See the *Ethics*, part III, propositions 6 and following (1:498): "Each thing, as far as it can by its own power, strives to persevere in its being (*unaquaeque res, quantam in se est, in suo esse perseverare conatur*)." I would like to try below to clarify indirectly the reasons why there is no such equivalent. Borrowed from pre-Newtonian dynamics, but reworked by Spinoza in an attempt to construct an analytic of psychic conflict, *conatus* connotes individuality but not subjectivity (thus the ambiguity of translating it as "effort"), power but not finality (thus the ambiguity of translating it as "tendency"). "Energy" would not be a bad translation, by paradoxically bringing together *both* of the two antithetical significations that this term has historically assumed.

10. Several recent commentators have corrected the error that consists in including Spinoza among "contract theorists," hence among the theorists of "natural right" in the sense initiated by Hobbes, hence among the founders of modern legal ideology, and have shown what confusions follow from this error. See Alexandre Matheron, *Individu et communauté*

chez Spinoza (Paris: Editions de minuit, 1969), 287–354; Deleuze, *Expressionism*, 255–72; and especially Negri, *The Savage Anomaly*, 191–210. It obviously does not follow from this that Spinoza's thought is a matter of organicism, nor that the use of the term "pact" in the *Theologico-Political Treatise* only has the significance of an atavism or an incoherence; on the contrary, it plays a central role in the analysis of the overdetermination of the political relation by the religious imaginary. See the very illuminating analyses of Sylvain Zac, *Philosophie, théologie, politique dans l'oeuvre de Spinoza* (Paris: Vrin, 1979), 145–76 and 203–14. I have tried to sustain and explain the dialectic of that overdetermination in my article, "*Jus-Pactum-Lex,* sur la constitution du sujet dans le *Traité théologico-politique,*" *Studia Spinozana* 1 (1985): 105–42.

11. On this aporia of Rousseau's theory, see Louis Althusser, "Rousseau: The Social Contract (The Discrepancies)," in *Montesquieu, Rousseau, Marx: Politics and History*, trans. Ben Brewster (London: Verso, 1982), 111–60.

12. These formulas concerning the deliberative capacity of the multitude echo a long tradition that goes back to Aristotle (*Politics*, III, 1281b). But they above all evoke directly certain arguments put forward by Machiavelli (*Discourses*, I, 47, and 57–58, in which the concept of the *multitude* arises precisely as another name of the *people*) which have always sustained the "democratic" reading of his work. It is to the extent that Spinoza both indirectly reconsiders the question of the imaginary structure of the multitude, and beyond that poses the problem of its organization, that he can go beyond the restriction Machiavelli placed on his own thesis. See the commentaries of Leo Strauss, *Thoughts on Machiavelli* (Glencoe, Ill.: The Free Press, 1958), and Claude Lefort, *Le travail de l'oeuvre Machiavel* (Paris: Gallimard, 1972), 520–31.

13. Lucien Mugnier-Pollet, *La philosophie politique de Spinoza* (Paris: Vrin, 1976), 226 (see also chapters 4 and 18); Matheron, *Individu et communauté,* 465–502; Pierre-François Moreau, "La notion d'*Imperium* dans le *Traité politique,*" in *Proceedings of the First Italian International Congress on Spinoza,* 355–66. To be convinced that, behind this speculation, there is a tradition and a precise historical problem (which is not only fiscal but has to do with the organization of social hierarchies in the monarchies and oligarchies of the sixteenth and seventeenth centuries), read the pages Fernand Braudel devotes to the scales of wealth and power in Venice, Genoa, and England in *The Wheels of Commerce*, vol. 2 of *Civilization and Capitalism, 15th-18th Century,* trans. Siân Reynolds (New York: Harper and Row, 1982), 466–70. See also later in the book (546–48) his clarification concerning the modalities of Dutch mercantilism, often denied. On this point, see Immanuel Wallerstein, *The Modern World System II: Mercantilism and the Consolidation of the European World Economy, 1600-1750* (New York: Academic Press, 1980), chapter 2, "The Period of Dutch Hegemony," 36–71. On statistics as "state science" and "science of the state," see Jacqueline Hecht, "L'idée de dénombrement jusqu'à la Révolution," in *Pour une histoire de la statistique,* vol. 1, ed. Jacques Mairesse (Paris: I.N.S.E.E., 1977), 21–81, which emphasizes the direct role of Jan de Witt and Christian Huyghens, close friends of Spinoza, in the development of Dutch statistics.

14. *Political Treatise*, VII, 27. The fact that this maxim (which comes from Tacitus, *Annals,* I, 29) figures here in the context of a refutation by Spinoza of antidemocratic arguments, generally prompts commentators to remark that Spinoza does not share the view it expresses. This is to erase all the ambivalence that, precisely, I seek to explain. The same formula, we shall see, figures in the *Ethics* under a hardly different form (*terret vulgus, nisi metuat*), assumed this time by the author.

15. The necessary exclusion of women from citizenship, under the same heading as foreigners and slaves, is of course a commonplace of political philosophy which goes back at least to Aristotle and is deeply rooted in the very history of institutions. But the *Political Treatise* is

"unfinished" precisely on this point, or, let us say, precisely at the point where the *fear of women*, a veritable metonymy of the fear of the masses, comes to block analysis and to leave the theoretical exposition unfinished, and this cannot be considered a simple contingency. It is a supplementary index in support of the hypothesis that I advanced above with respect to the final aporia characteristic of the *Political Treatise* and the death of its author.

16. See Martial Gueroult, *Spinoza, II: L'âme (Ethique II)* (Paris: Aubier-Montaigne, 1974), 110–15, 135–42, 165–70, and Macherey, *Hegel ou Spinoza*, 208–25. On all of this, Deleuze's discussion in *Expressionism*, 204–12, is obviously essential.

17. Naturally this critique, if that is what it is, has no meaning except to the extent that Spinoza himself—defining the good as essentially *communicable* (that is, as form rather than as object of collective communication) and wisdom as a *practical* affirmation—is obliged to ask himself what it has to do with *collective practice*. This is why, before any particular critique, Negri must be recognized as the first writer who has, on this point, systematically compared Spinoza with the history and exigencies of his own problematic. See my own interpretation in *Spinoza et la politique*, 114–18.

18. On the impossibility of distinguishing between "will" and "intellect" and on the absurdity of the voluntarist idea of a "free power to suspend judgment," see *Ethics*, II, propositions 48 and 49, with their scholia, which cannot be reproduced here. Spinoza's thesis is directed against Descartes but also, on the other hand, against Calvin. See *Institution de la religion chrétienne*, chapter II (1541 ed.), "De la connaissance de l'homme."

19. See Hobbes, *Leviathan*, chapters XXXIII and XLIII, and *De Cive*, chapter XVIII, 12–13. See also the invaluable commentary by Matheron, "Politique et religion chez Hobbes et Spinoza," in *Anthropologie et politique au XVIIᵉ siècle: Etudes sur Spinoza* (Paris: Vrin, 1986), 123–53.

20. Deleuze sketches a formulation of this principle, precisely regarding the way in which, in the finite mode, there is implied or expressed "a multitude exceeding any number. Spinoza suggests that *the relation that characterizes an existing mode* as a whole is endowed with a kind of elasticity. Here we see the full significance of the passages of the letter to Meyer which allude to the existence of a maximum and a minimum" (*Expressionism*, .)2–203 and 222–223, emphasis added). Earlier in the book he writes, "Individuation in Spinoza is neither qualitative nor extrinsic; it is quantitative and intrinsic, intensive" (197).

Chapter 2 • "Rights of Man" and "Rights of the Citizen"

1. Cf. Etienne Balibar, "Citizen Subject," in *Who Comes after the Subject?* ed. Eduardo Cadava *et al.* (New York: Routledge, 1991), 33–57.

2. Marcel Gauchet, *La Révolution des droits de l'homme* (Paris: Gallimard, 1989).

3. Now collected in Florence Gauthier, *Triomphe et mort du droit naturel en Révolution, 1789-1795-1802* (Paris: P.U.F., 1992).

4. Balibar, "Citizen Subject."

5. A similar view is held by Lucien Jaume, *Hobbes et l'Etat représentatif moderne* (Paris: P.U.F., 1986).

6. The eclipse of the contract in the final draft of the *Declaration*, a major index of its separation from any origins in the doctrine of natural right, is closely linked with the (provisional) abandonment of the idea of a declaration of rights *and duties*. In fact "duties" are the counterpart of "rights" if it is imagined that there is a "reciprocal engagement" between contracting parties, whether between individuals and "themselves," or between individuals and the "community," "society," or "the state."

7. It is well known that the inscription of this right was and continued to be the object of the most heated confrontations, both between the partisans of "order" (who immediately obtained its suppression in 1795) and those of the "continuous revolution" (who in 1793 sought to emphasize its decisive function), and between the supporters of a juridical logic (it would be "contradictory" for a constitutional state to codify its own negation) and those of a social logic (it would be "contradictory" for individuals who are collectively sovereign not to affirm that any government, any institution exists relative to their freedom). The inscription of "resistance to oppression" among the fundamental rights thus entirely confirms that the modality with which we are dealing here is that of the unity of opposites.

8. This is very much the way John Rawls is proceeding—so it seems to me—when, after having first "lexically ordered" his "two principles of justice" (the first, the principle of equal liberty; the second, the principle of difference), he goes on to reformulate the second as a principle of "fair opportunity," which alone is to give practical content to the otherwise formal notion of equality involved in the first principle (see Rawls, *A Theory of Justice* [Oxford: Oxford University Press, 1972], sections 11–13, 31ff., 82). My attention was first drawn to the similarity between the formulation I use ("the proposition of equaliberty") and Rawls's "principle of equal liberty," of which I was unaware, by Jacques Bidet (see his *Théorie de la modernité* [Paris: P.U.F., 1990]). But both formulations have precedents in the nineteenth century, notably in a famous passage of Tocqueville's *Democracy in America*, vol. 2 (1840), part 2, chapter 1. In fact, all this is simply the continuation of a much older and decisive "signifying chain," which traces back to the Roman notion of *aequa libertas* (cf. Cicero, *De Republica*, I, xxxi).

9. Marx did not quite understand this since he saw *community* as being entirely in the revolutionary camp, on account of his being a communist prior to being a socialist.

10. Cf. the studies of Jacques Rancière, most recently *The Ignorant Schoolmaster: Five Lessons in Intellectual Emancipation*, trans. Kristin Ross (Stanford: Stanford University Press, 1991).

Chapter 3 • Fichte and the Internal Border

1. It is Fichte (even more than Herder) who serves Louis Dumont (following so many others) as an example to elucidate the difference between French and German "subcultures" (and thus, whether he wants it or not, of the difference between the "Latin" and "German" characters) as "variants" of "modern individualism." See "A National Variant, I: German Identity: Herder's *Volk* and Fichte's *Nation*," in *Essays on Individualism: Modern Ideology in Anthropological Perspective* (Chicago: University of Chicago Press, 1986), 113–32.

2. In 1915 the German General Staff had printed hundreds of thousands of copies of *Addresses to the German Nation* in order for each German soldier leaving for the front to have one in his pack. Von Moltke is reported to have exclaimed, "Take Fichte into the trenches!" This story takes on its complete signification in light of the fact that Fichte unsuccessfully solicited the King of Prussia for a position as "preacher in the army" during the national war against Napoleon.

3. See, once again, Dumont, for whom the immemorial battle of egalitarianism and hierarchy is waged in Fichte at every moment (whence its "dialectic").

4. Johann Gottlieb Fichte, *Reden an die deutsche Nation*, 5th ed. (Hamburg: Felix Meiner Verlag, 1978), 207; *Addresses to the German Nation*, trans. R. F. Jones and G. H. Turnbull (Chicago: Open Court, 1922), 223–24. Page numbers for all further citations will be given parenthetically in the text: the German edition first, followed by a slash and the English

translation.

5. Fichte places himself here in a long tradition, marked by the texts of Saint-Pierre and Rousseau, but he precisely inverts their conclusions.

6. Fichte, *Der geschlossene Handelsstaat* (1800), in *Ausgewählte politische Schriften*, ed. Zwi Batscha and Richard Saage (Frankfurt a.M.: Suhrkamp, 1977), 59–167.

7. It should be recalled that in Kant's work, beyond any evolution in its themes, "cosmopolitanism" presents one constant: the strict association of the two forms of commerce (circulation of commodities *and* circulation of ideas, thus the free circulation of men as merchants *and* as intellectuals) as the natural (but not sufficient) condition of universal peace. See my article, "Ce qui fait qu'un peuple est un peuple: Rousseau et Kant," *Revue de synthèse* 110 (1989): 391–417.

8. Frederick II, who claimed not to know the German his subjects spoke, had had the "universality of the French language" proclaimed by the Academy of Berlin; see the complete history of this decisive episode in the constitution of "linguistic nationalism" in Germany in Ferdinand Brunot, *Histoire de la langue française* (Paris: Armand Colin, 1935), tome VIII.

9. Ernst Moritz Arndt, *Germanien und Europa* (1802), cited by Friedrich Meinecke, *Weltbürgertum und Nationalstaat: Studien zur Genesis des deutschen Nationalstaates*, 4th ed. (Munich and Berlin: R. Oldenbourg, 1917), 94, note 2.

10. Jean Lerond d'Alembert and Denis Diderot, *Encyclopédie, ou Dictionnaire raisonné des sciences, des arts et des métiers, par une société de gens de lettres* (1751–1767, reprint New York: Pergamon Press, n.d.), 5 vols., *s.v.* "Nation," 2:1003.

11. It is at exactly the same moment that Friedrich Schlegel publishes the inaugural work of historical philology, *Über die Sprache und Weisheit der Indier* (Heidelberg: Mohn und Zimmer, 1808).

12. Cf. Renée Balibar, *L'institution du français: Essai sur le colinguisme des carolingiens à la république* (Paris: P.U.F., 1985).

13. Cf. the "fragments" of a political text from 1813, responding to the king of Prussia's appeal to the people, "Aus dem Entwurfe zu einer politischen Schrift im Frühlinge 1813," *Sämtliche Werke*, ed. Immanuel Hermann Fichte (Berlin: Walter de Gruyter, 1971), 7: 546–73.

Chapter 4 • The Vacillation of Ideology in Marxism

1. Cf. Alain Badiou, *Peut-on penser la politique?* (Paris: Editions du Seuil, 1985).

2. I leave aside the question of Marx's retrieval of the term "ideology" from the French sensualist ideologues and the distortion it undergoes in the process. The most complete study I know of on this point is that of Patrick Quantin, *Les origines de l'idéologie* (Paris: Economica, 1987).

3. There is one notable exception to this schematic account: the reference made in the preface to *A Contribution to the Critique of Political Economy*, in *Karl Marx, Early Writings*, trans. Rodney Livingstone and Gregor Benton (New York: Vintage, 1975), 426, to "ideological forms," identified with "social consciousness." This text is explicitly retrospective, alluding in particular to *The German Ideology*, whose persistent trace it carries.

4. Marx is neither the first nor the last philosopher to take up the problem of the production of idealities, or the process of idealization, in this overdetermined form (see Spinoza before him and Freud after). It is remarkable that these three intellectual efforts, clearly related but formulated within entirely different concepts, have essentially surfaced *independently* of one another. Marx read Spinoza closely in his early years, but by way of an astonishing quid pro quo, inscribed him within the tradition of the *Aufklärung*, and in

his struggle against romantic pantheism, he sees in Spinoza only an apology for rationalism and democracy. On this point see Alexandre Matheron, "Le *Traité théologico-politique*
vu par le jeune Marx," *Cahiers Spinoza* 1 (1977): 159–212.

5. Karl Marx and Frederick Engels, *The German Ideology*, in *Collected Works* (New York:
   International Publishers, 1975—), 5:49. All further citations will be given in the text.

6. Both Marx and Engels bear witness to the true answer: we have seen this proletariat radically stripped of ideology. See the Dedication to Engels's *The Condition of the Working
   Class in England, Collected Works* 4:298: "I found you to be more than mere *English*men,
   members of a single, isolated nation, I found you to be *Men*."

7. I am thinking of a contemporary example, Michel Foucault's "episteme," and more generally of the universals of the culturalists. The common ancestor of all these notions is, of
   course, Hegel's concept of the *Zeitgeist*.

8. Marx, preface to *A Contribution to the Critique of Political Economy*, 426.

9. Marx and Engels, *Manifesto of the Communist Party*, in *The Revolutions of 1848*, ed. David
   Fernbach (New York: Vintage, 1974), 86. All further citations will be given in the text.

10. Indeed, Marx, who is faithful on this point to his own German ideology, suggests that the
    proletariat alone can save the classical culture of humanity (Homer, Dante, Shakespeare)
    from its degeneration into bourgeois philistinism. See S. S. Prawer, *Karl Marx and World
    Literature* (Oxford: The Clarendon Press, 1976).

11. See Marx and Engels, "Address of the Central Committee to the Communist League
    (March 1850)," in *Revolutions of 1848*, 319–30, and Marx, *The Class Struggles in France,
    1848 to 1850*, in *Surveys from Exile*, ed. David Fernbach (New York: Vintage, 1974), 123.

12. The then-dominant model in Marx's thought regarding this strategy is that of a "perma-
    nent revolution" which offers the long-term transformation of bourgeois revolutions into
    proletarian revolutions and the short-term transformation of the radical democratic pro-
    gram into the communist program (because the polarization of the class struggles anni-
    hilates the petty-bourgeoisie as an autonomous force). See Stanley Moore, *Three Tactics*
    (New York: Monthly Review Press, 1963), and my article, "Dictature du prolétariat," in
    Dictionnaire critique du marxisme, ed. Georges Labica and Gérard Bensussan (Paris:
    P.U.F., 1983), 266–74.

13. Although the pairs abstract/concrete and thought/real are not strictly commutative,
    Engels's formulations on this are clearly more empiricist than those of Marx in the
    (unpublished) 1857 introduction to the *Critique of Political Economy*, where it is the *sci-
    entific method*, inasmuch as it proceeds from the abstract to the "concrete in thought,"
    that *seems* to engender the real, starting from the concept, and thus creates an idealistic
    illusion. In his critical reading of Hegel, Marx touches on the idea of the conditions and
    ideological effects inherent in scientific practice itself, but he does not use the term. See
    Marx, Introduction to *Grundrisse: Foundations of the Critique of Political Economy*, trans.
    Martin Nicolaus (New York: Vintage, 1973), 100–02.

14. See Engels, *Anti-Dühring, Collected Works* 25:88–89. All further citations given in text.

15. From the *Grundrisse* to the "Critique of the Gotha Program," by way of books 1 and 3 of
    Capital, Marx presents a similar critical analysis of the categories "freedom" and "equali-
    ty" as an internal reflection of commodity production and circulation, which produces
    (for example, in the chapter on commodity fetishism) a comparison between legal and
    religious idealities (or abstractions) and a substitution of one for the other within history.
    However, what is never really clear in Marx is whether the law itself is ideological or
    whether a distinction ought to be made between law (property, contract, etc.) and legal
    ideology (freedom and equality).

16. See the examples given in Ulrich Dierse, "Ideologie," in *Geschichtliche Grundbegriffe:
    Historisches Lexicon zur politisch-sozialen Sprache in Deutschland*, ed. Otto Brunner,

Werner Conze, and Reinhart Koselleck (Stuttgart: Ernst Klett Verlag, 1972–1990), 3:131–69.

17. The "terminological" problem that Engels comes across here is far from idiosyncratic. At the same time, French positivists like Littré also posit a substitution of "worldview" for "philosophy" in order to designate the form in which the positivist spirit stops being spontaneous and unconscious and becomes self-conscious and systematic. Cf. Ernest Coumet, "La philosophie positive d'Emile Littré," *Revue de synthèse* 103 (1982): 177–214.

18. On the use of the term "Marxism" and on the ambivalent relations first Marx and then Engels had with it, see Georges Haupt's detailed account in "Marx and Marxism," in *History of Marxism*, ed. E. J. Hobsbawm *et al.*, (Bloomington: Indiana University Press, 1982), 1:265–89. On the "crisis of Marxism" after Engels's death, see Roberto Racinaro, *La crisi del marxismo nella revisione di fine secolo* (Bari: De Donato, 1978); Hans-Josef Steinberg, "Il partito e la formazione dell'ortodossia marxista," in *Storia del Marxismo*, ed. E. J. Hobsbawm *et al.* (Turin: Einaudi, 1982), 2:181–200.

19. Cf. Engels's article, "Social Classes—Necessary and Superfluous," *Collected Works* 24:415–18.

20. The first edition of Friedrich Albert Lange's *The History of Materialism*, which represents the union between "Marxist," "neo-Kantian," and "Darwinian" circles, was published in 1866. Engels rejects its epistemological theses, but borrows a scheme or rather a historical plan from it. It is only with Dilthey, at the end of the century, as we know, that the term *Weltanschauung*, of romantic origins (Schelling, Schleiermacher; Hegel to the contrary uses it very little) becomes the watchword of the philosophy of history and hermeneutics developed by the vitalist current of neo-Kantianism against the rationalist current (from Cohen to Cassirer).

21. The idea of a history of thought, understood in this way, obviously leads to several interpretations or research programs: that of an empirical history of the sciences and their effects upon philosophy; that of a "history of the theoretical" of the sort proposed by Althusser in *Reading Capital*, trans. Ben Brewster (London: Verso, 1979), 49–51, reviving an expression of Hegel's; and, finally, that of a history of "class struggle within theory," ultimately considered by the same Althusser as the proper terrain of philosophy and which we will come across later on in taking up Engels's text. See "Philosophy as a Revolutionary Weapon" and "Lenin and Philosophy," in *Lenin and Philosophy and Other Essays*, trans. Ben Brewster (New York: Monthly Review Press, 1971), 11–22 and 64–68, and "Reply to John Lewis" and "Elements of Self-Criticism," in *Essays in Self-Criticism*, trans. Grahame Lock (London: New Left Books, 1976), 37–39, 58–59, and 142.

22. B. M. Kedrov's study, *La classification des sciences*, vol. 1: *Engels et ses prédécesseurs*, (Moscow: Editions du progès, 1977), is unfortunately flawed by his persistent desire to present Engels's thinking in terms of "the Marxist solution" to "the problem of the classification of the sciences." It seems, by contrast, that there are some original ideas to be found in the highly documented study by Sven Eric Liedman, *Motsatsernas Spel: Friedrich Engels' filosofi och 1800-talets vetenskaper* ["The Game of Contradictions : The Philosophy of Friedrich Engels and the Sciences of the 19th Century"] (Lund: Bo Cavefors Bokförlag, 1977), 2 vols., but I have only been able to consult a short résumé of it in English.

23. See Engels to Pyotr Lavrov, 12 November 1875, *Collected Works* 45:106–9, and "Bruno Bauer and Early Christianity," *Collected Works* 24:435.

24. Georges Canguilhem, Georges Lapassade, Jacques Piquemal, and Jacques Ulmannn, *Du développement à l'évolution au XIXe siècle* (Paris: P.U.F., 1985) (reprinted from *Thalès* 11 [1960]), is far and away the most rigorous study of the history and concepts of evolutionism *before* and *after* Darwin. See Ernst Haeckel, *The History of Creation: or The Development of the Earth and Its Inhabitants by the Action of Natural Causes*, trans. E. Ray

Lankester (London: Henry S. King, 1876), 2 vols.

25. Engels, *Ludwig Feuerbach and the End of Classical German Philosophy* (1888), *Collected Works* 26:398. All further citations given in text.

26. A striking illustration of this theme can be found in H. G. Wells, *A Short History of the World*, which tells the story of humanity starting from the formation of the solar system and ending with socialism.

27. Marx, *Capital*, vol. 1, trans. Ben Fowkes (New York: Vintage, 1977), 929.

28. See Canguilhem, *Ideology and Rationality in the History of the Life Sciences*, trans. Arthur Goldhammer (Cambridge, Mass.: The MIT Press, 1988), as well as Yvette Conry, ed., *De Darwin au darwinisme, science et idéologie* (Paris: Vrin, 1983).

29. See, in particular, "Bruno Bauer and Early Christianity," *Collected Works* 24:427–35, which constructs a parallel between "modern ideologists," those of the ancient world (philosophers and jurists), and those of the medieval world (theologians and clerics). All these texts were first published in *Neue Zeit*, Kautsky's review and the bastion of orthodox "Marxism."

30. Let us judge here the extent of this progress in relation to Marx's formulations in *Capital*, vol. 1 (610), where it is the sole regulative intervention of the state (factory legislation) that is given as society's "conscious reaction" to its own "organism."

31. Gramsci, from this point of view, is not mistaken in posing together the problem of proletarian hegemony and that of the "crisis of the state" (ignored by Engels, if not by Lenin).

32. Engels and Karl Kautsky, "Lawyer's Socialism," *Collected Works* 26:597–98 (translation modified). It is to the credit of Peter Schöttler, who gives us an illuminating analysis of it, to have brought to our attention the importance of this text. See his study, "Friedrich Engels and Karl Kautsky as Critics of 'Legal Socialism,'" *International Journal for the Sociology of Law* 14 (1986): 1–32.

33. One constantly comes across this denial of the existence of a legal ideology, articulated from very different perspectives. The most delicate position to discuss would, or course, be that of "juridical positivism" (Kelsen), which explicitly posits an opposition of the norms of positive law and "legal ideology," against natural right. A recent example is in the work of Jean-François Lyotard, starting from his "pragmatic" analyses of the relations of communication in late capitalism. See, for example, *Instructions païennes* (Paris: Galilée, 1977), 55–56, "showing" that there is no bourgeois legal ideology because, generally speaking, there is no dominant ideology in capitalism; capital as such would be *indifferent to ideology* (to "semantics"), in contrast to archaic structures like the state, the party, the Church, and so on. Likewise *money*, as a *medium* of communication, would exclude ideology, even legal ideology (76).

34. See Engels "[On the Association of the Future]," *Collected Works* 26:553.

35. See my article cited above, "Dictature du prolétariat." It is striking that, during this period, Engels is moved to say something new about the ancient city (in *The Origin of the Family*) which clarifies the "civic" sense of the idea of community present within the term "communism." This clarifies the ulterior motive behind the curiously Aristotelian phrase in the *Critique of the Erfurt Program* (written against the anarchists), according to which "the workers are political by nature." More than a nostalgic definition of politics, by way of the Greek example, it is a question of thinking the crux of the proletarian worldview in reference to what, throughout the entire classical tradition, symbolizes politics as such. Following on the analysis of the Greek city as the first form, in its contradictory development, of the fusion of politics and the state [*du politique et de l'étatique*] in the history of class struggle, it is a way of showing that, in the transition to communism, the critical stake of struggle is the possibility of dissociating politics from the state [*dissocier le politique de l'étatique*] by associating (or fusing) politics with labor, *praxis* with *poiesis*: two

poles of a contradiction that cuts across all of history. See Etienne Balibar, Cesare Luporini, and André Tosel, *Marx et sa critique de la politique* (Paris: Maspero, 1979).

36. Engels, "On the History of Early Christianity," *Collected Works* 27:457–61. Michèle Bertrand is one of the few in France to have studied this text, in *Le statut de la religion chez Marx et Engels* (Paris: Editions sociales, 1979).

37. Gustave Le Bon's *The Psychology of Crowds*, which Freud was to discuss (for lack of anything better?) in *Group Psychology and the Analysis of the Ego*, was also published in 1895. Labriola and Plekhanov, in particular, were quite preoccupied by the question of the relation between the "theory of ideology" and "social psychology." Le Bon's social psychology was to have a particular influence on Sorel. It does not consider itself to be "materialist" but "determinist" and, correlatively, is not founded on the class struggle but on "races." See, despite its disputable method of pure "history of ideas," the highly documented study by Zeev Sternhell, *La droite révolutionnaire, 1885-1914: Les origines françaises du fascisme* (Paris: Editions du Seuil, 1978).

Chapter 5 • In Search of the Proletariat

1. Karl Marx, *Capital*, vol. 1, trans. Ben Fowkes (New York: Vintage, 1977). Hereafter cited in the text.

2. See my article, "Dictature du prolétariat," in *Dictionnaire critique du marxisme*, ed. Georges Labica and Gérard Bensussan (Paris: P.U.F., 1983), 266–74, and my essay, "Etat, parti, idéologie: esquisse d'un problème," in Etienne Balibar, Cesare Luporini, and André Tosel, *Marx et sa critique de la politique* (Paris: Maspero, 1979), 107–67.

3. Marx to Paul Lafargue, 19 April 1870, in Karl Marx and Frederick Engels, *Collected Works* (New York: International Publishers, 1975—), 43:490–91, emphasis added.

4. See the works of Elie Halévy and Charles Andler, and more recently of Bert Andreas, Henri Desroche, Jacques Grandjonc, Jacques Rancière, and Michael Löwy. The essential text is probably *The Doctrine of Saint-Simon: An Exposition* (1829), trans. George G. Iggers (Boston: Beacon Press, 1958).

5. *Cinq études du matérialisme historique* (Paris: Maspero, 1974).

6. See "The Alleged Splits in the International," *The First International and After*, ed. David Fernbach (New York: Vintage, 1974), 314. This more than ambiguous phrase largely determines Lenin's argument in *State and Revolution*. See my article, "Bakouninisme," in *Dictionnaire critique du marxisme*, 85–91.

7. *Anti-Dühring, Collected Works* 25:268.

8. *The Manifesto of the Communist Party*, in *The Revolutions of 1848*, ed. David Fernbach (New York: Vintage, 1974), 79.

9. On this point, see Oskar Negt's excellent indications in "Il marxismo e la teoria della rivoluzione nell'ultimo Engels," in *Storia del Marxismo*, ed. E. J. Hobsbawm, *et al.* (Turin: Einaudi, 1982), 2:107–79.

10. See Henri Lefebvre, *De l'état*, vol. 2: *Théorie marxiste de l'état de Hegel à Mao* (Paris: Union générale d'éditions, 1976), 272–93.

11. Marx to Joseph Weydemeyer, 5 March 1852, *Collected Works* 39:60–66.

12. *Capital*, vol. 3, trans. David Fernbach (New York: Vintage, 1981), 927; translation modified, emphasis added.

13. Credit must be given to Mario Tronti, *Operai e Capitale* (Turin: Einaudi, 1966), and to Italian *"operaismo"* for having stated in a very decisive way the political and technological unity of factory despotism. The Chinese cultural revolution, in its ascending phase, and the working-class struggles of the 1960s and 1970s, were to confirm the soundness of this point of view, but also to invalidate the "voluntarist catastrophism" which tended on such

a basis to reduce society to the factory, and class politics to "workers' self-organization." See also the collection of texts edited by André Gorz, *The Division of Labor: The Labor Process and Class-Struggle in Modern Capitalism* (Atlantic Highlands, N.J.: Humanities Press, 1976), as well as Robert Linhart, *The Assembly Line*, trans. Margaret Crosland (Amherst: University of Massachusetts Press, 1981), and *Lénine, les paysans, Taylor: Essai d'analyse matérialiste historique de la naissance du système productif soviétique* (Paris: Editions du Seuil, 1976).

14. Cf. my articles "Pouvoir" and "Appareil," in *Dictionnaire critique du marxisme*, 707–12 and 49–56.

15. See "Marx's Critique," in Louis Althusser and Etienne Balibar, *Reading Capital*, trans. Ben Brewster (London: Verso, 1979), 165–81.

16. A close confrontation would be very instructive in this respect between the text of *Capital* and that of J.-C.-L. Simonde de Sismondi's *New Principles of Political Economy* (1819 and 1827), trans. Richard Hyse (New Brunswick, N.J.: Transaction Publishers, 1991). Marx transposes a whole series of formulations from Sismondi's text. What characterizes Sismondi is his reformulation of the discourse of political economy in terms of a *capital/proletariat* antithesis. But this "proletariat" has a purely economistic significance (see, for example, his definition of impoverishment as a "disproportion of relations," resulting from the "wrong economic direction"). Cf. Jacques Grandjonc, *Communisme/Kommunismus/Communism: Origine et développement international de la terminologie communautaire prémarxiste des utopistes aux néo-babouvistes, 1785-1842* (Trier: Karl-Marx-Haus, 1989).

17. A beautiful comparison between Marx's use of metaphor—related to the idea of the role of the masses and the "deep" or "dark" side of history—and other nineteenth-century writers (Hugo, etc.) has been carried out by Pierre Macherey, "Autour de Victor Hugo: Figures de l'homme d'en bas," in *A quoi pense la littérature?* (Paris: P.U.F., 1990), 77–95.

18. Adolphe Quêtelet, *A Treatise on Man and the Development of his Faculties* (1835) (Gainesville, Fla.: Scholars' Facsimiles and Reprints, 1969). See the classical commentary by Maurice Halbwachs, *La théorie de l'homme moyen: Essai sur Quêtelet et la statistique morale* (Paris: Alcan, 1912).

19. See Engels to August Bebel, 18–28 March 1875, *Collected Works* 24:67–73. See also my commentary in *Marx et sa critique de la politique*.

20. I have resumed the discussion of this thesis in my essay, "From Class Struggle to Struggle without Classes?" in Etienne Balibar and Immanuel Wallerstein, *Race, Nation, Class: Ambiguous Identities*, trans. Chris Turner (London: Verso, 1991), 153–84.

Chapter 6 • Politics and Truth

1. The organizing "myth," Sorel would say. But, conversely, does not every organization have its own working myth? Gramsci, in particular, asked this question.

2. The disappearance of the "leader/theoretician" in the form this historical character took from Marx to Mao Zedong, which seems irreversible, is a particularly pertinent index of the crisis of the party form in the workers' movement.

3. Karl Marx, *Capital*, vol. 3, trans. David Fernbach (New York: Vintage, 1981), 927.

4. Althusser had analyzed Engels's theoretical construction (following the text of Engels's letter to Joseph Bloch of 21 September 1890) in the appendix to his study on "Contradiction and Overdetermination," the publication of which was delayed "to spare certain susceptibilities." See Louis Althusser, *For Marx*, trans. Ben Brewster (London: New Left Books, 1977), 117–28.

5. Cf. Solange Mercier-Josa, "Esprit du peuple et idéologie," in *Pour lire Hegel et Marx* (Paris:

Editions sociales, 1980), 69–116. See my own commentary on the symmetry of the "great man" and the "masses" in Hegel, in "Marx, the Joker in the Pack (or the Excluded Middle)," trans. David Watson, *Economy and Society* 14 (1985): 1–27.

6. In this situation each word becomes a double-edged weapon. The notion of a "proletarian worldview" can act as an index for working-class ideologies (in the sense of practices rather than opinions) irreducible to the dominant ideology. See, in an analogous fashion, the opposition between "*bürgerliche*" and "*proletarische Öffentlichkeit*" proposed by Oskar Negt and Alexander Kluge, against Habermas, in *Öffentlichkeit und Erfahrung: Zur Organisationsanalyse von bürgerliche und proletarisher Öffentlichkeit* (Frankfurt: Suhrkamp, 1972). But it can also prevent any critical elaboration of these ideologies upon themselves to the extent that, according to the logic of speculative empiricism, it posits these ideologies as direct "representatives" of the universal (and uses them to forge the ahistorical archetype of the worker). Conversely, it is not at all clear that the fact of speaking about *working-class ideology*, as Marx and Engels do not do, is enough to ruin the specular relation. "The worker" is a place in the capitalist labor process; in the guise of "giving the power" of words or ideas to the workers, such a notion perpetuates them *in their place* (even "puts" them in it, in the sense of "putting someone in his place"). It can thus be the instrument of a "new bourgeoisie" (including a new party bourgeoisie, subaltern but tenacious). To a large extent, this would explain how, in "really existing socialism," workers could be dominated (and condemned to silence) *in their own name*.

7. Marx, *The Poverty of Philosophy*, in Karl Marx and Frederick Engels, *Collected Works* (New York: International Publishers, 1975—), 6:174.

8. Classical political theory from Machiavelli to Hobbes and Rousseau (with its conformists and its heretics) is an example of this vacillation of ideology from the theological to the juridical, with the moment of political recognition of the real state that it involves. This moment, however, is never "pure" (even in Machiavelli), since the untwisting movement of the theological cover is always already the twisting motion of the juridical cover.

9. Marx, "Critique of the Gotha Program," in *The First International and After*, ed. David Fernbach (New York: Vintage, 1974), 359.

10. See Engels to Wilhelm Bracke, 11 October 1875, and to August Bebel, 12 October 1875, *Collected Works* 45:94–98.

11. See the collection *Le retrait du politique* (Paris: Galilée, 1983), and particularly the essay by Denis Kambouchner, "De la condition la plus générale de la philosophie politique," 113–58, which vigorously contests this possibility.

12. *Collected Works* 25:268.

13. This does not mean that proletarian ideology has become "dominant" in the modern state; but it undoubtedly has played a determining role in its transformations, both before and, even more, after the Soviet revolution, the lessons of which bourgeois capitalists have been assimilating and preaching against ever since. Every bourgeois state today, even in the "capitalist world," is in a strong sense *postrevolutionary*. Negri is correct on this point; see *La classe ouvrière contre l'état* (Paris: Galilée, 1976).

14. Of course it is *for us* that there is a contradiction in seeing Marx and Engels incapable of suspecting that the politics of class struggle—able to tear off the "masks" of religion and law—should also be, by another turn of reason's screws, able *to engender its own masks*. As a consequence, *no absolute end* can be assigned to the dialectic of the relations between the dominant or state ideology and revolutionary ideology. As for the implications of such a position for a theory of discourse, see the studies of Michel Pêcheux: *Language, Semantics, and Ideology*, trans. Harbans Nagpal (New York: St. Martin's Press, 1982); and (with Françoise Gadet), *La langue introuvable* (Paris: Maspero, 1981).

15. Cf. "XXX," "L'idéologie technocratique et le teilhardisme," *Les temps modernes* 243

(August 1966): 245–95. (The actual author was François Regnault).

16. Engels to Karl Kautsky, 8 November 1884, in Karl Marx and Friedrich Engels, *Werke* (Berlin: Dietz Verlag, 1964–1969), 36:230.

17. I refer here to the analyses of Dominique Lecourt, *L'ordre et les jeux: Le positivisme logique en question* (Paris: Grasset, 1981); and *La philosophie sans feinte* (Paris: J.-E. Hallier/Albin Michel, 1982).

18. See V. I. Lenin, "Kommunismus," in *Collected Works* (London: Lawrence and Wishart, 1960–1970), 45 vols., 31:166, and *Philosophical Notebooks, Collected Works* 38:360.

19. This is Althusser's thesis of the "overdetermination" and "underdetermination" of contradictions. Cf. "Contradiction and Overdetermination," in *For Marx*, 87–116, and "Is It Simple to Be a Marxist in Philosophy," in *Philosophy and the Spontaneous Philosophy of the Scientists and Other Essays*, ed. Gregory Elliott (London: Verso, 1990), 221–23.

20. This is what Althusser tried to express by constructing a Marxist topography around the paradoxical concept of an "absent cause," a term inspired by psychoanalysis and Spinozism. See "Marx's Immense Theoretical Revolution," in Louis Althusser and Etienne Balibar, *Reading Capital*, trans. Ben Brewster (London: Verso, 1979), 182–93. On "practical correctness," see *Philosophy and the Spontaneous Philosophy of the Scientists*, 102–5.

Chapter 7 • Fascism, Psychoanalysis, Freudo-Marxism

1. This was pointed out in 1973 by Elisabeth Roudinesco: "But the question left hanging by Reich remains" (*Un discours au réel* [Tours: Editions Mame, 1973], 35).

2. I have developed this notion in my book, written in collaboration with Immanuel Wallerstein, *Race, Nation, Class: Ambiguous Identities*, trans. Chris Turner (London: Verso, 1991).

3. Sigmund Freud, *Group Psychology and the Analysis of the Ego*, in *The Standard Edition of the Complete Psychological Works of Sigmund Freud*, ed. James Strachey (London: Hogarth Press, 1955), 18:116.

4. On the contrary, could it not be suggested that the Oedipal complex is not the *foundation* of the familial structure but the inscription of the conflict and variability of subjective positions within the familial institution, which thus forbids the roles it prescribes from being imposed as simple functions "normally" fulfilled by individuals (except in case of "abnormality")?

5. Wilhelm Reich, *The Mass Psychology of Fascism*, trans. Vincent R. Carfagno (New York: Farrar, Strauss & Giroux, 1970), 101.

6. It is known that, at the limit, in the policy proposed by Himmler (and enacted by him within the S.S.), the "legitimate" family no longer has any importance with respect to the "racial purity" of "biological" filiations, which leads to the encouragement of state-controlled prostitution. Cf. George L. Mosse, *Nationalism and Sexuality: Respectability and Abnormal Sexuality in Modern Europe* (New York: Howard Fertig, 1985).

7. Freud, *Group Psychology*, 18:123.

Chapter 8 • Racism as Universalism

This chapter was originally delivered as a paper at the New School for Social Research, New York, on October 6, 1988, at the request of the departments of Philosophy and Political Science. I want to thank the chairpersons of the two departments, Dr. Agnes Heller and Dr. Elizabeth Sanders, and all the colleagues and students who took part in this discussion.

1. I refer to my book, in collaboration with Immanuel Wallerstein, *Race, Nation, Class:*

Ambiguous Identities, trans. Chris Turner (London: Verso, 1991).

2. Let us mention in passing that the notion of *class*, although even more explicitly conflictual in a sense, does not work exactly the same way, at least not necessarily: in the guise of a concept of *class struggle*, as it was used by the socialist, and especially by the Marxist tradition, it has an immediately universalistic orientation.

3. Derrida's concept of "phallogocentrism" is probably the most sophisticated version of this argument.

4. Ordinarily, one eventually "chooses" the gender which is proposed or imposed by the family, the society—but not always. Let me mention in passing that the English language, by distinguishing between *sex* and *gender*, is clearer, but also more conciliatory than the French: the distinction blurs the paradox which lies in the fact that individuals have to "choose"—by completely dedicating themselves to that task—something which is unavoidable, or compulsory. This is the core of the problem of "identity," which explains why it is always communicated with the sensation of "destiny."

5. National revolutions are privileged circumstances in this respect, and a comparative study going from the English Revolution to the American, the French, the Russian, the Chinese, etc., would be most instructive.

6. See chapter 3 above.

7. I upheld this argument in a previous paper, "Sujets ou citoyens? (pour l'égalité)," *Les frontières de la démocratie* (Paris: La Découverte, 1992), 42–71.

8. See in particular the recent book by Louis Sala-Molins, *Le code noir ou le calvaire de Canaan* (Paris: P.U.F., 1987).

9. See my paper, "Ce qui fait qu'un peuple est un peuple: Rousseau et Kant," *Revue de synthèse* 110 (1989): 391–417.

10. That is, no more than saying, for example, Lévi-Strauss today "is a racist" because his concept of universality has a prerequisite that human "cultures" are incompatible (although he has now drawn for this prerequisite the conclusion that their "difference"—practically amounting to their remaining unbred or uncrossed—is a condition for the survival of the species or civilization).

11. The idea of contemporary "neo-racism" as being essentially a "differentialist" ideology (relying not so much upon alleged biological inequalities but upon the idea that "cultural differences" *indirectly* create inequalities and conflicts) was originally put forward in France by Colette Guillaumin, *L'idéologie raciste, genèse et langage actuel* (Paris: Mouton, 1972), and later on elaborated by Pierre-André Taguieff, *La force du préjugé: Essai sur le racisme et ses doubles* (Paris: La Découverte, 1988).

12. See his two papers, "The Ideological Tensions of Capitalism: Universalism versus Racism and Sexism," in *Race, Nation, Class*, 29–36, and "Culture as the Ideological Battleground of the Modern World-System," in *Geopolitics and Geoculture: Essays on the Changing World-System* (Cambridge: Cambridge University Press, and Paris: Editions de la Maison des sciences de l'homme, 1991), 158–83.

13. Theodor W. Adorno, Else Frenkel-Brunswik, Daniel J. Levinson and R. Nevitt Sanford, *The Authoritarian Personality* (New York: Harper and Row, 1950), 2 vols.

14. I have started to develop this point in "The Nation Form: History and Ideology," in *Race, Nation, Class*, 86–106.

15. The desire for knowledge is always individual, although it can never be fulfilled individually. It seems to me that the notion of a "collective desire" is meaningless. But an isolated, self-satisfying desire is impossible, as Spinoza, among others, already knew.

16. See my chapter on "Racism and Nationalism," in *Race, Nation, Class*, 37–67.

17. You might think that the difference lies in the fact that "patriotism" requires *dying* for one's country, whereas nationalism requires *killing* for it, but it is precisely on this point

that the distinction practically collapses: "killing, not murder" (when it is for the country's sake).

18. Even the European Community is trying to build itself as the same sort of quasi-national state: for that purpose it relied initially upon the ideology of collective resistance to the totalitarian threat from the East, now it is more and more relying upon the ideology of cultural, religious, and economic resistance to the South.

19. For the French case, see Renée Balibar, *L'institution du français: Essai sur le colinguisme des carolingiens à la République* (Paris: P.U.F., 1985).

20. For example if you take France and the United States (two countries which have their population made up of immigrants on a massive scale over a long period, the two "melting pots" of the Western world), they display completely different patterns. In order to be a "true" American, you must belong to some "ethnic community," or simply remember that your roots were in some ethnic community; you are an Irish-American, or Polish, or Jewish, or Hispanic (not very easy), or Black (not very easy either), or WASP (no problem). In order to be a true Frenchman, you must belong to some "province" or simply remember that your roots were in some local community; you are French because, although you may live in Paris, you are "from" Marseilles, or Brittany, or Auvergne, or even "lost" Algiers.

21. Only after I had proposed this notion of a "fictitious ethnicity" (in *Race, Nation, Class*) did I discover that it lies at the heart of Americo Castro's great book, *La Realidad Histórica de España*, 3rd ed. (Mexico City: Editorial Porrúa, 1966). From a different (Lacanian) angle, see also the remarkable chapter on "gatherings" (*rassemblements*) in Jean-Claude Milner, *Les noms indistincts* (Paris: Editions du Seuil, 1983), 105–15.

Chapter 9 • What Is a Politics of the Rights of Man?

The point of departure of this text is a lecture given in July 1991 at the Institut français of Santiago and the University of Playa Ancha in Valparaiso, Chile.

1. Among the notable exceptions it is obviously necessary to cite Claude Lefort, "Politics and Human Rights," in *The Political Forms of Modern Society*, ed. John B. Thompson (Cambridge, Mass.: The MIT Press, 1986), 239–72.

2. Marcel Gauchet, *La Révolution des droits de l'homme* (Paris: Gallimard, 1989), xxv: "the imperative of the rights of man has been *definitively* dissociated from political forms" (emphasis added).

3. Cf. E. P. Thompson *et al.*, *Exterminism and Cold War* (London: Verso, 1982), including my own contribution to the debate of 1981–1982, "The Long March for Peace," 135–52.

4. [Dirección Nacional de Inteligencia, the Chilean secret police from 1974 to 1977. — Translators note.]

5. Cf. Emmanuel Terray, *La politique dans la caverne* (Paris: Editions du Seuil, 1990).

6. I can only agree with Claude Lefort's formulations on this fundamental point: the rights of man "go beyond any particular formulation which has been given of them; and this means that their formulation contains the demand for their reformulation, or that acquired rights are necessarily called upon to support new rights....The democratic state goes beyond the limits traditionally assigned to the *état de droit*. It tests out rights which have not yet been incorporated in it . . ." ("Politics and Human Rights," 258).

7. Cf. Etienne Balibar, *Spinoza et la politique* (Paris: P.U.F., 1985); Antonio Negri, *The Savage Anomaly: The Power of Spinoza's Metaphysics and Politics*, trans. Michael Hardt (Minneapolis: University of Minnesota Press, 1991).

8. Karl Marx, "Provisional Rules of the International Association of Working Men" (1864), in *The First International and After*, ed. David Fernbach (New York: Vintage, 1974), 82.

9. Cf. also Jacques Rancière, "Les usages de la démocratie," in *Aux bords du politique* (Paris: Osiris, 1990), 62: "Thus is defined a labor of equality that can never be simply a demand made or a pressure exerted upon the other, but must always be, at the same time, a proof given to oneself. This is what *emancipation* means. Emancipation is leaving a tutelage. But no one leaves a social tutelage except by him or herself. . . ." It would be interesting to discuss this reversal of the etymological signification of the term emancipation (which comes from Roman law). Cf. also, as far as women (before the workers) are concerned, Elisabeth G. Sledziewski, "Révolution française: le tournant," in *Histoire des femmes en occident*, ed. George Duby and Michèle Perrot (Paris: Plon, 1991), 4:49: "integrating female citizens into the political body makes them decision-makers, active subjects of the revolution on a level with men: a hypothesis that many find unbearable at the time. On the other hand the idea of men making civil laws that emancipate women is more reassuring, since women then remain in the position of objects. . . ."

10. Pierre-Joseph Proudhon, *What Is Property? An Inquiry into the Principle of Right and of Government* (1840), trans. Benjamin R. Tucker (New York: Dover, 1970), 44–53.

11. It is precisely on this path that, each in its own way and motivated by divergent intentions, the declarations of Year I (1793) and Year III (1795) set out, immediately bringing into play the notions of goods, revenues, labor, industry, service, employment, production, social order....

12. Cf. Florence Gauthier, *Triomphe et mort du droit naturel en Révolution 1789–1795–1802* (Paris: P.U.F., 1992), which in particular recalls how, beginning in 1789, the proclamation of martial law is associated with the defense of economic freedom against popular claims for subsistence goods. On the opposite side, faced with the "new despotism" of the rich, Robespierre gives "the first theorization of the natural universal right to existence, and explodes the contradiction between political freedom and the natural right of private property in material goods....(He) clearly exposes the way that proprietors put themselves in contradiction with the *Declaration*-Constitution by restraining *the general idea of property* to material goods alone (...)." Cf. also E. P. Thompson *et al.*, *La guerre du blé au XVIIIe siècle: La critique populaire contre le libéralisme économique au XVIIIe siècle* (Paris: Editions de la passion, 1988).

13. This is why the ethico-political legitimacy of pure liberalism is entirely dependent on the postulate that every individual will *always* be able to live from his or her work.

14. Cf. Albert Soboul, "Utopie et Révolution française," in *Histoire générale du socialisme*, ed. J. Droz (Paris: P.U.F., 1972), 1:195–254.

15. Babeuf had already spoken of a "right to employment." See Viktor Moiseevich Dalin, *Gracchus Babeuf à la veille et pendant la Révolution française 1785-1794* (Moscow: Progress, 1987), 281ff. In Fourier see in particular the *Théorie des quatre mouvements et des destinées générales* (1808), ed. S. Debout (Paris: J.-J. Pauvert, 1967), 219: "I will limit myself to indicating the subject that would have to be discussed, the *right to employment*. I have no intention of entering a debate on these daydreams of a renewed Greece, on these entirely ridiculous rights of man. After the revolutions that their reign has caused us, will it be believed that we are headed for new troubles, for having forgotten the first and only useful one of these rights: the right to employment, which our politicians, following their habit of omitting the primordial questions of each branch of study, never mention. . . ."

16. See the text of the debate of 11 and 13 September 1848 at the National Assembly in *Ainsi parlait la France: Les heures chaudes de l'Assemblée Nationale*, ed. Jean-François Kahn (Paris: Editions Jean-Claude Simoën, 1978).

17. It is well known that, surrounded by diverse qualifications, the right to employment is symbolically inscribed in the preamble to the French Constitution of 1946 (confirmed in 1958), as well as in the Universal Declaration of Human Rights adopted by the United

Nations in 1948. Considered as the counterpart of the duty to work, it obviously formed one of the pillars of the successive Soviet constitutions.

18. The confrontation with the French Civil Code of 1804 is instructive: "Property is the right to enjoy and to dispose of things in the most absolute fashion, provided that a use prohibited by laws or regulations is not made of them" (art. 544). Read, on this point, the brilliant commentary by Elisabeth G. Sledziewski, who emphasizes the distance between this "Roman" formula and the text of 1789, concluding that the major function of properly bourgeois "individualism" (that of the Civil Code) is to "economize on politics by applying 'state power' directly to the treatment of individual interests" (*Révolutions du sujet* [Paris: Meridiens-Klincksieck, 1989], 44–59).

19. At the heart of the expropriation of workers (better: of individuals *qua* workers), there is thus the division of "manual labor" and "intellectual labor" in its different forms and with all its conditions: inequalities of formation, parcelling of tasks, prohibition of "horizontal" communication. This, by contrast, points up the organic function filled by intellectual activity in all effective appropriation, thus in property itself.

20. Cf. Karl Marx, *Capital*, vol. 1, trans. Ben Fowkes (New York: Vintage, 1977), 927–30.

21. Or of total *taking possession*: *Besitznahme* in German. Hegel distinguishes between possession (*Besitz*) or taking possession, and property (*Eigentum*), but he establishes a strict correlation between the two, making property the juridical, that is, "objective" form of subjective possession. See G. W. F. Hegel, *Elements of the Philosophy of Right*, §45, ed. Allen W. Wood, trans. H. B. Nisbet (Cambridge: Cambridge University Press, 1991), 76–77: "To have even external power over something (*in meiner selbst äußeren Gewalt*) constitutes *possession*, just as the particular circumstance that I make something my own (*zu dem Meinigem mache*) out of natural need, drive, and arbitrary will is the particular interest of possession (*das besondere Interesse des Besitzes*). But the circumstance that I, as free will, am an object (*gegenständlich*) to myself in what I possess and only become an actual will by this means constitutes the genuine and rightful element in possession, the determination of *property*." Marx on the other hand, in *Capital*, takes up the same concepts while inverting their positions, which allows him to think possession as a "social relation" of appropriation. Cf. Etienne Balibar, "On the Basic Concepts of Historical Materialism," in Louis Althusser and Etienne Balibar, *Reading Capital*, trans. Ben Brewster (London: Verso, 1979), 226–33; and, more recently, Tony Andréani, *De la société à l'histoire* (Paris: Méridiens-Klincksieck, 1989), 2 vols., 1:397–403.

22. The considerations that follow owe much to the idea exposed some time ago by C. B. Macpherson of a "political theory of property," even though they diverge in the detail, principally on account of the change in historical context. Macpherson's idea is that the political foundations of the right of property are put back into play from the moment that, in the "quasi-market" societies in which we live, economic and social evolution requires a movement from property as a "right to exclude" to property as a "right not to be excluded" from access to certain goods, and thence to property as a "right to a kind of society." Cf. *Democratic Theory, Essays in Retrieval* (Oxford: The Clarendon Press, 1973), 133–40, as well as the commentary by Carlos Ruiz, "Tres Criticas a la Teoria Elitista de la Democracia," *Opciones* (Revista de Centro de Estudios de la Realidad Contemporanea, Academia de Humanismo cristiano, Santiago, Chile) 6 (1985): 87–105, which shows how the blockage of reflection on property maintains the illusion of a separation between economics and politics.

23. Cf. René-Jean Dupuy, *La communauté internationale entre le mythe et l'histoire* (Paris: Economica/UNESCO, 1986), 159–70. Cf. also, by the same author, "Réflexions sur le patrimoine commun de l'humanité," *Droits* 1 (1986): 63–71.

24. Dupuy speaks on this count of a "conflictual community." The "subject" is then the pro-

cedures of agreement and reciprocal control, supported by a particular balance of power, between individual and above all collective subjects (firms, states, possibly associations).

25. Cf. Etienne Balibar, "Intellectuels, idéologues, idéologie," *Raison présente* 73 (1985): 23–38.

26. "On ne remplace pas un cerveau par une machine," in *Intelligence des mécanismes, mécanismes de l'intelligence*, ed. Jean-Louis Le Moigne (Paris: Fayard/Fondation Diderot, 1986). Cf. also Pierre Lévy, *Les technologies de l'intelligence: l'avenir de la pensée à l'ère informatique* (Paris: La Découverte, 1990), 193–94, "Consciousness is individual, but thought is collective."

27. I will have to come back to this question: in a sense it contains, in its turn, the totality of the aporias of a politics of the rights of man. It is the tomb of moralism and legalism as well as of their abstract reversals. In a world in which the disproportion of wealth goes hand in hand, now more than ever, with that of the capability of annihilating the adversary, a world in which the principal frontier (whether it is called North/South or otherwise, for the "South" is everywhere) tends to separate *two humanities*, one which is constantly subjected to violence and one which is constantly girding itself against it, a politics of the rights of man cannot be "nonviolent" *in principle*. Nor however can it fail to go beyond the idea that, according to the famous saying, (the) violence (of the masses, of the oppressed) is "the midwife of every old society which is pregnant with a new one" (*Capital*, vol. 1, 916). This is not only because the oppressors seem to have found the means to make the violence of the oppressed systematically turn around against them, but because violence can no longer—if it ever could—be considered as a *means*, and tends to become a *condition* of existence. Once the distinctions between security and insecurity, public and private violence, military and economic violence, and even between human violence and "natural" disasters start to become effaced, the problem can no longer be either simply to regulate violence (by law), to drive it out (by the state), or to eliminate its causes (by revolution): it is to organize an "antiviolence," that is, to install in the center of politics the collective "struggle" against the both multiple and interdependent forms of violence. I would be tempted to believe that what is today called the passivity or the political discouragement of the masses is to be attributed not so much to some "end of ideologies" or of history as to the extreme uncertainty of perspectives and of strategies in this new kind of "struggle." (On these question, see a first attempt at discussion in my paper, "Violence et politique: Quelques questions," in *Le passage des frontières: Autour de l'oeuvre de Jacques Derrida*, ed. Marie-Louise Mallet [Paris: Galilée, forthcoming].)

INDEX

ACKNOWLEDGMENTS

Chapter 1 originally appeared in *Les temps modernes*, Paris, September 1985. English version first published in *Rethinking Marxism*, Fall 1989, trans. Ted Stolze. Revised by J. Swenson and E. Balibar and reprinted with permission of The Guilford Press.

Chapter 2 originally appeared as "Droits de l'homme et droits du citoyen" in *Actuel Marx*, Paris, no. 8, 1990. Reprinted in Etienne Balibar, *Les frontières de la démocratie*, (Paris: Éditions la Découverte, 1992), and is translated by J. Swenson and published with permission.

Chapter 3 first appeared in *Cahiers de Fontenay*, Paris, June 1990. Translated by J. Swenson.

An earlier version of Chapter 4 and Chapter 6 appeared as "The Vacillation of Ideology in Marxism" in *Raison présent*, Paris, no. 66, 1983. First English version, trans. Andrew Ross and Constance Penley, appeared in *Marxism and the Interpretation of Culture*, (Champaign, Illinois: University of Illinois Press, 1988). Material revised by J. Swenson and E. Balibar and reprinted with permission of the University of Illinois Press.

Chapter 5 was first published in *Les temps modernes*, Paris, no. 451, 1984. First English version of Chapter 5 appeared as "The Notion of Class Politics in Marx," in *Rethinking Marxism*, Summer 1988, trans. Dominique Parent-Ruccio and Frank R. Annunziato. Revised by J. Swenson and E. Balibar and reprinted with permission of The Guilford Press.

Chapter 7 was first published in *Psychanalyse et nazisme*, Actes du Colloque International de Montpellier, revue *Dires* (Université Paul Valéry, Montpellier), 1990. Translated by J. Swenson.

Chapter 8 was first published in *New Political Science*, Fall/Winter 1989. Reprinted with permission.

Chapter 9 originally appeared as "Qu'est-ce qu'une politique des droits de l'homme?" in Etienne Balibar, *Les frontières de la démocratie*, (Paris: Éditions la Découverte, 1992), and is translated by J. Swenson and published with permission.

The author wishes to thank Éditions la Découverte for their kind cooperation.